A WALK IN THE SKY

CLIMBING HIDDEN PEAK

NICHOLAS CLINCH

THE MOUNTAINEERS
THE AMERICAN ALPINE CLUB

THE MOUNTAINEERS: Organized 1906
"...to encourage a spirit of good fellowship
among all lovers of outdoor life."

THE AMERICAN ALPINE CLUB, founded in 1902, is
a public foundation dedicated to the promotion and
dissemination of knowledge pertaining to
mountains and mountaineering.

Published by The Mountaineers
715 Pike Street, Seattle, Washington 98101
and The American Alpine Club, Inc.
113 East 90th Street, New York, New York 10028

Published simultaneously in Canada by Douglas & McIntyre, Ltd.
1615 Venables Street, Vancouver, British Columbia V5L 2H1

Manufactured in the United States of America
Cover photo: Author leaving Camp III on reconnaissance
Title photo: Hidden Peak (Gasherbrum I), from Gasherbrum IV (Fosco Maraini photo)
Designed by Elizabeth Watson
Photos by members of the expedition unless otherwise credited
Photos edited by Jim Stuart
Map by Dee Molenaar

Library of Congress Cataloging in Publication Data

Clinch, Nicholas, 1930-
    A walk in the sky.

    1. Mountaineering—Pakistan—Gasherbrum I.
2. Gasherbrum I (Pakistan)—Description.
I. Title.
GV199.44.P182G373   1982   796.5'22'0954913   82-18778
ISBN 0-89886-042-3

*Dedicated to the memory of
Othmar Gurtner and Jean Couzy,
two of our friends*

CONTENTS

PREFACE

This book was written in the summer of 1959. Except for this preface and the epilogue, everything from the title, dedication, and introduction to the last sentence of the text was written twenty-three years ago. This book cannot be used as a guide to the Karakoram—many things have changed. Even some of my opinions have changed. It is not a primer on what it takes to organize an American expedition today, although there will be more than a few similarities. It is not even a retrospective history of an episode in American mountaineering. It is simply the account, as recalled by me the following summer, of how we organized an expedition and climbed Hidden Peak in the summer of 1958.

There is a story as to why this book was written and why it remained unpublished for so long. I wanted to return to the Karakoram in 1960 and climb Masherbrum. George Bell and I were working to put together an expedition, and I did not want to take a job and then have to leave it. I also wanted to write a book about the Hidden Peak trip, for as I had always wondered what it was like to organize a major expedition and climb in the Himalaya, I wanted to share my experience with others who might have a similar curiosity. So I went to Seattle in the summer of 1959, displaced Pete Schoening's sister-in-law from her apartment, and wrote the book. I was in no particular hurry to finish it because I needed an excuse to keep me gainfully occupied before I had to buckle down to organize the Masherbrum trip. Besides, the mountains around Seattle and Mary Lou Schoening's cooking and hospitality were further inducements for slow, considered writing. But eventually it was done and I even got Pete Schoening to write the chapter about the summit climb.

Meanwhile, I obtained the services of a literary agent, who did a fine job of getting the manuscript around to the publishers. Several of them expressed great interest. However, in the late 1950s the warehouses were full of remaindered books about climbing expeditions and there was not much room for another one, especially about a trip where no one had gotten hurt. After the initial pass through the publishing world had been made, I found myself busily employed and had no overwhelming desire to get the book published.

Time passed, the climbing world in the United States greatly expanded, mountaineers began running over the Himalaya the way they used to run over the Alps, and all the while the manuscript rested safely somewhere in my library.

Then in 1977 Pete Schoening, in a moment of good-hearted weakness, mentioned the existence of the book to The Mountaineers. By then I was somewhat reluctant to have it printed. After all, the expedition had been a private affair and my account seemed quite personal to share with others. Certainly our efforts did not come up to modern mountaineering standards. Perhaps I was vaguely aware of the biblical admonition "would that mine adversary had written a book." After some hesitation I sent the manuscript to The Mountaineers. To my surprise they wanted to publish it. Twenty years before I would have been excited, but in 1977 I did not know. I mumbled a little, hoping that the whole thing would go away. The Mountaineers sent me back a first-rate edited copy of the manuscript, but I was too busy to give the manuscript the attention it needed. John Pollock, director of The Mountaineers Books and a most gracious gentleman, kept reminding me about it and even Pete Schoening made a few casual remarks (I found out later that he had forgotten he had written the summit chapter), so with all excuses exhausted, I finished the task.

My key decision was that the manuscript was to be edited but not rewritten with twenty years' hindsight. I feel this decision most keenly in regard to the dedication since a lot of my friends are gone now, especially Mohd Akram, Fernande Spichiger and Lawrence Coveney. But to express my strong feelings today in the dedication would make it a necrology of world mountaineering for the past two decades. I am not the same person I was in 1959. It is not just the maturing of years; it is the passing of friends, most of whom were killed in the mountains. When one is young and has been climbing only a few years, one's experience is limited and death is abstract. After having been around a while, things are different. Mountains are still magnificent and mountaineering is worthwhile, but there is an overtone of what is at risk that one cannot completely forget.

I have used the epilogue to bring the story of the mountain and the members of the expedition up to date. I have omitted the obligatory equipment list since I doubt if very many people are interested in what we considered in 1958 to be the world's finest equipment. When I offered to contribute some of it to a 1974 venture, Tom Hornbein looked at it and said, "That's all right, Nick. You just take it back to your museum and we will buy some new gear."

Despite my initial misgivings about all this, I do want to thank the kind people who have contributed to this work. Most of the persons who helped with the expedition are mentioned in the book. My opinion about my companions and all of our many friends should be quite clear. I am not going to thank Pete Schoening in print for bringing this manuscript to the attention of The Mountaineers, because it might encourage him in similar ventures. On the other hand, I appreciate the help and support of John Pollock, Jim Sanford, Connie Pious, Donna DeShazo, Ann Cleeland, and Betsy Fulwiler of The Mountaineers. My friends Fosco Maraini and

PREFACE

André Roch have kindly allowed us to grace this book with some of their photographs. I also want to thank my friends at the National Geographic Society for making a rare exception to their policy and permitting us to use some pictures belonging to the society. Finally, I want to thank my wife, Betsy, who formerly did editorial research at *National Geographic* magazine, for leaving no nit unpicked.

For the dedicated reader who has struggled this far, I know that you cannot have as much fun reading about our expedition as we had living it, but I hope that you understand some of the feelings we had, as wearing our cowboy hats and whistling the theme from "The Bridge on the River Kwai," we went walking into the Karakoram.

Palo Alto, California   Nick Clinch
August, 1982

INTRODUCTION

Smothered beneath the layers of rationality in every human mind there lies the urge to attempt the impossible. In striving to accomplish this, the individual rises above petty annoyances and for a brief moment his character assumes the epic nature of the struggle in which he is engaged. That the objective may be intrinsically useless is immaterial. The important thing is that it demand the last reserves of his physical, mental, and emotional resources.

To every mountaineer, neophyte or veteran, this desire for self-fulfillment usually is the unexpressed ambition to make the first ascent of an "Eight Thousander," one of the fourteen highest mountains in the world over 8,000 meters (26,268 feet) high. For years these select peaks stood as symbols of invincibility, and the failure of expedition after expedition to climb them merely intensified their challenge. But the ascent of Annapurna (26,492 feet) by the 1950 French Himalayan Expedition broke the magic barrier of these hitherto inviolate summits and in 1953 the British success on Mount Everest and the German-Austrian ascent of Nanga Parbat reversed the previous pattern of failure. By using new techniques and new equipment, and in many instances by discovering better routes, expeditions began to climb these giants at the rate of more than one a year. The frontier of high-altitude mountaineering closed in with the relentlessness of a hydraulic press, and if one failed to act immediately, the opportunity to participate in the pioneering of these magnificent mountains would be gone forever. The only answer was to organize an expedition, a solution as difficult as it was certain.

Like most words, the noun "expedition" possesses a grandeur that is missing from the actuality it represents. The letterhead, the magazine article, and the book unconsciously inspire visions of supermen, backed by vast organizations, pitting themselves against the malignant forces of implacable Nature. The dimensions of everyday living seem to be lost in such titanic efforts, which obviously are beyond the powers of normal mortals. Even mountaineers who know that the only thing extraordinary about themselves or their friends is the desire to climb mountains tend to regard more famous climbers as being different and upon meeting such celebrities are surprised to discover that they too are just human beings. We forget how amazingly adaptable the individual is. In our world of reliable plumbing, automobiles, and other such benefits of a technical civilization, the contrast between our pleasant lives and the supposedly incredible hardships endured by participants of expeditions appears greatly increased. Yet the great mass of humanity exists without such comforts.

Expeditions are remarkable, not because they consist of "heroes," but because they consist of ordinary men trying to achieve what to them appears almost impossible. Climbing expeditions are a dramatic demonstration of man's defiance of his destiny.

This is not the official account of the 1958 American Karakoram Expedition sponsored by the American Alpine Club, as there never was anything very official about our undertaking. This is merely the story of how an idea, surviving many crises, became a few dedicated friends who struggled together to climb Hidden Peak, which at 26,470 feet was the second highest unclimbed mountain in the world.

Hidden Peak

1

AN IDEA

Frequently while in the hills the mountaineer
will survey his surroundings with joy, whether
they are the quiet meadows beneath his practice
cliff, the valleys and familiar peaks of his neighboring mountains, or an array of spectacular
giants in a distant range that few men are privi-
leged to behold. As he contemplates the solitude
that engulfs him, he is grateful that he should be
there so far from his habitual routine. During
the evenings at the high camps on Hidden Peak,

I would look out across the peaks of the Karakoram as the glow of the sun faded from the snow and wonder how my friends and I, of all people, had managed to get halfway around the world from our homes and up the flanks of this magnificent mountain to witness these unforgettable scenes. The succession of improbable events that had led us there formed a tortuous trail, but every step was deeply engraved in my memory like a series of sustained pitches on a difficult climb.

It all began in a wet tent in the middle of a storm. In the spring of 1954, six of us, students at Stanford University and members of the Stanford Alpine Club, decided to organize an expedition to the rugged Mount Waddington region of the British Columbia Coast Range. Although we had climbed for years throughout the United States and Canada, this was our first trip that required any more planning than merely throwing some food into a rucksack and heading into the bush. We enthusiastically tackled the many details involved and even held weekly meetings discussing every minute point about the trip. Soon we were joined by Andy Kauffman, a graduate of Harvard University and State Department official, who had made the second ascent of Alaska's Mount Saint Elias in 1948. Now we had someone who had done this sort of thing before.

The seven of us flew to Dumbbell Lake (named after its shape rather than the mentality of people who land aircraft on it) and packed sixty-five-pound loads for three days until we reached a rock outcrop 10,000 feet high on the Tellot Glacier. "This is Base Camp," said Kauffman. An overcast delayed our airdrop and we amused ourselves by building a snowhouse while waiting for it. Suddenly a plane scooted under the clouds and dropped our supplies. We happily gathered in the boxes just before dark. That night the first blizzard struck.

As cloth ripped and poles snapped in the fury of the icy blast, we debated about retreating. Over the whine of the wind, someone yelled, "And we have forty days of this before the planes return." But if we retreated, our first expedition would fail and the thought of failure was intolerable. Again and again we sallied forth from our snowhouse to rescue the tents and sink them deep into the glacier behind high snow walls to protect them from the gale. Watching my companions backing into the white sheet, I excitedly thought, "This is just like Little America." Then the tent pole I was holding broke. It was terrible work but eventually we salvaged everything.

For the first two days we were miserable and unhappy, but as the storm continued our morale rose. We were adjusting. By the fifth day of our confinement we were in a happy mood. Surely the Himalaya could not be worse than this. Why not go there? We had only the vaguest idea about how to organize such an expedition, but that did not faze us. If the Italian party that was then attempting to climb K2 in the Karakoram range of

Northwest Pakistan failed, Dr. Charles Houston, leader of the 1938 and 1953 American expeditions to K2, would be returning to that mountain in 1955. All we would have to do would be to copy Dr. Houston. Our little band would march up the Baltoro Glacier into the heart of the Karakoram under his protective supervision. Our objective was uncertain, as we were hesitant about tackling one of the Eight Thousanders in the region; however, there would be many other mountains to choose from. As we would be near K2 and could serve as reinforcements in the event of an emergency, we were confident that "Good Ole Charlie," whom none of us knew personally of course, would be delighted to handle all the little details of our trip, such as obtaining permission from the Pakistani government, hiring porters, and arranging transportation. He would have to do this for his own expedition, and it would not be any trouble to include our modest needs. "And just how do you propose to finance this thing?" asked Kauffman in one of our more rational moments. "Oh, lots of people would be glad to contribute to such a worthy cause," I replied. My companions agreed. It was obvious that our judgment was beginning to be affected by the prolonged inactivity.

Fortunately there were a few clear days when the wind reversed its direction, in order to go back for more snow. During these brief intervals we exploded from the tents in groups of two and three and tried to climb everything in sight before being forced back into our sleeping bags. When the planes finally arrived at Dumbbell Lake to evacuate us, we had made thirty ascents of twenty-five peaks and were elated by our success. Off to the Karakoram!

When we arrived back in Seattle we were greeted by Burge Bickford, who had been rash enough to be our host. "Did you hear?" he said. "The Italians have climbed K2." Our dreams dissolved instantly and Dr. Houston never learned what he had been spared. It had been a short-lived Himalayan expedition.

A year later in the summer of 1955, Andy Kauffman and I were invited to participate in an expedition to the Cordillera Blanca of Peru. After five days of wandering up and down over the Andes prodding our lethargic burros into greater activity, we arrived at the base of unclimbed North Pucahirca (20,300 feet). Fixed rope was attached to difficult sections of the mountain by others, and Kauffman and I made an attempt to reach the top. By eleven on the morning of July 11, we were standing twenty feet away from the summit of North Pucahirca under a large mushroom cornice on a high-angle snow slope that threatened to avalanche. Andy and I debated whether we could claim a first ascent when we could touch only the bottom of the summit and not the top of it. As the mist rising from the Amazon basin enveloped us, we recalled many precedents for retreating and prudently followed tradition.

3

I had always been afraid that I might not be able to adjust to high altitude, but Andy and I had climbed to 20,000 feet without difficulty. Now I was confident that we could climb even higher in the Himalaya.

By the fall of 1955 I had finished my studies at Stanford Law School, and was awaiting orders to active duty in the air force. At this time I obtained a copy of Professor G. O. Dyhrenfurth's book *To the Third Pole*. Upon reading this history of the fourteen Eight Thousanders, my old desire to climb in the Himalaya was reawakened, and I began to think about the situation.

If I were ever going to climb in the Himalaya it would have to be in 1958, when my two-year tour of duty with the air force would be over. Assuming that I would decide to organize an expedition, what should be the objective: an Eight Thousander or a lesser mountain that offered a greater chance of success? There had been four American attempts on Eight Thousanders, three to K2 in 1938, 1939, and 1953, and one to Makalu in 1954. However, the nearest any American ever approached to the summit of one of these giants was in 1939 when Fritz Wiessner, one of our most brilliant mountaineers, climbed to within 750 feet of the top of K2, the second highest mountain in the world. Although these expeditions did not obtain their objectives, they did not fail, for merely to get into the field and climb high on such a mountain is a triumph. The finest moment in the history of American mountaineering was the Homeric retreat of Dr. Houston's party off K2 in 1953. Besieged high on that mountain by the monsoon, they refused to abandon a mortally ill companion, Art Gilkey, and courageously tried to lower him down the ice-coated slabs. After an incredible accident in which the last man on the rope held five falling men, followed by an avalanche that swept Gilkey to his death, the party reached their base camp completely exhausted.

In addition to the difficulty involved in climbing an Eight Thousander, there is the problem of financing such an expedition. There would be little public support. The 1954 California Himalayan expedition to Makalu had demonstrated that. It was sponsored by the Sierra Club of California, an extremely vigorous organization, which tried to obtain support from its own members and the public. After a tremendous effort the expedition reached its mountain, but when it was time to return, the climbers were stranded in Base Camp, flat broke. Their wives learned about their plight and, anxious to see their husbands again, raised enough money to pay the wages of the porters needed to bring the expedition back to civilization. In contrast to this, a well-financed and well-equipped French expedition efficiently climbed Makalu the following year. This outstanding success in which every member of the climbing team reached the summit accented American indifference.

Despite these difficulties I thought that an Eight Thousander should be the objective. The cost of flying halfway around the world to India is the largest single item in the budget of any American expedition to the Himalaya. The additional expense of attempting an Eight Thousander as compared with a lesser mountain is relatively small, and the chances of raising money are better. Also, while the success or failure of a country's mountaineers upon Eight Thousanders does not necessarily reflect upon the ability of the climbers involved, much less an entire nationality, people tend to think in terms of stereotypes and believe emotionally what they rationally know to be false. The ascent of an Eight Thousander proves absolutely nothing, but it does resolve an emotional doubt posing as an empirical truth. Finally, like many other things in life, an Eight Thousander is to be respected but not feared. In the past only outstanding mountaineers have climbed such mountains. However, this has been due as much to a process of selection as to one of elimination. Mountains are not a track course. In a race there can be only one winner. On a mountain everyone beyond a certain indefinite standard of ability and strength can reach the summit. The standard varies with the mountain and the condi- tions. I was convinced that experienced mountaineers do not have to be supermen to climb an Eight Thousander provided they are properly equipped and willing to work.

Now, which Eight Thousander? In the fall of 1955 there were four unclimbed Eight Thousanders in Nepal and three in the Karakoram of Pakistan. The Karakoram seemed to be the best choice. Nepal had been steadily increasing its restrictions on mountaineering while Pakistan had a more liberal policy. Moreover, the monsoon strikes the eastern Himalaya around the first of June, while if it strikes the Karakoram at all it is usually after the middle of July. As many American mountaineers are students and teachers who cannot leave until the latter part of May, it would be easier to get a party for the Karakoram. Most important, the three unclimbed Eight Thousanders in the Karakoram were within one day's march of each other at the head of the Baltoro Glacier. Thus, an expedition could be planned to either Gasherbrum I (Hidden Peak, 26,470 feet), Broad Peak (26,400 feet), or Gasherbrum II (26,360 feet), and shifted from one to another with a minimum of difficulty. Undoubtedly, all three mountains would be tried by European expeditions in 1956 and 1957, but perhaps if we were lucky one of them might remain unclimbed by 1958. Of these three peaks, Hidden Peak was my first choice. It was the highest.

I began to study my proposed objective. The main Himalaya extends for over 1,500 miles from the Brahmaputra River in Assam on the east to the Indus Gorge near Nanga Parbat (26,620 feet) on the west. The Kara- koram is a separate range that lies north and slightly west of the Himalaya. The region stretches for over 300 miles from the Shyok River on the east to the Hindu Kush range on the west, and is bounded by the Indus River to the south and the Shaksgam tributary of the Yarkand River on the north. It contains nineteen peaks over 25,000 feet, including six peaks over 26,000 feet, the greatest concentration of high mountains in the world. The word Karakoram itself means black gravel. This was the name of the Mongol capital in Chinese Turkestan under the emperor Genghis Khan. Since that great city disappeared under desert sands and was not rediscovered until 1889, it is believed that the mountains received their name from historic Karakoram Pass to the east.

The main group of the Karakoram, which forms the continental divide, is called the Baltoro Muztagh—*muz* meaning ice and *tagh*, mountain. It lies in the territory of Baltistan, almost exactly on the opposite side of the Northern Hemisphere from Denver, Colorado. It is about 900 miles north and west of Mount Everest. In the midst of this Baltoro Muztagh stands Hidden Peak, the second highest mountain in the Karakoram and the eleventh highest mountain in the world.

In *To the Third Pole* Dyhrenfurth gave a concise history of the mountain. Gasherbrum I was first explored in 1892 by an expedition led by Sir Martin Conway. He believed that the mountain could not be seen from the Baltoro Glacier because of intervening peaks and gave it the name Hidden Peak. This name is generally used today to avoid confusion with surrounding mountains that also bear the name of Gasherbrum. In 1909 Vittorio Sella, the incomparable mountain photographer, who was with the Duke of Abruzzi's Italian expedition, obtained some excellent photographs of the mountain and in 1929 another Italian expedition climbed the nearby Conway Saddle. However, the mountain was not reconnoitered until 1934, when the International Himalayan Expedition under Professor Dyhrenfurth tried to discover a route up the mountain. First, Dyhrenfurth and André Roch explored the South Gasherbrum Glacier under the great northwest face of Hidden Peak, but they were unable to find a promising route. Then Roch and Hans Ertl tried the southwest spur and climbed to an altitude of 20,600 feet. Their Balti porters refused to follow—they had no Sherpas with them—so the expedition turned its attention to lesser neighbors. Members of the expedition reached the eastern summit of Baltoro Kangri (23,761 feet) and the western summit of Sia Kangri (23,500 feet). Hidden Peak remained virtually untouched.

In 1936, Hidden Peak was the objective of the first French expedition to the Himalaya. It was patterned after the early British attempts on Everest and was a large and ponderous affair compared with many recent expeditions. More than 650 porters were needed to carry its baggage from the last village of Askole to a base camp on the upper Baltoro Glacier. Led by Henry De Segogne, the party consisted of the finest French alpinists of that day, who were supported by thirty-five Sherpas. The French rejected the ridge explored by Roch and Ertl as being too long and tried to climb the mountain by a nearer shoulder that they called Hidden South. Displaying great ability and courage, they established four camps on the south spur before an early monsoon defeated them. During the retreat two Sherpas fell over 2,000 feet down a snow couloir. Miraculously, both men survived, but they had to be carried out from the mountain on litters.

The fact that such a fine French party had reached a height of only 22,000 feet on Hidden Peak was discouraging. However, Dyhrenfurth said that the southwest ridge was straightforward. Why not give it a try? No one had looked at the mountain since 1936.

Where to begin? There were three fundamental elements to the expedition that had to be obtained—money, permission, and personnel. It was impossible to raise funds without having received permission from the Pakistani government. It was equally impossible to get the permission without having a party and in the United States it was difficult to get personnel without having the money. There was no choice. I had to find five other climbers plus a climbing doctor who would allow me to use their names in applying for permission.

Accounts of other expeditions relate how the members were selected from the cream of the nation's mountaineers, who rushed forward en masse to volunteer. In this country there were many competent mountaineers who would be eager to participate in such an undertaking, but everyone was rightly afraid of the repercussions if the public, employers, clients, patients, business associates, and immediate family should learn that such an irrational and irresponsible act was even being contemplated. The odds were so great that the trip would never occur, that to become a member just was not worth the risk to one's reputation. Although I promised to keep the matter as confidential as possible to protect the persons who allowed me to use their names, I had to proceed with the caution of a criminal conspiracy.

While the primary qualification for membership in the expedition was availability, a certain amount of care had to be exercised in inviting climbers since, if we did receive permission, it would be desirable to have a party capable of climbing the mountain. One must always remember that a good expedition is stronger than the sum of its parts. While technical ability and physical strength are essential in an expedition member, determination and judgment are even more important. A strong man who will not get out of the sack in the morning is useless, and a fool is dangerous. The best antidote for high-altitude lassitude is an all-consuming passion to climb. Above all, an expedition member must have the ability to work with others under the most trying conditions. Unlike mountains in the Alps, the Rockies, and the Andes, or even lesser peaks in the Himalaya, an Eight Thousander is so huge that one outstanding mountaineer cannot climb it and pull his companions up behind him. He may spearhead the

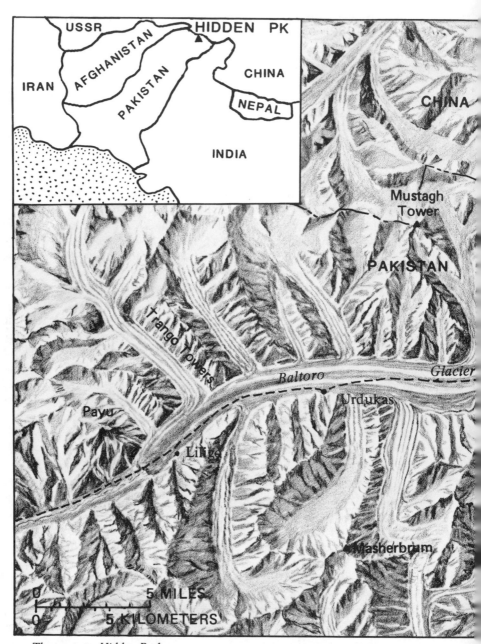

The route to Hidden Peak

assault, but it takes a team working together to succeed on such a peak, as even the most outstanding feats of a single man are swallowed up by the immensity of these giants. Contrary to popular concept, climbing in the Himalaya is unglamorous, backbreaking work. A Himalayan mountaineer must be willing to exhaust himself in anonymous toil and, if he is selected to represent his companions on the summit team, he must have a personality that will inspire them to use their last reserves of strength to help him. With these qualities in mind I began to assemble a team.

Both Gary Driggs, who had been a member of the Coast Range expedition and was now a Mormon missionary in Finland, and Andy Kauffman, in Washington, D.C., wrote that they were interested. Felix Knauth, a teacher in Menlo Park, California, was enthusiastic instead of incredulous when I asked him to join. Bruce Meyer, an orthopedic surgeon in Carmel, California, allowed me to list him as the medical officer. He had performed exceedingly well as the climbing doctor for the California Makalu expedition.

Still looking for volunteers, I went to the Union Court at Stanford University, where members of the Stanford Alpine Club gathered every noon to discuss new forays to Yosemite Valley, and plan further escapades on campus buildings. "Who wants to climb Hidden Peak?" I announced. Over a mixture of shocked silence and suppressed laughter, I heard someone say, "You've come up with some wild ideas, but this takes it." Then Gil Roberts, who had also been on the Coast Range trip, said, "I'd be interested in a trip to the Karakoram in '58 if I can get free from medical school." This was encouraging, for Gil is an extremely strong and capable mountaineer. Now only two more names and I would have a party.

Up in the hills of Berkeley, California, there was a nondescript house that was called Toad Hall by five mountaineers who were renting it. I dropped by one evening for dinner and, after everyone was pleasantly full of spaghetti, I casually mentioned the possibility of climbing Hidden Peak. They did not even laugh. "Aw, come on, all I want is just two more names so I can apply for permission," I pleaded. From the kitchen where Bob Swift and Dick Irvin were washing the dishes came Swift's voice, "I'll go with you," followed by Irvin's chuckling, "Sure, count me in." Dick Irvin and I had started climbing together in 1951 when we spent the entire summer climbing in the Tetons and the Canadian Rockies. Since then he had climbed throughout the western United States and Canada, as well as Alaska and Peru. Besides being an excellent mountaineer, he is the finest artist in cooking over a Primus stove I have ever known. His meals are a pleasure, not a necessity for survival. Also, no expedition with Irvin is ever dull.

I had first met Bob Swift in the spring of 1954 when he, Dick Irvin, Gary Driggs, and I climbed the Lost Arrow. He was a veteran of some of the most difficult two- and three-day rock climbs in Yosemite Valley, and had also climbed in the Coast Range of British Columbia, where he had been a human packhorse. He has a sharp sense of humor and, like Irvin, enlivens any trip in which he participates. Normally I would have been elated by the addition of these two fine mountaineers; however, Irvin and Swift had recently achieved some local notoriety by planning an attempt on the legendary Muztagh Tower in the Karakoram with two British climbers on a total budget of $5,000. Only the most fanatic mountaineers were volunteering for my proposed expedition. Now we had a party—on paper.

Then there was the question of science. Only by invoking its holy name could the expedition become a respectable venture worthy of support. Yet it is almost impossible to mix serious scientific research with difficult climbing, for if mountaineers are distracted by having to pick wild flowers or chase butterflies in order to justify the affair, then both mountaineering and science suffer. A scientific program must function independently from the climbing team. Our problem was to find an important scientific project that could be safely incorporated into the expedition with a minimum of effort and expense. The study of high-altitude physiology fitted this requirement. It is of increasing importance in the present space age, and the tests do not interfere with the climbing program. Also, only one scientist is required. Furthermore, Dr. Nello Pace of the University of California, a recognized authority in the field, was a friend. Dr. Pace expressed great interest in the expedition and enrolled tentatively as a member.

I decided to call our enterprise the "1958 American Karakoram Expedition," which adequately disguised its real nature, and assumed the title of "director" because it sounded impressive. There was no competition for the job. Andy Kauffman was listed as the climbing leader. Despite our distinguished appearance on paper, I was not too certain how the mountaineering world would react to our group, so I showed the roster to my friend and mentor, Dr. David Harrah, assistant professor of philosophy at the University of California at Riverside and a veteran of the Andes. Harrah is noted for his blunt honesty, and while this trait does not always enhance his popularity, it makes his opinions highly respected. "What do you think of it?" I timidly asked. "It's a strong party," he replied. The expedition had survived its first test.

By then it was November and I received a long-distance call from Dallas, Texas. I recognized my mother's distraught voice. "What assignment did you request?" Slightly taken aback I answered, "Germany. Why?" "Are you sure you didn't volunteer for Iceland?" she demanded. My air force orders had arrived.

Time was limited and I still did not know how to proceed when suddenly I got the inspiration that Dr. Charles Houston must have faced the same difficulties in 1938 and 1953 that now were confronting me. I wrote

11

him confessing that the grand "1958 American Karakoram Expedition" consisted of me and my typewriter, and asked him what I should do. Fortunately my naive candor impressed him favorably and he invited me to visit him in Exeter, New Hampshire, in early December, when I would be in the East for the annual meeting of the American Alpine Club. Dr. Houston was extremely encouraging. I was worried that we would never get permission from the Pakistani government, since we were supposed to furnish proof of adequate finances, which at this stage were entirely lacking. "Don't worry. You'll get permission," he reassured me. "Merely state that the party will be privately financed. That gives the impression of wealthy American millionaires and there will be no difficulty."

Also, we needed sponsorship from a recognized alpine club to assure the Pakistani government that we were a moderately competent party. Since we were going to attempt an unclimbed Eight Thousander, we felt that the American Alpine Club would be the logical sponsor for such an enterprise. Most of the members of our proposed expedition belonged to it and we planned to infiltrate the organization with those who did not. The American Alpine Club had sponsored the three expeditions to K2, but the leaders had been Dr. Houston and Fritz Wiessner, two of the United States' most distinguished mountaineers, who had previously climbed in the Himalaya. We, on the other hand, were relatively unknown. If our ragged group received sponsorship and support and then managed to get wiped out, it would be damaging to the club's reputation. However, the members of the governing council were a reasonable group and I knew most of them personally. Besides, the secretary, Lawrence Coveney, and I were very close friends. I had met Coveney in 1952 at a section meeting of the American Alpine Club in Berkeley. After a short conversation, we both realized that he had been my father's bunkmate in flight school in 1918. He had last seen my father in 1926, four years before I was born. This fortunate coincidence became of great importance to our efforts, as in 1953 Coveney moved to New Jersey and became a member of the governing council of the club.

On my way from Dallas to Iceland I stopped to visit Coveney and outlined my entire plan for the expedition. He was extremely enthusiastic about it and promised to do everything he could to help. Coveney became our staunchest supporter; without him, our expedition would never have been more than a pile of papers inside a manila folder. After saying goodbye to Lawrence, I departed for Iceland.

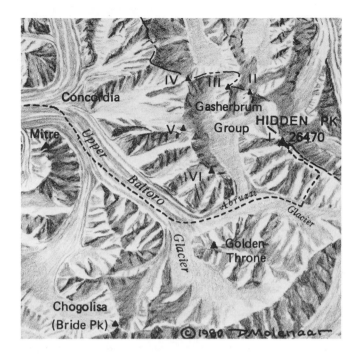

2

A FEW
PRELIMINARIES

On January 22, 1956, I stepped off the military transport plane at Keflavik Airport, Iceland. Because of the difficulty involved in getting out of the Keflavik Airport Agreed Area, most American servicemen stationed there considered their tour of duty in Iceland a year lost from their lives. Fortunately I was assigned to the base legal office, and my duties included being the observer for all hearings held on American personnel in the local Icelandic court off the base. I also was able to make contact with the mountaineers of the Icelandic Air Ground Rescue team and the Icelandic Glaciological Society. Soon I was invited to join an Icelandic expedition across the Vatnajokull, the largest ice field in the world outside the polar regions. For two and a half marvelous weeks, twelve Icelanders and I rode to and fro across the vast snowcap in our snowmobiles, erecting survey cairns on the highest mountains of the island.

I made other climbs with my Icelandic friends, including a first ascent of a moss-covered lava spire on the north coast called Hraundrangi. Sigurdur Waage, Finnur Eyolfsson, and I spent six hours climbing 300 feet. The rock was exceedingly rotten and I was constantly afraid that one of the large blocks I kept dislodging would strike my companions on the head. When we reached the summit Sigurdur turned to me and said, semijokingly, "You do know how to get down, don't you?" The next morning I walked into the dining room of the local hotel in my filthy climbing clothes and came face to face with the commanding general of the defense force! Fortunately he was an understanding gentleman.

Iceland was an ideal place to organize the preliminaries of an expedition. Despite frequent delays in receiving mail, there were few outside distractions. Dr. Houston sent me a draft of a request for permission from the Pakistani government, which I submitted through the American embassy in Karachi.

Time passed quickly. Dick Irvin wrote from Pakistan that their British-American Karakoram Expedition was going to attempt Rakaposhi instead of the Muztagh Tower. The Japanese climbed Manaslu (26,658 feet); the Austrians, under Fritz Moravec, climbed Gasherbrum II, a neighbor of Hidden Peak; and the Swiss in a brilliantly conducted expedition made the first ascent of Lhotse (28,028 feet), the fourth highest mountain in the world, and then climbed Everest twice on successive days. Soon after I learned of the success of these expeditions, I received a letter from the American Alpine Club stating that while the council was extremely sympathetic with our plans, it could not assist us in the manner I had requested. There were legal complications. Hesitating to request full sponsorship for fear we could not get it, I had made the most innocuous proposal I could. Now that was rejected.

At this time there was a tragic collision between two airliners over the Grand Canyon, and as a gracious gesture Swiss Airlines flew a mountain rescue team to the United States from Switzerland to participate in the recovery of the victims from the canyon. The Swiss did a wonderful job; however the newspaper headlines were most unfortunate for American mountaineering. One night on the way from Keflavik Airport into Reykjavik to attend a meeting of the Air Ground Rescue team, I picked up an Icelandic hitchhiker. The first thing the stranger asked was, "Aren't there any mountaineers in the United States?" I said nothing, although my car struck the next chuckhole squarely.

Expeditions are born in the minds of men and more of them die there than are defeated by avalanches, bad weather, and misfortune combined. I was ready to throw the entire expedition file into the wastebasket and would have done so except that I received several letters of encouragement from Lawrence Coveney, Gil Roberts, and Felix Knauth. Coveney instructed me to request full sponsorship from the American Alpine Club. I did not think the club would take such a risk; nevertheless, in October, 1956, the council did grant us full support, subject only to our obtaining the necessary permission from the Pakistani government. I realized that we were an experiment, and that the manner in which we ran our trip would determine the club's attitude toward expeditions and the future of American mountaineering in the Himalaya.

Meanwhile, as I had always wanted to climb in the French Alps, I carefully hoarded my fifteen-day leave until the middle of August, when I headed for Chamonix. There it rained for twelve days straight. Splashing through the puddles on the way to the post office I heard someone call me. Spinning around I spotted an emaciated figure with a blond beard approaching me. It was Dick Irvin.

"I'm glad I finally found you. You wrote that you would be in the Alps last part of August, and I've been looking all over for you. Just came from Zermatt," he said.

"How was Rakaposhi?" I asked.

"Interesting. We got to within 1,500 feet of the summit before the monsoon caught us. On the way down Swift took a hundred-foot tumble. Then he was almost struck by lightning. He tried to avoid the blast by throwing his pack down, but it took a bad bounce and fell to the Biro Glacier instead. We spent the night in Camp II with one sleeping bag for the two of us. The next day I fell thirty feet unroped, but I managed to grab a protruding rock on the edge of a 4,000 foot drop-off. Everyone contracted dengue fever. We didn't retreat off that mountain—we escaped!"

As I looked at Irvin and listened to his story, I realized that he was still very sick and should be hospitalized as quickly as possible. We left Chamonix for London where we could contact Captain Mike Banks, who had been the leader of the Rakaposhi expedition.

On our retreat to England, Irvin and I stopped momentarily in Paris to have lunch with Jean Couzy, veteran of Annapurna and Makalu and one of the finest mountaineers in the world. As we sat around the table in the sidewalk cafe, Couzy, oxygen expert for the French Makalu expedition, explained how well their oxygen apparatus worked, how light it was, and, above all, how fast they were able to climb using it. Couzy's expression brightened as he warmed to his subject. "Mountaineers are making a mistake. They use oxygen only on such extremely high mountains as

Everest, K2, and Kangchenjunga. They have not used it on the petit Eight Thousanders, the ones between 26,268 and 27,000 feet. Yet it would be much more effective on such mountains. On Makalu we climbed at a high rate of speed between 23,000 and 26,000 feet, using a reduced flow rate of three liters of oxygen a minute instead of four. This means that two bottles of oxygen will last longer, and, therefore, only a few bottles are needed to ensure an adequate supply for the summit assault parties on the lesser Eight Thousanders. The cost would not be excessive and it would greatly increase the safety and mobility of any expedition using it. Although such tactics have not yet been used on the lesser Eight Thousanders, I am absolutely convinced not only that it will prove successful but also that it is necessary to ensure the safety of the party."

Irvin and I absorbed every word he said without daring to hint at what we were planning. Hidden Peak really belonged to French mountaineers due to their prior expedition. However, the French were so well organized and efficient that we were afraid if they decided to make another attempt, the mountain was as good as climbed. We wanted very much to try an unclimbed Eight Thousander and there were few left. As we said good-bye to Jean Couzy and thanked him for the lunch, we were determined that his theory was going to be tested—by us.

In every activity there are always a few places where the participants seem to congregate almost by instinct. In Cambridge, Massachusetts, the house of Henry Hall, a past president of the American Alpine Club, is such a lodestone for mountaineers. Upon returning to the United States from Iceland in January, 1957, I went to Cambridge to see Henry and also Dick Irvin, who was working in Boston. My roommate on the third floor of Hall's house was a quiet blond Swiss who had received a Ph.D. in chemistry. Dr. Jürg Marmet had also made the second ascent of Mount Everest with the Swiss expedition the previous summer, a fact he would reluctantly admit after being confronted with it. As Irvin and I related our aspirations and our difficulties in trying to fulfill them, Marmet became very sympathetic. Once he asked Irvin, "How far from the summit of Rakaposhi were you?" Irvin's answer summed up the history of American mountaineering in the Himalaya. "We were $5,000 short," he replied.

Marmet, who had been the oxygen expert for the Swiss expedition, Dick Irvin, and I gathered around pictures of the Karakoram and, with mounting enthusiasm, Marmet carefully picked out a possible route up Broad Peak. "I'm sure that will go," he said. He was right. The Austrians climbed the mountain by that route during the coming summer. Before I left him, Marmet, in an unguarded moment, casually said, "If there is ever anything I can do for you, just let me know." He will never make that offer again.

The air force sent me to Long Beach, California, to be the claims officer in the base legal office. It was a busy job. Supersonic jets belonging to the air force, the navy, the marines, and various aircraft companies flew across the Los Angeles basin breaking the sound barrier. Down below were two and a half million irate citizens and taxpayers. Windows broke and ceilings cracked, and it was up to me to handle the complaints. Finally, I could no longer endure the routine of standing ankle-deep in fallen plaster and saying, "I'm very sorry, madam, but our tests prove conclusively that this could not possibly have happened." I had a thirty-day leave coming and there was only one place to go—back to the Cordillera Blanca of Peru where there were no telephones.

I contacted Tom McCormack, a rancher in Rio Vista, California, who is an old climbing friend of mine from Stanford. Years before I had taken McCormack on his first climb in Yosemite Valley, but overcoming this initial handicap he had developed into an exceedingly fine rock climber. Since then he had done many difficult ascents throughout the United States and Canada. Despite his tremendous drive he is always cheerful and good humored.

McCormack had already been thinking about going to the Andes and he and Rick Tidrick flew to Peru to handle the preliminary arrangements. When Virgil Day, who was on leave from the army, and I joined them we went straight to the mountains. We decided to attempt Nevado San Juan (19,000 feet), which was unclimbed although it looked easy in the photographs we had. After several false starts, Tidrick and I reached the top of the mountain late in the afternoon of July 3. We bivouacked in a crevasse 500 feet below the summit, and six days later I was back in the base legal office in Long Beach with two days of leave left.

Meanwhile the 1958 American Karakoram Expedition was slowly being decimated. Neither Dr. Nello Pace nor Dr. Bruce Meyer could go and Felix Knauth could not get away from his teaching. It was apparent that our party would be quite small to tackle such a massive mountain as Hidden Peak. All previous expeditions had been accompanied by a Pakistani army officer, who handled the important function of transportation. We, too, would have such an officer, and he would require the identical clothing and equipment that we would use. In the past some of these liaison officers had been interested in mountaineering and had performed well on their own initiative. Others had not. It was largely a matter of luck whether the officer assigned to an expedition would want to climb. We needed climbers badly and could not afford to have anyone, American or Pakistani, in the party who would not do his share toward climbing the mountain. Having just spent a very successful year in Iceland climbing with the local mountaineers, I suddenly realized that the trouble was not with the individual officer who did not want to climb, but with the expedition for not making the trip a joint venture with the Pakistanis. For years

17

foreign expeditions had gone into Pakistan, which had been a courteous host, but few expeditions had ever invited Pakistani mountaineers to join as full-fledged partners in climbing their own mountains. Why should the officers have done anything more than their duty when they were not given an equal chance to go high on the mountain? We promptly invited the Pakistani army to send not just a liaison officer but two men who wanted to climb with the rest of us as full members in the climbing team. While in retrospect it seems like a very obvious step, at the time it was considered a great gamble.

There were other problems. The Austrians succeeded in climbing Broad Peak although their leader, the incredible Hermann Buhl, was killed later when he fell through a cornice on Chogolisa, a neighboring mountain. Of the three unclimbed Eight Thousanders that were in the Karakoram when I started organizing the expedition, only Hidden Peak still remained untouched. Several friends of mine applied for permission to attempt K2 and were turned down. Still we had no word from the Pakistani government concerning our application. If we had sufficient funds there would be plenty of time to organize our trip, but we could not begin to raise money effectively until we received the permission. I explained our predicament to Major General M. Hayaud-Din, the Pakistani military and naval attache in Washington, D.C. General Din, who is a mountaineer himself, had constantly helped us when we needed it most and once again he began to check into the matter.

Always there was the difficulty of finances. Mountaineering is a personal sport and does not lend itself well to international competition. Any experienced mountaineer knows that, given the same conditions and equipment, any competent party of any nationality can climb these mountains. However, in a desperate attempt to obtain money, I decided to "wave the flag" a little and see what would happen. With the aid of Dewey Linze, a sympathetic staff writer at the *Los Angeles Times*, I made a thinly veiled appeal for help. The one thing worse than selling your soul to the devil of expediency is not getting anything for it. The only results from the article were a phone call from two men who had climbed the Matterhorn with a guide and wanted to join the expedition, and a letter from an ex-paratrooper "with guts" who was willing to lead the charge. While this response demonstrated that the automobile has not completely stifled all spirit of adventure in the United States, I realized that I might as well stick to my principles and struggle along with a clear conscience since I was going to have to struggle along regardless.

Soon it was the first week of November. The annual meeting of the American Alpine Club was only a month away and still we had received no word as to the status of our request for permission. It was becoming increasingly difficult to convince people that we were going to climb Hidden Peak when I was beginning to doubt it myself.

Earlier I had taken Jürg Marmet up on his ill-considered offer of assistance and requested him to supervise the procurement of our oxygen supplies. Marmet replied that, as the manufacturing process required months, the oxygen bottles being made out of a special aluminum alloy and reinforced by piano wire, we would have to order the apparatus immediately in order to be certain of having it. Using this information about the flow rates needed for climbing and sleeping at various altitudes contained in Albert Eggler's book *The Everest-Lhotse Adventure*, I calculated that at least four breathing sets and twenty-five bottles of oxygen were needed to ensure our success and safety. It would cost over $1,500, but this was the opportunity of a lifetime, and if we did not gamble we would never get started, so I instructed Marmet to go ahead and order the necessary equipment. But I began to wonder if I would end up stuck with twenty-five bottles of oxygen that were useless below 23,000 feet.

In the middle of November the air force released me from active duty. I was delayed for five days from leaving Long Beach in order to complete some unfinished business. The same afternoon that I began my postponed trip to New York for the crucial meeting of the American Alpine Club I instinctively checked my mailbox. Inside was the familiar envelope of the United States Foreign Service. We had received permission.

3

GET IT TO THE
PORT ON TIME

The granting of permission by the Pakistani
government was not an unmixed blessing. If
our request had been denied we could have
relaxed and consoled ourselves with the thought
that we had tried. Now we had our long desired
opportunity and little else.

Like all expeditions to the Himalaya our
schedule was determined by weather and climatic

conditions. Mountaineers have argued for years over whether the monsoon ever penetrates the Karakoram. It is evident that prolonged bad weather does strike the region and although certain experts say it cannot be the monsoon, it suspiciously resembles that phenomenon. Regardless of nomenclature, a long storm can be disastrous to any party caught high on an Eight Thousander. Accounts of prior expeditions to the Karakoram and neighboring Nanga Parbat indicated that summit attempts should be made before the middle of July, as the weather tends to deteriorate after that time. In some years there were unsettled conditions early in the summer that eventually improved, while in other years the weather remained fair throughout. However, June and early July seemed to offer the greatest chance of good weather.

In order to be in a position to make the summit assault on Hidden Peak during the first week of July, we should reach Base Camp no later than the end of May. Calculating back from that date, and allowing sufficient time for the 135-mile approach march from Skardu and the delays inherent in shipping supplies halfway around the world, we learned that our equipment would have to be at the port of New York no later than the middle of March. We had exactly three and a half months to raise the money, enlist personnel, order equipment, and get everything to the dock properly crated.

Not only did we lack funds, but the entire party also had to be reorganized. We had not heard from the Pakistani army concerning our two Pakistani mountaineers. Dr. Nello Pace, Dr. Bruce Meyer, and Felix Knauth definitely could not participate. Gary Driggs was practically out, Gil Roberts and Dick Irwin were doubtful, and Andy Kauffman, though eager, was hesitant. Only Bob Swift and I were certain that we could go. Swift had had a special clause inserted into his teaching contract that permitted him to leave his duties early if our expedition became a reality. The principal of the Half Moon Bay Union High School had agreed to this only after Swift assured him that the chances of the expedition taking place were extremely remote. Swift had told him the absolute truth, although I doubt that the principal ever believed it. I was not confronted with such difficulties. I was out of the air force and unemployed.

Upon learning that we had received permission, I dispatched telegrams to all members of the expedition, to John Oberlin, president of the American Alpine Club, and to Lawrence Coveney. Also, as I suspected that Jürg Marmet, a very practical Swiss, would wait a while to see what developed before ordering our oxygen, I sent him a cablegram saying that permission had been received and requested him to increase our oxygen order to twenty-nine bottles and five regulators.

Next, Roberts, Swift, and I held an emergency conference in Roberts's apartment in San Francisco. The general tenor of the meeting was aptly summed up by Swift's comment, "That's good news. Now what do we do with it?" The response among nonmountaineers was even less enthusiastic. One person who was told about the permission remarked, "Wonderful. How much can you sell it for?" Any illusions about our expedition suddenly becoming a popular crusade were quickly dispelled.

At the annual meeting of the American Alpine Club I told the members of the council that we would put at least a small party into the field, without bothering them with minor details such as just how small the party was going to be. I was not fooling anyone, but the club was completely behind the project and lent us their entire expedition fund of $6,000. Although the reputation of the club was at stake, during the critical months that followed the council gave us complete control in the organization and execution of the expedition, a demonstration of trust that greatly increased our confidence. Frequently we had to ask the impossible from the club and its individual members and somehow they always fulfilled our requests.

I now was studying for the California bar examination that was to be given for three days early in March. I still lived in an alley a block and a half from the Pacific Ocean in Long Beach in the same small house that I had rented primarily because the nearby beach was an inconspicuous place for me to run in an effort to get into physical condition. My portable typewriter could not make sufficient carbon copies of the weekly bulletin I had to send to all concerned informing them of the expedition's lack of progress, so I made a deal with my former air force boss. In exchange for having access to the legal office and its electric typewriter, I spent several hours a day helping to process claims.

By December of 1957, Dick Irvin, despite his experiences on Rakaposhi, was eager to return to the Karakoram, and in one fourteen-hour effort he compiled two tentative food and equipment lists for a four-month expedition. One list was for an optimum budget of $45,000 and the other was for the probable budget of $25,000.

Despite the general lack of interest in mountaineering in the United States, there is one source of support that all American Himalayan expeditions have relied upon for the last ten years—*The Saturday Evening Post.* I contacted Martin Sommers, the foreign editor, and by return mail I received a much-needed option for the story of the trip. Jokes such as, "John, will you please fall into the next crevasse for the benefit of our *Post* article?" are a constant source of amusement to American mountaineers, but mountaineers are very thankful for this one bright spot in an otherwise dismal picture. With the receipt of the *Post* option, our project started to become respectable. Then at the end of December the bottom fell out.

First, Gary Driggs wrote that he definitely could not go. This was a terrific blow, not only because he is an extremely fine mountaineer and I was counting heavily upon his ability and strength, but also because he is a close friend with whom I have done some of my finest climbs. I have absolute confidence in him. Next, the Austrians announced that they had received permission from the Pakistani government to attempt Hidden Peak. Their expedition was under the leadership of Fritz Moravec, who had climbed Gasherbrum II, and was supposed to leave Austria in February for the Karakoram. This seemed incredible, as one reason official permission is required is to prevent two parties from engaging in a race up the same mountain. While I found this difficult to believe, in 1956 a French and a British party were climbing the Muztagh Tower simultaneously from opposite sides, so anything was possible. The Austrian announcement meant that our expedition could not approach prospective backers by saying we had exclusive permission to attempt Hidden Peak, since if the Austrians also had permission they would beat us to the mountain as they were closer and had the necessary money. I immediately sent letters to the American embassy in Karachi and to General Hayaud-Din in Washington requesting them to check into this situation. Six weeks later the American embassy learned that the Austrians did not have permission after all, but by then it was too late for us to obtain outside backing.

Finally, I received from the French company that was making our oxygen regulators a letter stating that the firm manufacturing the oxygen bottles could not produce them until the end of March, which would be too late for our expedition. There has been much discussion about the ethics of using oxygen to climb high mountains and no prior American expedition had ever used it except for medical purposes. The use of oxygen is the same as the use of pitons for safety. It has been proven that Eight Thousanders can be climbed without oxygen. However, the use of oxygen not only increases the chance for success but also definitely protects the health of the mountaineers who use it. Parties that systematically use oxygen above 23,000 feet almost always return without permanent injury. Expeditions that do not use oxygen often suffer severely from frostbite. Thus, while the loss of our oxygen equipment would not necessarily doom us to failure, it would greatly increase the risk of someone's getting hurt. I knew exactly one French and one Swiss mountaineer, but Jean Couzy and Jürg Marmet happened to be the oxygen experts for the French Alpine Club and the Swiss Foundation for Alpine Research, and I wrote them pleading letters requesting that they do everything in their power to try to speed up the production of our bottles. Also, I phoned Andy Kauffman at the American embassy in Paris. We had one of those garbled connections in which I could hear Kauffman's voice clear as a bell saying over and over again, "I can't understand you." Later during the long evenings of the approach march Kauffman would regale us with imitations of the squawks and gurgles at his end of that ill-fated phone call. This was the nadir of the expedition: no oxygen, no party, and the Austrians were going to climb the mountain.

By the middle of January the situation began to improve. Jean Couzy and Jürg Marmet simultaneously jumped on the bottle manufacturer in the name of French and Swiss mountaineering and the impossible deadline was moved up to the end of February, which gave us sufficient time to have the bottles filled and shipped to Pakistan. Several members of the American Alpine Club offered to donate enough money to the expedition that, combined with the loan from the club and the assets of the members of the party, would permit us to operate a trip on a budget of about $25,000, which was adequate but did not allow luxuries such as mail runners.

On January 25, 1958, Swift, Irvin, and I met to thrash out more details. Both Irvin and Gil Roberts could not be in the main party. Irvin could not leave his teaching duties and Roberts could not leave medical school early. At this point we invited Tom McCormack to join the expedition. McCormack accepted our invitation and the 1958 American Karakoram Expedition consisted of four climbers: Swift, Kauffman, McCormack, and me.

Meanwhile Jürg Marmet wrote that the Bally Shoe Company would furnish us with the same type of handmade climbing boots and high-altitude reindeer boots that the 1956 Swiss Everest Expedition had used. It would take eight weeks to make the boots; therefore the fifteenth of February, which was the last day the Bally company could receive the foot outlines and still make the boots in time for the trip, was the deadline for having a definite party. With this deadline only two and a half weeks away, we still needed another climber and a climbing doctor. By now I had an impressive file of letters from the most distinguished mountaineers and climbing doctors in the United States who could not participate in the expedition. I began to call various physicians long-distance. Once I heard myself callously saying, "My heartiest congratulations on your first son, Fred, and when you return to the hospital to see your wife, tell her you want to go to the Karakoram. I'll call you back Sunday." Needless to say, Dr. Fred Dunn could not go.

Dunn suggested Dr. Tom Nevison. It is amazing how one can overlook the obvious. I had first met Nevison in 1952 when he came to Stanford University for advanced study after graduating from Harvard University. He had been the president of the Harvard Mountaineering Club and had participated in an expedition to the Windy Range of the Northern Selkirks in British Columbia. In the spring of 1952 while on a ski tour to Ostrander Lake in Yosemite National Park, I miscalculated the snow texture and broke my left leg. It took my friends and the park rangers twenty-four hours to haul me out. Nevison participated in the rescue and he remained in Yosemite Valley bolstering my morale by soundly beating me at various card games until I was in condition to return to Stanford. I had not seen Nevison since that spring, and while I was going to law school he was attending Harvard Medical School. My invitation to join the expedition caught him by surprise. "Isn't it a bit late to be asking me?" he responded. But Tom is a strong man and an eager mountaineer, and I was not going to let him get away that easily. "Look," I repeated, "we've got the permission and we will never get another opportunity." "Okay, I'll see if I can get away and then I'll let you know," he replied. "While you're checking send me an outline of your feet with two pairs of heavy wool socks on," I added. Nevison became the medical officer.

In the summer of 1957 when it became apparent that our expedition would need more men, I conducted a letter poll of the members for suggestions as to whom we should invite to join us. The first choice of every member was identical—Pete Schoening, a thirty-one-year-old chemical engineer from Seattle, Washington. In 1952 Schoening had led a highly successful expedition to King Peak near Mount Logan in the Yukon. He had been a member of the 1953 American expedition to K2 and it was his belay that held five falling men above 25,000 feet during the retreat off that mountain. In response to our invitation Schoening said that he could not go. In December, when I saw him at the annual meeting of the American Alpine Club and again tried to persuade him to join us, he still insisted that it was impossible for him to break away. For the next two months I kept putting pressure on him, but he still had other commitments. Finally in one of his letters I detected slight signs that he was beginning to waver and I bombarded him with special-delivery letters and long-distance phone calls. With the boot deadline only a few days away he reluctantly agreed to join the expedition. The leader of an expedition should always be the man whom other mountaineers will blame for the results of the trip regardless of whether he is in a position of authority. By unanimous consent of the members of the party, Pete Schoening was elected leader.

Just before Schoening agreed to go I received a letter from the Sports Control Committee of the Pakistani army stating that Lieutenant Mohd Akram and Captain N. A. Soofi would be our Pakistani mountaineers. Enclosed in the letter were the officers' measurements and the precious foot outlines. We had our team.

With the exception of Pete Schoening, it was our first try at an Eight Thousander so we relied upon the experience of recent European expeditions. A pattern of success over these mountains had been established, which we intended to follow closely. As we could not count on contributions of equipment and would have to pay for almost everything, we decided to use the finest equipment in the world, regardless of its source. The foot outlines were rushed to Bally. Jürg Marmet and the extremely efficient Swiss Foundation for Alpine Research went to work to obtain our oxygen masks, helmets, and breathing tubes, as well as less exotic equipment such as ice-axes, crampons, snow glasses, silk gloves, and countless other articles. In Paris, Andy Kauffman, assisted by Guido Magnone and Raymond Leininger, ordered butane-gas stoves and the equipment for our high-altitude porters. Kauffman also monitored the progress of our oxygen bottles. Schoening contacted the Weyerhaeuser Timber Company and they agreed to furnish plywood for the porters' boxes we needed to carry our equipment during the approach march. Nevison obtained radios and medical supplies. We also received a transistor shortwave receiver from the Zenith Radio Corporation to pick up weather broadcasts, and Bradford Washburn, director of the Museum of Science in Boston and veteran Alaskan mountaineer, lent us three walkie-talkie radios for inter-camp communication.

Almost every night I stayed up until three in the morning typing coordination bulletins, letters, and appeals for help on the indispensable electric typewriter. There were so many faint carbon copies of the bulletin that most of the recipients were unable to tell exactly what was happening. I had a strict priority system for determining who got legible copies. John Oberlin got the original by virtue of being president of the American Alpine Club. I kept the first carbon and distributed the other copies in accordance with the importance of each person's task in that particular bulletin. Nevison began to flood the mail with medical bulletins and Lawrence Coveney, who had been head of the New York office of an international trading company before he retired, sent out numerous reports concerning the impending shipping deadlines. At the bottom of my copy of one bulletin in which he pleaded with everyone to hurry up and get the supplies to the transfer company in New York, Coveney scrawled, "Do you really think that it is all going to get here on time?"

Already it was too late to order our food in the United States and still have it packaged into approach march, base camp, and high-altitude rations. I remembered Len Frank, a book dealer and member of the Alpine Club, whom I had met when I went through England in 1956. I had been overweight for the plane flight back to Iceland and he graciously shipped my pitons and other hardware to me without any facetious remarks about the decadence of the younger generation. Len readily agreed to help procure our food as well as our air mattresses and wind suits. Originally I had hoped that the firm that had furnished the food for the British Everest and Kangchenjunga expeditions would handle our order, as both those expeditions had been eminently successful and I had never heard any violent complaints about the food. However, Len Frank and I quickly learned that once a company has gone through the ordeal of furnishing and packaging food for a three-month trip, it never wants to do it again.

Len was getting desperate when his wife woke him up in the middle of the night and said, "Why not try Hudson Brothers?" Hudson Brothers referred him to its subsidiary firm, Peter Keevil & Sons, which did not realize what it was getting into and agreed to handle the order.

The previously hectic pace became more frenzied as the shipping deadlines approached. Crisis after crisis broke over us in ever increasing waves as this phase of the expeditionary tide swelled toward its crest, sweeping all of us before it. The bar examination began to descend upon me like the blade of a guillotine. Every expedition member was instructed as to what items he should beg, borrow, or, as a last resort, buy; and in the United States, England, France, and Switzerland lamps burned late into the night. Schoening took charge of the remaining details of the United States shipment and he and Coveney nipped at the heels of our suppliers like a couple of hungry wolves after a herd of deer. Gerry Cunningham shipped his eight high-altitude tents at the last minute. Allen Steck of the Ski Hut in Berkeley barely managed to get our rucksacks to the port. The Eddie Bauer Company in Seattle put our sleeping bags and down clothing on a fast truck heading east. Swift checked into our order of mountain pants and wrote, "They mailed them yesterday, which was fortunate. You should have seen their faces when they found out that we aren't being sponsored by the government. I suggest you pay them as soon as we get some money." Drugs, film, pitons, rappel pickets, pliers, and other small but indispensable items poured into the transfer warehouse to be crated for immediate overseas shipment. Despite Coveney's premonition of disaster, when the S.S. *Flying Enterprise II* sailed from New York, all of our equipment from the United States was on board.

In London Len Frank was having trouble getting our food properly packaged in time to make the early boat, the S.S. *Kulladu.* With my bar examination a week away we exchanged daily cablegrams. Finally I instructed him to ship the food in bulk. They could dump it down the hatch, as long as the food got on board. On Monday morning, March 11, the day before the examination began, I received another cablegram, which read, "All well, food will be on Kallada, Len." I breathed a sigh of relief, picked up some law outlines, and began to cram furiously. Then workmen from the city street department began to tear up the alley with jackhammers.

When I returned to my house from the bar examination, there was just a small stack of letters and telegrams to add to the twenty pounds of paper piled on top of my letter that began, "Dear Dr. Houston. . ."

I put thirty-five crates of mountaineering books and one record player into storage and began the long trip to Orosi, San Francisco, Dallas, and points east. I was to be the vanguard of the expedition. After checking on our shipments from England, France, and Switzerland and learning from

Jürg Marmet how to use the oxygen equipment, I was supposed to arrive in Karachi sufficiently ahead of the rest of the party to get our equipment out of customs and sent to Rawalpindi. Perhaps with a little luck I could even get the equipment flown to Skardu before May 13, when the rest of the party was scheduled to reach Pakistan.

Although Dick Irvin and Gil Roberts could not leave the United States until June 6, we had been promised a special contribution for the specific purpose of having them come in later to reinforce us. First we had to find out if they would be allowed to make a separate approach march. On March 22, when I visited Irvin in Orosi, California, he and I agreed that I would send him a cablegram from Karachi if it was all right for the two of them to join the main party.

That night I left Irvin's house and drove to Swift's cottage in Moss Beach. On the way I stopped for gasoline at a service station near Fresno. I have been in the mountains since I was nine years old and although I once broke my leg skiing, I have never been injured climbing. Reentering my car I was completely preoccupied with the problems of the expedition and failed to open the door wide enough, with the result that I gashed my forehead against the edge of the window and had to have the wound sewed up at the local hospital. As I drove on to Swift's house I suddenly realized how dangerous Himalayan expeditions are. Already I had three stitches in my head and I was still in the United States!

When I got to Dallas there was the usual pile of correspondence. Andy Kauffman wanted to know how many butane-gas stoves we could afford to buy. I instructed him to get as many stoves as he thought necessary and Kauffman promptly got the stoves, oxygen bottles, and other equipment shipped out of France. The Pakistan Army Sports Control Committee wrote that Captain Soofi could not participate but that Captain S. T. H. Rizvi, who had been with the 1957 Manchester Himalayan Expedition that attempted Masherbrum (25,660 feet) would take his place. Rizvi had climbed to 22,500 feet on that mountain and knew the region extremely well. His measurements were the same as Captain Soofi's, except that his feet were a size larger. It was impossible to change the order for our boots so it seemed that Rizvi was going to get sore feet. Also there was a personal letter from Rizvi, which contained much useful information. His most important advice was that we should have two persons who could use the expedition's letter of credit. The treasurer of his prior expedition had died of pneumonia.

I established an expedition bank account and had all the members of the party sign waivers of liability in the event of an accident. Also everyone agreed that if by a miracle the expedition made a profit it would go to the expedition fund of the American Alpine Club.

There was one more problem. Every major Himalayan expedition has to have a treasurer who stays behind to handle the accounts and stall off the creditors. There were no volunteers for this job, so I gave it to my long-suffering father. Like most responsible citizens, my parents are unenthusiastic about mountaineering. However, they learned years ago that I was going to climb anyway so they have tried to make my various trips successful. Besides, I could always end my father's occasional remonstrances by reminding him that at the age of seventeen he had run off and joined the French army as an ambulance driver in World War I. After presenting the expedition files to my father, I was ready to leave for Pakistan.

4

TO SKARDU

My parents and grandmother have had considerable experience in watching me depart from the Dallas airport on various expeditions; they now maintain a cheerful countenance at such farewells. "Be careful," was my mother's final advice as I turned to board the aircraft on April 4. With my blue air force bag, my overloaded briefcase, my wooden box that contained the movie camera, and other cameras and binoculars slung across my father's partially-mildewed

World War II trench coat, I was a parody of the American tourist. But my cowboy hat really made all the bystanders stare and shake their heads. I had obtained ten-gallon hats for all members of the expedition, not only to protect us against the sun and rain during the approach march but also to give us a feeling of common identity. The hats proved to be an excellent source of morale, but it was a mental strain to have to wear them all the way to Karachi, especially for Bob Swift and Pete Schoening, who wore two hats each on their heads because there was no other way to deliver the hats that were earmarked for Rizvi and Akram. "We would have attracted less attention if we had had two heads," commented Swift at the end of his ordeal. Sometimes the strain was not merely mental. One hotel that I had previously visited wearing my air force uniform doubled the rate on me for a room that was identical to my prior accommodation.

I spent several days in Summit, New Jersey, with Lawrence Coveney, checking last-minute details about our shipping invoices. After promising Coveney, who had been the expedition's champion from its inception, that we would not quit until the mountain was climbed or our food ran out, I left for Europe.

Len Frank met me in London with a briefcase full of shipping documents, customs declarations, and food lists. He had good news. By working twenty-four hours a day, our food suppliers had packaged our food into approach march, base camp, and high-altitude rations. This would save us at least one day at Base Camp since we now would not have to reorganize the food.

There was still the matter of obtaining insurance for our high-altitude porters, a typical detail that makes expeditions such time-consuming monsters. As I did not know what indemnity was required if a high-altitude porter was killed or injured, I went over to the Alpine Club where I was referred to the Everest Foundation, which has a room in the basement of the same building. A very nice lady courteously dug through stacks of documents that occupied cabinets, closets, the desk, and even overflowed onto the floor. Although she produced enough information on mountaineering in Nepal to document a Ph.D. dissertation, she found nothing about insurance rates for high-altitude porters in the Karakoram. Making a wild guess I insured the men for 1,000 rupees (approximately $213) each. Later I learned that it should have been 2,000 rupees.

After thanking Len once again for his assistance, I flew to Paris. My two days there with Andy Kauffman were spent pounding the keyboard of a typewriter and visiting a few mountaineers. M. Vergne of L'Appareil Medical de Precision, the company that filled our oxygen bottles and manufactured our regulators, took Andy and me on a tour through his shop, where craftsmen were filling and checking the oxygen bottles for our future neighbors in the Karakoram, an Italian expedition that was going to

East meets West. Tom Nevison shares an instant picture with his train steward.

attempt Gasherbrum IV. That evening we had dinner at the home of Kauffman's friend Raymond Leininger, who had been invaluable in assisting Andy with our supplies in France. The next day I had lunch with Jean Couzy and his charming wife, Lise. Couzy had done a superb job in getting our oxygen bottles produced soon enough for us to use them. The genuine enthusiasm displayed by these French mountaineers for the success of our expedition on a mountain their countrymen had pioneered demonstrated how the common bond of mountaineering transcends national frontiers.

Jürg Marmet had promised to teach us how the oxygen apparatus worked and on April 19 Kauffman and I went on our different ways to Basel, Switzerland. We had reserved one oxygen bottle for instructional purposes. It was pressurized beyond all legal limits so Andy had to take the train, cuddling the menace in his arms, while I flew. Marmet had never seen Kauffman, but he had no difficulty in spotting a yellow bottle of oxygen in the Basel train station. My plane arrived later that evening.

Marmet spread helmets, masks, breathing bags, rubber tubes, valves, gauges, and oxygen regulators over the dining room table in his apartment and began to brief us on the equipment that he had so painstakingly obtained for our expedition. Outside, the Rhine flowed quietly toward the sea; inside the conversation never dipped below 23,000 feet.

The total oxygen apparatus for one man weighed 14½ pounds. It consisted of a cylindrical oxygen container that was made of aluminum alloy and wrapped with piano wire for greater strength and held 4 liters, at a pressure of approximately 230 atmospheres. Thus each bottle contained about 920 liters of oxygen at sea level. The regulator screwed directly to the container and could be adjusted to allow a flow rate of ½, 1, 2, 3, or 4 liters to the minute. It also had a built-in manometer, which measured the amount of pressure remaining in the bottle. A hose led from the regulator to a bladder, which served as a reservoir for a continual supply of oxygen and attached directly to the oxygen mask. The oxygen entered the mask through an intake valve and mixed with air that entered through three separate intake valves, one of which was made out of mica and was mounted in the nose of the mask; the other two were rubber valves located on each side. The mask attached to a light flying helmet by snaps on one side and a wire hook on the other. Jürg pointed out all the places where stoppages might occur, as well as how to diagnose the trouble and then correct it. We were drilled in reading the manometer and calculating instantly how many minutes of oxygen remained in the bottle at a given flow rate. After a lengthy discussion about flow rates for climbing and sleeping at different altitudes, Jürg said, "The main thing is to use the amount of oxygen that makes you feel comfortable." He also emphasized that we should move the oxygen equipment up the mountain together with the food and other essential supplies instead of waiting to bring it up at the last minute for the final assault. This would enable us to take advantage of any sudden favorable break in the weather.

We were greatly worried about pneumonia, which is a swift killer in the thin air of the Himalaya, but Marmet finished his lecture by telling me that a climber on his expedition to Everest in 1956 was cured by antibiotics and a steady administration of oxygen. "Of course, you will have to write off six bottles of oxygen for every pneumonia case, but a friend's life is worth it," he said dryly. Andy Kauffman was selected to be the oxygen officer for the expedition. He then returned to Paris while I remained with the Marmets for another week.

After the skiing accident in 1952, my left leg had never returned to normal strength; however, it did not bother me until January, 1958, when my left knee began to feel as if there were sand in the joint. I ignored it, hoping that the pain was temporary and would go away. But by the time I reached Switzerland I could barely walk up the three flights of stairs to the Marmets' apartment. I went to the Burgerspital in Basel where my knee was X-rayed. Apparently the only thing wrong was a little osteoarthritis in the kneecap. Dr. Hans Baumann gave me several injections of cortisone and said that I could go on the expedition with his blessing. I was going regardless, but it was reassuring to have medical approval.

I had always imagined the Swiss Foundation for Alpine Research as a large impersonal organization that ran model Himalayan expeditions and published the finest mountaineering annual in the world as a matter of course. So when I went to Zurich to visit the foundation, which had taken such an interest in our expedition, I was surprised to discover that its public front consisted of two people. There was the usual indispensably efficient secretary, Fernande Spichiger, who kept insisting that she was merely the "lucky instrument" of the foundation as she dispatched numerous wires and letters in our behalf, and Othmar Gurtner, the editor of *The Mountain World.* Other people behind the scenes included Dr. Karl Weber, the founder and president, and Ernst Feuz, the manager, who helped to obtain our equipment.

Miss Spichiger took me to the warehouse where our climbing boots were being crated. The reindeer boots were quite impressive. There was no difficulty in spotting the pair for Bob Swift. They could have substituted for snowshoes. As I gazed upon them lovingly, I remembered Marmet's words: "No mountaineer wearing reindeer boots has ever been frostbitten—yet!"

Despite everything the foundation had already done for us I was still unprepared for the shock when Mr. Gurtner said, "Don't worry about our bill. You can wait and see how your financial situation is at the end of the trip before anything is done about payment. We know how it is with expeditions." It was a great temptation to accept this generous offer, but I insisted that we pay for everything immediately. Just as I was leaving his office Gurtner added, "All of us hope that your expedition is successful. You deserve it after all the pioneering Americans have done in the Himalaya."

American mountaineers generally dislike flag-waving on summits, but people expect flags to be hauled to the top of unclimbed Himalayan mountains, so we had obtained some small American, Pakistani, and Texas pennants. Besides, the Swiss took flags to the top of Everest and they usually do not do things that are in bad taste. However, British, Swiss, and French mountaineers had done everything they could to get our expedition into the field and by coincidence Hidden Peak had been explored by mountaineers of the same nationalities. In order to emphasize that our expedition not only stood on the shoulders of its predecessors but also was the result of a tremendous international effort, we now added British, French, and Swiss pennants to our collection. Later, the higher camps on Hidden Peak resembled a United Nations conference building, as a multitude of flags waved in the breeze from the tent poles.

Before I left Switzerland there was one other important thing I had to do. The last expedition to Hidden Peak had been in 1936 and we had very little information about the mountain. What was the high snow plateau like? And what was the best route for reaching it? The French spur seemed extremely difficult and the southwest ridge pioneered by André Roch seemed extremely long. Roch was serving his annual tour of military service in the Swiss army, but Jürg Marmet made arrangements for me to meet him in Pontresina.

Upon arriving in that village I went straight to my hotel room and began to study some photographs of Hidden Peak. Suddenly I became aware of someone in a military uniform standing quietly in the doorway. It was André Roch, veteran of five Himalayan expeditions and the man who knew more about Hidden Peak than any other person. After several minutes of friendly conversation I was forced to call him André instead of Mr. Roch. "This is the way the French went," he said, pointing at the photograph I was holding, "but I think our way here is better. Hans Ertl and I climbed to 20,600 feet in only a few hours and without wearing crampons. You can establish a dump halfway up the slope. Of course, it must be anchored so that small avalanches will not carry it away. From a camp here," he continued, still pointing at the photograph, "you can climb to the top of the ridge. You will have to put in fixed ropes, but then it should be all right." Although André thought that his southwest ridge could be climbed, he also suggested that we carefully reconnoiter the entire mountain before making a final decision on the route. Listening to him I tried diplomatically to phrase my fundamental doubt about his route. Professor Dyhrenfurth had said that the southwest ridge was straightforward and now so did André, but still I was uncertain. Mountaineers of the ability of Roch and Hans Ertl do not turn back on easy routes. André continued to describe the advantages of the southwest ridge and finally I could no longer contain myself. "If it's so simple, why didn't you and Ertl push it?" I blurted. "Oh, it was our first trip to the Himalaya and we weren't sure about what we were doing," he replied with a broad grin. By this honest statement André Roch put our expedition on the route that we followed to the summit.

The trouble with visiting Switzerland is that one has to leave it. Unfortunately between tender farewells and heroic welcomes it is considered customary to make at least an attempt at one's objective so I resumed my journey to Karachi. There was a flurry of last-minute activity when I remembered that the expedition did not have an altimeter. Just before I departed from Zurich, Fernande Spichiger located an aneroid altimeter in a cardboard container that had the notation "8,000 meters" on it. Grabbing it, I assured her that we could guess at the last 68 meters on the mountain.

It was April 29 when I reached Karachi and with the remainder of the expedition due to arrive in only two weeks, I promptly phoned our shipping agents. John Mouat, a Scotsman with a dry sense of humor, who was the head of the shipping department, and his assistant, Waheed, immediately came to my hotel room and over the inevitable cup of tea and under the useless ceiling fan, they began to describe graphically the vagaries of the shipping industry and business conditions in Karachi generally. "It's like shoveling sand against the tide," said Mouat resignedly. Not only was the *Flying Enterprise II* a few days behind schedule but there also was a five-day berthing delay for all freighters at the port as some of the wharves were being repaired and others were occupied by wheat boats from the United States, which required ten days to unload. However, our supplies from Europe had arrived and were sitting around somewhere in the hot customs shed. All that had to be done was to obtain a customs clearance.

I had requested that Captain Rizvi meet me in Karachi and that evening he arrived. He was a twenty-five-year-old officer in the Twentieth Lancers Regiment of the Pakistan Army Armored Corps and a descendant of the Prophet Mohammed. His full name is Syed Tasawer Hussein Shah Rizvi Khaurazmi. We called him Tas. An outgoing individual, he knew every important official in Rawalpindi and Skardu, exactly what governmental permits we still needed, and how to purchase supplies from the army quartermaster in Skardu. He was an important addition to the party, and during the critical days of the approach he would prove absolutely indispensable. When we met he had more advice. "Don't ship the food and equipment to Rawalpindi on a freight train. Our Masherbrum expedition did that last year and we spent two weeks trying to locate our food while it sat on a siding in the Sind desert in the 110-degree heat, slowly rotting!" After Rizvi and I made up a list of what had to be done in Karachi and Rawalpindi, we decided that he should return to the latter city and start making the necessary arrangements there. "I'll fly up in a few days as soon as we get the gear out of customs," I said naively.

Every year in Karachi during the last two weeks of April and the first two weeks in May a few harassed individuals can be seen scurrying from governmental ministries to foreign embassies at a frantic pace. These are the advance men for the various expeditions to the Karakoram who are trying to smooth the way for the main party. When the paths of these persons cross, they stop and exchange heartrending stories of unobtained permits, misshipped supplies, and other tales of woe. The first two weeks in May of 1958 were no exception.

There was Mike Banks, who was trying to get his governmental permit switched from Distaghil Sar ("It's an avalanche trap") to Rakaposhi. He had just about accomplished this when several crates of his supplies were unloaded at Bombay by mistake. When I last saw him, he was disappearing into the depths of the British High Commission in an effort to straighten this out. Then there was Dr. Hans-Jochen Schneider from Munich, who was attempting to get permission for a German Alpine Club expedition into the Batura region of the Karakoram. Dr. Schneider was a constant source of inspiration. No matter how badly I had fared during the day, he had done worse. We always had lunch together and he invariably greeted me with, "In Karachi, we learn the virtues of patience." He had been there two weeks before I arrived, learning the virtues of patience, and eventually left Pakistan without obtaining his permit. Finally there was Dr. Fosco Maraini. A highly educated journalist who speaks many languages fluently, and who had made several expeditions into Tibet, he was the advance man for the Italian expedition to Gasherbrum IV. Both our expeditions would be making the identical approach march up the Baltoro Glacier, and when Fosco and I met we cautiously exchanged information. "We wanted Hidden Peak originally," he said, "but you had the permission so now we have to attempt Gasherbrum IV instead. We felt that there was a way up Hidden Peak, but our mountain. . .!" I sympathized with him but pointed out that their party was extremely strong and that both expeditions were on mountains that were suited to their capabilities. After this pleasant banter we got down to more fundamental questions. "How much equipment do you have?" Fosco asked. "About three tons," I replied. "And your party?" "Seven tons," he answered. At this moment it became apparent to both of us that our expeditions could not march in together because of the shortage of men in Baltistan needed to carry ten tons of supplies and that someone would have to be first. There was only one way the issue could be determined. We politely wished each other the best of luck and the race was on.

The entire Italian expedition with their seven tons of equipment was not due to arrive until May 12, while two tons of our gear was already in Karachi. But the Italians were on the express ship—S.S. *Victoria* out of Genoa—which, as a passenger vessel, would get a berth immediately upon arrival, while the *Flying Enterprise II* would have to wait for space. Also, the rest of our expedition would not arrive until May 13. It was going to be close. Dr. Maraini and I danced a lively minuet through the various governmental ministries. Upon meeting we would exchange polite inquiries into each other's progress and then dash off in opposite directions in a desperate effort to expedite matters. Occasionally we would have dinner together and console each other about our respective lack of progress.

Every day I made the tour of governmental ministries to obtain our customs clearance. Every noon I returned to John Mouat's office to be greeted by his cheery, "And what did you accomplish this morning?" The routine was always the same. Starting with the foreign ministry we would have an appointment with a deputy minister, who always was extremely polite. After we had tea together, the official would make a phone call and within a few minutes a subordinate would arrive with our papers. The deputy minister would sign them, wish us the very best of luck, and say that our papers would be forwarded to the next ministry in the chain. We would thank him very much and after taking the precaution of obtaining the reference number of the letter of transmittal, would depart. For eight days Waheed and I followed our clearance papers. Meanwhile the *Flying Enterprise II* arrived off port; Fosco, his customs difficulties solved, left for Rawalpindi; and Rizvi kept meeting every evening flight of Pakistan International Airlines only to return to his quarters and find the daily telegram that I dispatched every morning saying that I was delayed "for one more day."

On May 8 Mouat had just sent a cablegram to New York saying that the *Flying Enterprise II* would be sitting off port for another three days when the harbormaster phoned and said the vessel could have an immediate berth but that it would have to leave the dock by Saturday night, May 10, to make way for the S.S. *Victoria*. Captain Kurt Carlsen had maintained steam in some of the boilers and he brought the freighter into port at once. Slowly the longshoremen began to unload the cargo.

By Friday, May 9, our clearance papers arrived in the last ministry before going to the chief collector of customs, but the minister concerned was out of his office. Now desperate, Waheed and I went to the chief collector and explained our situation. "Of course, I'll give you a customs clearance pending formalities," he said. "Just give me a list of all your supplies." I was stunned. If we had done this in the first place, our equipment would have been cleared within twenty-four hours after arriving in Karachi.

I returned to Mouat's office and collapsed in a chair. There was a pile of letters for me stacked on his desk and I opened the top one, which was from Jürg Marmet. "Probably just a reply to my thank-you note," I thought, ripping open the envelope. It was a carbon copy of a letter sent to Andy Kauffman. Our crate of boots had been put on a slow freighter by mistake. Impossible! I went back and read the letter again carefully. Our boots were to have been shipped on the S.S. *Victoria*, but the shipping company had reserved all space for the Italian expedition's supplies and the local agent of the freight forwarder failed to explain the importance of our crate of footwear. The agent tried to phone the forwarding company and the Swiss Foundation for Alpine Research, but it was May Day and no one was there. So the crate of boots was loaded on the next ship heading for Karachi, a tramp steamer called the S.S. *Erria*, which was out on the Mediterranean crawling toward the Suez Canal at six knots before the Swiss Foundation was informed of the error.

My little world exploded. The freighter was not due in Karachi until May 21. I looked up at Mouat. "There'll still be a five-day berthing delay here, won't there?" "Yes, I'm afraid so," he answered quietly. Our only hope was to get the boots off the freighter at Port Said and have them flown to Karachi. Already the Swiss Foundation and the forwarding agency were bombarding the captain of the S.S. *Erria* with letter-length radiograms pleading with him to unload the crate of boots at all cost. Looking up at Mouat again, I said, "That crate probably will be buried in the hold under tons of other cargo, won't it?" "I would say that most likely it is," he replied. Then I glanced up at the calendar and realized to my horror that the freighter was due in Port Said the next day, May 10. Fervently wishing that American and Egyptian relations were not so strained, I dashed over to the American embassy and spilled out my troubles to Goodwin Cooke, the second secretary. We sent a message to the American consul in Port Said and our shipping agents also sent a telegram to their correspondents to check into the situation.

Other difficulties suddenly arose. Up in Lahore, a servant to a political leader shoved a knife through the ribs of his employer. There were demonstrations in Karachi and the police reserves were called out. Also, the longshoremen decided to go on a one-day sympathy strike and there would not be enough time to unload the *Flying Enterprise II* completely before the *Victoria* preempted the berth. "Please try to get our ton of gear out, John," I feebly begged. "We'll do the best we can," he sighed.

On Saturday, May 10, Waheed and I made the rounds once more. I wanted to make the Chenab Express, which left that night for Rawalpindi, and we needed special permission in order to get the first two tons of our equipment into a baggage car. It was eleven o'clock when we visited the stationmaster. "Please submit your request in writing," he said. Thinking, "Here we go again," I scrawled out the request on a piece of expedition stationery. To my amazement he simply stamped it "Approved" and we had our special permit.

Except for the equipment on the *Flying Enterprise II*, all the supplies were brought down to the depot and weighed. I made one last check of my papers, sent a wire telling Irvin and Roberts it was all right for them to march in separately, requested Mouat to keep me informed as to what happened to our boots, and went down to the station. "After all this, it will really be something if your party climbs the mountain," said John as we parted. "Especially if we climb it barefooted," I replied. As the Chenab Express pulled out of the station, Waheed, who was trotting alongside, instructed the dining-car steward to serve me eggs, toast, and tea for the duration of the journey and as he disappeared amid the mass of humanity crowding the platform, I heard him shout, "Good luck!"

The 900-mile train ride across the Sind desert to Rawalpindi was hot and dusty and lasted two days. An overhead fan that blew directly down upon a block of ice mounted inside a washtub was a slight help. There were no inside passageways on the cars and at every stop the dining-car stewards ran along outside the train taking orders and shoving trays through the compartment windows. The Express stopped so frequently that there never was any delay in getting meals. As the train picked up speed there would be a half-dozen waiters holding stacks of trays waiting along the track to swing aboard the dining car as it flew by. Watching this never-ending phenomenon, I began to wonder how many waiters went under the wheels of the train during one trip. Rizvi met me at the Rawalpindi station with a truck, which carried us and the two tons of equipment out to his quarters at the Twentieth Lancers Officers' Mess.

The next problem was to get the expedition flown from Rawalpindi to Skardu. Before World War II all expeditions had reached Skardu by marching from Srinagar, Kashmir, over the Zoji-la and down the Indus River. After the partition of the subcontinent into the countries of India and Pakistan, there was a struggle for Kashmir, which left that country divided by a cease-fire line that no one could pass. This line cuts off the regular trade routes between the upper part of Kashmir, known as Baltistan, and the rest of the world. As Baltistan is a barren country with a submarginal economy, it must import large quantities of food, especially wheat, and the only connecting link between it and Pakistan is by air. Old DC-3s owned and operated by Pakistan International Airlines constantly fly the 190 miles from Rawalpindi to Skardu through some of the highest mountains in the world. All priorities for the flights are determined by the air transport officer of the Ministry of Kashmir Affairs. Already Fosco had been making arrangements to have the Italian expedition flown into Skardu, but as we had two-thirds of our baggage with us, we could get it booked. After Rizvi and I went to the main office of the Ministry of Kashmir Affairs where they checked our papers and wished us luck, we went down to the office of the air transport officer. Our horse-drawn tonga pulled up in front of a building that was completely hidden by piles of boxes and flour sacks stacked up even with the roof.

Malik H. Naseem, the air transport officer for the Ministry of Kashmir Affairs, had long since resigned himself to being eternally unpopular. He was a former all-India boxing champion and this spirit seemed to be his only support. He was not afraid of anyone. "There is a 400-plane backlog on freight and I have the names of 300 people on the passenger list," he said over the usual cup of tea. "Also, the planes are not flying and have not been flying for weeks because of the weather. To get to Skardu they must fly up the Indus Gorge, which is so narrow that a plane cannot turn around, so the pilots are reluctant to enter it when there is even the smallest cloud hovering inside. However, expeditions have top priority so bring your stuff down and we will see what can be done for you."

When Rizvi and I returned to the officers' mess we met Lieutenant Mohd Akram, who was looking for us. Like Rizvi, Akram graduated from the Pakistan Military Academy and was in an infantry regiment stationed at Lahore. Although he attended the Pakistan army's mountain warfare school, this was his first expedition. In contrast to Rizvi, he is extremely quiet and reserved. He would have an initial period of bad luck on the expedition, but toward the end of the trip he would prove to be extremely tough and capable, and an ideal man for an expedition. As we discussed plans in the officers' mess he said little but agreed to fly to Skardu with our first two tons of equipment and begin to make arrangements for the approach march.

That evening Rizvi and I went over to the house of Bill and Buster Goodwin, who have entertained every mountaineering expedition that has gone through Rawalpindi in recent years. A dust storm hung 500 feet in the air over the city, casting a weird amber glow on everything. The four of us together with R. Trevor Braham of the Himalayan Club, who was joining a British expedition to Minapin, sat on the front porch in the yellow light as it tried to rain. Suddenly a bolt of lightning flashed through the gloom and struck a tree about a hundred yards away. The lightning increased but only a few drops of moist dust fell. "Strangest winter we've had in years," said Buster Goodwin, as our moods began to match the surrounding atmosphere. "It's been a late winter in the Karakoram, which means that the monsoon should be late or perhaps not even strike the range at all this year," said Rizvi, trying to cheer us up. "Can we depend on that?" I asked. "No," he said, and then it was quiet as the five of us became absorbed in our private speculations, punctuated by the thunder. But on Wednesday, two days later, the first aircraft in weeks slipped through the Himalaya to Skardu, carrying Akram and our first two tons of supplies.

On Thursday morning, May 15, Schoening, Swift, Kauffman, and Nevison arrived, looking like apparitions from a sheriff's nightmare as they stepped off the Khyber Mail wearing ten-gallon hats. "Howdy, pardner," drawled Seattleite Schoening. "Got a surprise for you," added Swift, pulling his right arm from behind his back to reveal a cast that reached to his elbow. Two days before leaving California Bob had smitten his desk trying to restore decorum to his classroom. To the delight of the students, he accidentally struck the edge instead of the center of the desk and broke his little finger. "The cast can be taken off when we reach Base Camp," chirped Nevison. "He has to wear it for only three weeks." Normally I would have been upset by this development, but I knew that the only lasting effect it would have on Swift would be to make him more determined to climb the mountain.

They had the one ton of equipment from the *Flying Enterprise II* with them and Tom McCormack was following them one day later with our wayward crate of boots. Once again the Swiss Foundation had accomplished the impossible. The boots had been off-loaded at Port Said and flown to Karachi in time to avoid delaying our expedition.

My companions' journeys to Karachi had not been without incident. Schoening and Swift were delayed in leaving New York for Paris when the airline company with which they had booked passage claimed that someone had canceled their reservations. Catching a later plane, they arrived in Paris barely in time to join Kauffman and Nevison for the flight to Karachi. The day after the four of them departed for Pakistan, the French army in Algeria revolted and all plane flights over France were temporarily halted. As usual we were proceeding smoothly just one step ahead of disaster.

Tom McCormack arrived the next day with the boots. At twenty-three, the youngest member of the party, Tom has the misfortune of being good-natured, and so got saddled with many of the unpleasant tasks of the expedition. When other methods of persuasion such as the rigged flipping of coins failed, the rest of us would appeal to his sense of duty and team spirit, which always worked.

By now the entire Italian expedition had arrived in Rawalpindi and was staying at Flachmanns Hotel. Friday evening, reinforced by the arrival of McCormack, which put our expedition at full strength, we descended upon them like outlaws on a wagon train. We caught the Italians in the dining room just as they were finishing dinner. They were extremely cordial and all of us adjourned to a neighboring room, where we sat alternately at a long table. Then we groped for a language that the person nearest us could understand. Fosco Maraini was the principal center of communications while Andy Kauffman conversed in French at the far end of the table. Several of the Italians knew a little English and McCormack and I tried out our inadequate Spanish on Carlo Mauri, who spoke it also. Riccardo Cassin, the leader of the Italian expedition and veteran of some of the most difficult climbs in the Alps, gave the impression that any granite block that fell on him would come out second best. The appearance of Walter Bonatti, Carlo Mauri, Toni Gobbi, and the rest of the members of the expedition belied their fantastic reputations, but we knew that if this group of Italians could not climb Gasherbrum IV, given a break in the weather, that mountain was going to remain unclimbed for a long, long time. After a very pleasant evening we wished them the best of luck and walked back to our quarters in the Twentieth Lancers mess.

On Saturday afternoon on the eve of our departure to Skardu the entire expedition, with the exception of Akram who had gone ahead, gathered in Rizvi's room in the officers' mess. Swift and Kauffman were sitting on the couch. Schoening and Nevison were lying on the floor with their heads propped up against the wall. McCormack and I were sprawled over one bed while Rizvi was sprawled over the other. We were congratulating ourselves on our brilliant job of organization in obtaining such excellent equipment and getting it to Rawalpindi on schedule when suddenly Rizvi said, "Say, you wanted to buy some *dekshis* here. It's getting late and the bazaars will soon close. How many do you want?" This gave us a jolt since we had planned on using these locally made cooking pots and as a consequence had brought little else. I turned to Schoening and said, "How many pressure cookers do we have?" "One," he answered. "How many other cooking pots do we have?" I asked. As I had the master checklists I should have known, but this item had escaped me. No one answered. Finally Nevison said, "I brought my Boy Scout cooking kit," and everyone laughed nervously. "But I just brought it in the event of an emergency," he continued. "Do you mean to say it and one pressure cooker are all we have?" A rapid glance at the master equipment list confirmed that we had nothing else. The mess sergeant was promptly dispatched down to the bazaar to purchase twenty-five *dekshis,* which nestled into two-pot kits. Within an hour he returned with our cooking pots and everyone relaxed again.

The next morning, May 18, when Rizvi and I went down to the air transport office, we discovered that for some reason the expedition members had not been booked as passengers although our freight had been cleared. However, Naseem was able to arrange for four of us to fly in to Skardu, while three of us would have to wait until Monday. This was unfortunate because the weather might change and the three men left behind could remain stranded in Rawalpindi indefinitely. We decided to send Rizvi, Schoening, Nevison, and Swift to Skardu first so that they could assist Akram in making arrangements for obtaining porters and start repacking our equipment into sixty-pound loads for the approach march.

The hiring wall, Rest House, Skardu

The four of them, together with Fosco Maraini, left at 9:00 A.M. for Skardu on the first passenger plane. Most of our freight had already been flown in earlier that morning on a cargo aircraft. After the first group departed I was sitting very disconsolately in Naseem's office when he made a phone call to Captain Sahib Zada, a chief pilot for Pakistan International Airlines. Already Captain Zada had made one sortie to Skardu and was getting ready to fly to Gilgit and back, but Naseem persuaded Captain Zada to make a third sortie. Hanging up the receiver Naseem turned to me and said, "Get ready. The three of you will leave for Skardu at two o'clock."

Naseem lent us his jeep and we hurriedly brought our personal baggage to the air transport office to be weighed and then we went to the airport. Earlier we had received a note from Nevison saying that his suitcase and our container of color film had been removed from his aircraft because of overweight and put in the airline office. Arriving at the airport we discovered that the film and suitcase had been sent back to the warehouse at the air transport building. It was too late to retrieve the articles, but the officials promised to send them in on the next flight and we boarded our aircraft.

The flight to Skardu has been accurately described as "the most thrilling commercial plane ride in the world." As Captain Sahib Zada pulled the nose of our heavily laden DC-3 off the runway and pointed it toward the menacing layer of cumulus clouds that was building up over the Himalaya, I thought, "We're never going to make it. The gorge will not be clear." The parched brown earth of the plains gave way to verdant foothills, which merged into the snow-covered rock of the Himalaya. Bare ridges and dull white glaciers reached up toward us as we wallowed through the sky between cloud-shrouded mountains. The plane strained for more altitude as higher peaks loomed ahead. Across the aisle five Baltis sat motionless in their bucket seats. As we reached 17,000 feet Andy Kauffman, who was in the seat behind me, said, "Try to write your name." But already I could feel my fingertips beginning to tingle as my mind became fuzzy and I began systematically to breathe deeply to force more oxygen into my lungs. Off the right wing Nanga Parbat slid by, its summit lost in clouds. After scraping over another ridge we made a diving turn into the Indus Gorge. The bottom of the aircraft seemed to fall out and two brown blurs that were the walls of the canyon raced by the windows. Then the gorge widened into a barren valley surrounded by snow-capped peaks. A dirt runway appeared in the sand below. Cutting the throttles, Captain Zada touched the plane down at the end of the strip and we rolled to a stop in front of a solitary white building. Except for a box of film and a suitcase, the expedition had arrived at Skardu.

5

SUN, SAND,
AND BLISTERS

While the cargo was being unloaded from the plane, McCormack, Kauffman, and I joined the crew in the airport office for a cup of tea, which was hastily downed. The airstrip at Skardu has no facilities for servicing aircraft and Captain Zada was afraid of being grounded by the rapidly descending clouds. The last crate was removed from the DC-3, the doors were slammed shut, the engines started, and the plane began to roll. A few minutes later it was airborne and flying back to Rawalpindi.

Skardu is nine miles from the field, and the airport manager, Mushtag Ahmad, lent us his jeep and trailer to haul our baggage into town. The trailer could not carry all our equipment so McCormack volunteered to remain with the boxes that had to be left behind while Kauffman and I made the first trip. The dirt road was rough and the jeep bounced violently. We were surrounded by peaks 17,000 feet high, with the winter's snow still covering their crests. As we rode through orchards of apricot trees and past irrigated fields of barley, all my past doubts about whether the expedition was worth the effort and sacrifice involved in it disappeared in the overwhelming joy of just being there. Sitting in the back seat, Andy kept saying over and over, "Isn't this something! It's marvelous! Look at them. They're tremendous. This is worth absolutely everything!" At this moment eventual success or failure meant nothing. To be there meant everything.

The rest house in Skardu is probably the most distinguished mountaineering hut in the world. Originally built to accommodate official visitors to Baltistan, it has been the headquarters for most of the expeditions that have visited the town on their way to the Karakoram. That afternoon when Andy and I arrived at the rest house the white mud walls that enclosed it were lined with Baltis who wanted employment as porters for our expedition. Inside the fence our comrades had begun the task of repacking our supplies for the approach march, and the yard was littered with empty crates and equipment. The food and the oxygen did not require repackaging but everything else did. The seven oxygen crates were overweight, but we were permitted to increase the compensation of the men who carried them rather than have to recrate the bottles into lighter loads, which would have been almost impossible.

Back in the United States our biggest problem in obtaining porter boxes had been to find a container that combined a maximum of strength with a minimum of weight. When the porters rest, they drop the boxes on the ground and collapse upon them. Only the most durable materials can take such treatment day after day. Yet every pound of deadweight in the form of containers costs heavily in porters' wages. Pete Schoening had recommended plywood veneer and the Weyerhaeuser Timber Company donated the material, which the Pennsylvania Box and Lumber Company manufactured into boxes according to our specifications. Now under Schoening's vigorous supervision, everyone was building the flattened containers at a rapid pace. I noticed a group of Baltis helping to put the boxes together and asked Rizvi who these men were. "Oh, they're candidates for high-altitude porters who just wanted to help us out," he replied with a wink.

The expedition had been organized so hurriedly that most of our equipment had gone straight from the manufacturers to the ports, and this was the first time we had seen all of it. Sleeping bags, down clothing, wind suits, boots, crampons, climbing pants, and other made-to-order items were issued to each member and placed in individual piles. Community equipment such as tents, stoves, *dekshis*, radios, and climbing ropes were stacked separately. Buried behind an array of pills, bandages, splints, and surgical instruments, Tom Nevison checked and sorted the medical supplies with professional efficiency. Everyone was impressed with the quality of the equipment and even Fosco Maraini, who was an interested spectator, said, "Your equipment is the best I have ever seen."

After the supplies had been checked and arranged into their proper groupings, we established an assembly line to pack them into the plywood veneer containers. As each box was filled an inventory was made of its contents. Then it was either nailed shut or secured with padlocks and banded with fiberglass tape, which was extremely strong and could be removed only by cutting it. The next step was to weigh the container and its contents on a scale that we made by attaching a wooden platform to a spring scale, which was suspended from the beam of the rest house door. As it was difficult to get sixty pounds of equipment, especially the light personal gear, into each box, we either combined two boxes, or a box and another item of supply such as a coil of rope, into one porter load. The articles and boxes that formed one load were fastened together with the fiberglass tape. Finally every load, including the food and oxygen crates, was given a master number, which we painted on each article, together

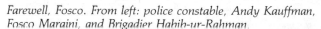

Farewell, Fosco. From left: police constable, Andy Kauffman, Fosco Maraini, and Brigadier Habib-ur-Rahman.

with a symbol of its general contents, by using a can of yellow spray paint that Nevison had brought, and stencils cut out of cardboard. When all the loads had been numbered, a master inventory was typed up in three copies on our portable typewriter.

Watching the boxes pass with machinelike efficiency from the men who packed them, to Schoening and Nevison who banded them, to Kauffman who weighed them, and finally to Swift and McCormack who painted on the master numbers and stacked them ready to be assigned to the porters, an observer could detect one of the underlying themes of the expedition—movement. From the beginning of the trip we were on the move unless prevented from being so by outside circumstances. This constant drive, which became apparent in everything that was done, was probably due to two factors: Schoening's relentless energy, which permeated the entire party, and the belief in everyone's mind that we were racing with the monsoon. Perhaps the monsoon would be late or not even reach the Karakoram at all, but it could strike, and the sooner we reached Hidden Peak the greater our chances of success. A day saved was priceless. Delay was synonymous with failure.

Two-thirds of our supplies were crated and arranged into porter loads before dinner. Messing arrangements at the rest house were simple. We told the cook and his assistant what was wanted, and they obtained the food in the local market and prepared it. Our diet generally consisted of curried lamb or chicken, rice, tea, and apricots for dessert. For bread we ate chupattis, which are pancakes made out of atta, a flour that is the staple of the people of Baltistan. In addition Rizvi usually obtained a few cans of vegetables and fruits from the officers' mess of the local unit of the Northern Scouts. We spent our first dinner trying to persuade Fosco to join our expedition. He, in turn, retaliated by showing us a picture of his pretty daughter. "Does she speak English?" asked McCormack, always quick to grasp the fundamental problems of such a situation.

The territory of Baltistan is governed by a political agent who resides in Skardu. It is a poor barren country of 150,000 inhabitants, and Indian and Pakistani sentries patrol a cease-fire line across the country's trade route to Srinagar so that the submarginal economy has to be supplemented by the airlift from Rawalpindi to Skardu, a precarious undertaking. About twenty Pakistani army officers and governmental officials, who lead lonely lives, run all the public services of the territory. The burden of trying to improve the lot of the inhabitants of Baltistan falls directly upon the shoulders of Brigadier Habib-ur-Rahman Khan, the political agent. It is a Herculean task because the people are illiterate, there is no concept of public sanitation, and communication facilities are nonexistent in that rugged land. Yet progress is being made because of the determination of this remarkable man.

Brigadier Rahman was inspecting the village of Shigar when we arrived in Skardu, but upon returning that evening he invited us to tea at his home, which is next to the rest house. As we sat around his living room, he expressed his belief that only education can break the vicious circle of poverty and ignorance that engulfs the people. He talked with great pride of the six Balti pupils who had just taken their matriculations to allow them to continue with their education. Tomorrow they were going to open the first high school building in Baltistan and he invited us to attend the ceremonies. When our visit was over Schoening gave the brigadier a few packages of seeds of various crops that might flourish in the arid climate of Baltistan.

The next morning we put our assembly line into operation again. While this was being done Schoening, Rizvi, and Akram went down to the supply depot of the Northern Scouts and picked up kerosene, atta, ghee (a form of rancid butter), and the other supplies that we had arranged to purchase for our high-altitude porters. Later, Nevison, Rizvi, and I represented the expedition at the opening of the two-room high school. The political agent cut the ribbon; the pupils, wearing their school uniforms, passed in review accompanied by the roll of drums, and then there were the usual speeches. Nevison photographed the ceremony with a Polaroid camera lent to the expedition by Carlton Fuller, treasurer of the American Alpine Club and a vice-president of Polaroid. Only the night before, the political agent had mentioned how much he would like a portfolio of expedition photographs and when Nevison presented him with pictures of the opening of the high school immediately after the ceremony, he was delighted. The Polaroid camera turned out to be one of the most useful instruments on the entire trip. Whenever we wanted the impossible from our high-altitude porters, we always promised to take photographs that they could send home to their wives. As soon as the local Baltis discovered that Nevison had a camera that produced a finished print, his popularity soared and he was followed constantly by hordes of people who wanted their pictures taken.

That afternoon we had to choose six high-altitude porters from the approximately twenty applicants. Expeditions have gone into the Karakoram continually since 1953 and a corps of experienced HAPs, as we nicknamed the high-altitude porters, is slowly being developed although the quality is still extremely uneven. Brigadier Rahman, who encourages mountaineering expeditions as a means of bolstering the economy, furnished us with a list of names of all the Baltis who had participated in various trips as high-altitude porters. The selection involved quite a ceremony. All the candidates had letters of recommendation from prior expeditions and each man would step forward and present his credentials for Schoening, Rizvi, and me to inspect. These tattered pieces of paper seemed

49

to be their greatest possessions even though they were ignorant of the contents. The recommendations had to be scrutinized with the greatest of care, and a knowledge of what every earlier party had accomplished was extremely important. One expedition had praised all its Baltis in identical glowing language. Four candidates from an expedition that had done some glacier surveying had recommendations stating that each man was the best porter on the trip. We even read a negative report while the Balti concerned stood proudly before us, eagerly awaiting selection. Rizvi knew most of the best men from his Masherbrum expedition, and finally we were able to choose the six men who were to be our constant companions and the backbone of the expedition.

There was Rahim Khan from Khapalu. Extremely powerful, he had carried a seventy-pound load to 23,000 feet on Masherbrum. Tas was inclined to think that he was somewhat dull because of his habit of carrying heavy loads between high camps on his own initiative. If this is stupidity we could have used an army of fools. Mild-mannered Abdul Rahim was the perfect butler as well as a good load-carrier. Mahkmal was a quiet man who never complained. He had made a pilgrimage to a Moslem shrine that was revered almost as much as Mecca itself by his fellow villagers, who, justifiably or not, had given him the title of Haji. Hussein, who had a gray beard, was our oldest HAP. Supposedly he had been on James Waller's expedition to Masherbrum in 1938; and indeed we called him "'38 model." Issac was a husky youngster who had received high recommendations from other expeditions. He was the only HAP who had not been with Rizvi on Masherbrum the year before.

There was only one choice for the critical position of sirdar and that was Ghulam Razul. He knew climbing technique and could keep the other HAPs under control. Moreover, he had some education and understood and spoke a little English. Razul had one disconcerting habit. A former noncommissioned officer in the Pakistani army, he always stood at attention when addressing any of the sahibs. This always made us feel as if we were giving orders for a bayonet charge instead of instructions about what loads should be carried up to the next camp. But there was one drawback. While the other HAPs were farmers or herdsmen back in their local villages, Razul was the chief fireman at the Skardu airstrip and would have to obtain a leave of absence. We considered him invaluable but Mushtag Ahmad was hesitant about letting him go. However, Brigadier Rahman, who by now had taken our expedition under his protective custody, spent fifteen minutes persuading the airport manager to grant Razul the necessary leave and we had our sirdar. Two months later when we returned to Skardu we discovered that Mushtag was in the hospital recovering from a heart attack, which he had sustained a few days after our expedition had departed for Hidden Peak.

Nevison gave the HAPs a complete physical examination and then we issued clothing and low-altitude equipment. All the men had complete sets of climbing clothing from prior trips, but they kept them at home and wore the typical Balti dress of long pajama-style shirts, thin baggy pants, and circular caps. Several of them had light sandals, but most of them were barefoot. The transformation wrought in the appearance of these HAPs by our clothes was amazing. The change was mental also, and from that moment on they identified themselves with the expedition instead of with their fellow Baltis who carried our loads only to Base Camp. There was the usual difficulty in trying to get the clothes and boots to fit them. The clothes were too large and most of the boots were too small. Several of the HAPs had small feet but most of them had the short broad feet that have been the despair of expeditions for years. Eventually we juggled the boots around until everyone could squeeze into a pair without suffering permanent damage to his toes.

That evening Brigadier Rahman gave us a farewell dinner. We had anticipated this and each of us had brought a suit and tie although it was a strong temptation to leave them in Rawalpindi. All the local officials were present at the affair, and about thirty men crowded into the political agent's living room. There was a brief minor crisis when the orange and strawberry punch was brought out and mixed with water. Up to this point we had been very careful to drink only water that we knew had been boiled. It seemed to be a question of insulting our gracious host or taking a chance of becoming disabled. I glanced at Nevison and he shrugged his shoulders noncommittally. Rizvi downed the contents of his glass immediately. Finally all of us decided that politeness was of the utmost importance, especially since we were quite thirsty and the punch looked extremely tempting. Like all forbidden fruit it was delicious, and there were no unhappy consequences. After the punch we had a magnificent dinner of curried chicken, curried lamb, ibex meat, vegetables, boiled rice, salad, fruit, ice cream, and green tea. Brigadier Rahman, who is an excellent hunter, had shot the ibex personally, and the ice cream was made from ice brought down from the nearby mountains by special runner. It was a wonderful evening but everyone had to leave by 9:15 since all the lights went out at 9:30. The electricity for both the rest house and the political agent's home is supplied by a generator in the hospital. Unless there is an emergency operation, the generator is turned off at night in order to save fuel oil, which has to be flown up the Indus Gorge like everything else in Skardu.

Baltistan is a desert country with very little normal precipitation, but when we woke up the next morning it was raining hard. As it continued to pour, we began to wonder how long this freakish weather would keep up.

A plane had brought in our film and Nevison's suitcase the day before and now that everything was packed Schoening wanted to leave immediately for Shigar, which was the end of the first day's march. The rest of us felt that it was impossible to hire all the porters and still move out in time to reach that village before dark. Skardu is near the confluence of the Indus and Shigar rivers and we had to cross the Indus at a point directly in front of the rest house in order to begin our march. It would take at least half a day to shuttle our 112 loads across on an ancient collection of rotting wood that is known as Alexander's Barge, named after an early Balti ruler.

By noon the rain stopped and we decided to hire twenty-five men, which was the absolute maximum the barge could carry on one trip, to relay our loads to the opposite shore. Then we could hire the rest of the porters and instruct them to meet us across the river the next morning, which would give us a good start on the first stage of our march. Rizvi and the police constable, whom the political agent assigned to our expedition to assist us on the march, selected twenty-five porters from the shouting, shoving throng of Baltis who were waiting outside the gates of the fence. These men began carrying our loads down the cliff beyond the rest house. The barge lay on the Indus River below. Kauffman and Rizvi went across with the first boatload of supplies to supervise the operation on the north bank.

Alexander's Barge was shallow and flat-bottomed, and was propelled by four men with long poles whose primary function was to push it far enough out into the current to start it merrily on its way downstream. The rudder man was a tall Balti with long, gray whiskers and a World War II U.S. Army trench coat. Once in a while he would make a feeble attempt to steer. The barge finally ran aground far downstream on the opposite side of the river, and after the twenty-five porters had disembarked, the four bargemen hauled it up the river to make the return crossing. Swift and I took movies of the first two crossings from the top of the bluff, and then I decided to go across on the third run to take closeup shots. Fosco joined me and we had a wonderfully wild ride down the river, which was only slightly marred by the fact that we had to jump out into knee-deep water on the far side. After the fourth trip there were 100 loads across the river, and Andy and Tas returned while Razul and several of the other HAPs unrolled their sleeping bags beside the supply dump.

So far everything had gone smoothly except that we were a group of invalids. Besides my knee and Swift's hand, Schoening, who had never been sick a day in his life, had developed a racking cough just before he left the United States, and he did not get rid of it during the entire trip. Now Akram came down with a fever and a severe attack of bronchitis and had to be hospitalized. He would have to march in later with the Italians. Because of the small size of our party this was a serious loss. However, our collective ill health gave Nevison an unprecedented opportunity to be the first expedition doctor in the history of Himalayan mountaineering to bring his party back in better health than when they had started.

We were up by five the next morning, May 21. The sky was still overcast and scattered clouds hung low upon the surrounding peaks, but it was not raining. After breakfast the political agent arrived to wish us good luck. The day before, I had misplaced our one small Pakistani banner, so I had requested several Pakistani flags from Brigadier Rahman. Now he gave us two banners that some schoolchildren had sat up all night to make.

After one last crossing on Alexander's Barge, we joined the swirling mob of men swarming over our loads on the north side of the Indus. Rizvi and the police constable had drawn up a list of 112 names from the hordes of Baltis who had marched in from miles around looking for a job. The constable called out the name of the first porter, and when the Balti stepped forward, Nevison handed him a metal disk stamped with the number one. Then the HAPs helped him to locate his load. The number on the porter list, the disk number, and the load number had to match. Many Balti names, such as Abdul, Ali, Mohammed, Khan, and combinations thereof, are extremely common and it would have been impossible to keep track of the men by using only the porter roster, although we tried to learn the name of each man's father as well as his home village. Before he was paid, each man had to surrender his metal disk. This prevented us from paying imposters who might claim to have carried a load, only to have to pay the amount again to the real porter when he appeared. Also, at the beginning of each day's march a porter could show us his disk and we could help him find his load.

It took an hour and a half to pass out disks and assign loads to the porters. The men wrapped up their loads with rope made out of goat hair and fastened them in the back with a small piece of wood. Then they shouldered the boxes and propped T-shaped resting-sticks under them. Bob Swift and I were standing apart from the group of porters in order to take movies when the entire mass began to quiver. "Get ready," Bob said. "Somebody stepped on the anthill." The constable's voice rang out, "Mohammed Ali, Mushtag Khan, Ali Mohammed," and a single file of barefoot men streamed out from the mob and began to shuffle across the sand for Hidden Peak, 135 miles away.

The trail climbed up over a rock ridge and entered the Shigar Valley. About halfway through the day's fourteen-mile march I noticed Pete Schoening perched atop a large rock. "Just resting," he lied diplomatically while waiting for me to catch up. Pete had taken it upon himself to carry all our paper money, which amounted to 18,000 rupees and weighed almost fifty pounds. Only the other sahibs knew where our money was and Schoening's welfare suddenly became of vital concern to all of us. Pete and I continued together along the trail, and after walking across more sandy riverbanks and climbing small bluffs, we reached the green irrigated fields and poplar trees that mark the outskirts of the village of Shigar. We arrived at the polo grounds where Schoening had camped in 1953, but our companions were not there. Wandering through the town, Pete and I pointed to our cowboy hats whenever we met an intelligent-looking Balti, who thereupon invariably smiled knowingly and waved us on down the street. Eventually we found our lost comrades on the second floor of the police station, the newest building in the village. They were munching on dried apricots and flipping the pits out the window onto the roofs of neighboring mud houses.

About three in the afternoon there was a loud commotion outside; our porters were arriving. Although stealing is heavily punished in Balti-stan, theft was a special concern to us during the first week of the approach march, since our caravan had to pass through many villages that would be convenient places to dispose of any loot. However, the constable, his assistant, and Ghulam Razul kept the porters' ranks closed, which reduced any opportunity for trifling with the loads. The sight of the long column of men marching through the street below filled us with a sense of awe at the enormousness of our undertaking. They entered the neighboring yard and dropped their boxes.

Rizvi and Kauffman went downstairs to assist the constable in checking the loads. The porters whose boxes contained articles such as cooking utensils and medical supplies that had to be used every day during the approach march were instructed to take them up to the second floor of the police station. The others just stacked their loads in the yard. Nevison and McCormack dug out the transistor receiver and, placing the radio on the balcony rail, turned it on. We had brought this along for the primary purpose of listening to special weather broadcasts from Radio Pakistan, but the receiver, which was our only immediate contact with the outside world, turned out to be more important as a morale booster. Now a great crowd of Baltis, both porters and villagers, gathered underneath the balcony and gaped at the little black box that played music. Nevison spun the dial to pick up a station broadcasting in Urdu and the stares changed to grins. As long as we played the radio, the crowd below remained undiminished.

Some of us had worn light walk-in shoes while others broke in their new climbing boots; at the end of the day's march, only the barefoot porters did not have blisters. Swift's feet were the worst. His right heel was almost raw. "And we're supposed to be going to climb an Eight Thousander," said McCormack. "A week of this and we'll be lucky even to reach the mountain."

"Back in 1953 when I arrived in Shigar, all of us then thought that we were in pretty bad shape, but there was a reporter who had accompanied us for the first stage and his feet were so bad that he had to ride on a *zahk* [raft] back to Skardu," chimed in Pete Schoening merrily. Meanwhile Tom Nevison quietly and methodically bandaged everyone's blisters. When he had finished with our feet, Tom began to arrange empty bottles, needles,

Organized confusion. Porters outside Shigar police station await word from Sahibs on balcony.

and syringes along the top of the medical box. In reply to our suspicious glances he said, "Remember my telling you that in order to get permission to leave my studies I promised that I would do research on this trip. Well, this is going to be my first analysis of blood samples. Who wants to be first?" Volunteers were not immediately forthcoming, but finally Bob Swift, who realized the advantage of getting it over with and then being able to heckle the other unfortunates, stepped forward. Nevison did a fine job or at least I thought so. However, Schoening's veins proved difficult to find and although Tom drew blood after several unsuccessful tries, it left such a black and blue mark on Pete's arm that he was thereafter exempt from the experiment. While a few people thought that Nevison had blundered, most of us suspected that this was just another one of Schoening's many talents. Even Rizvi did not escape and he began to realize exactly what being a member of the climbing team entailed as the needle was rammed into his arm. Despite all the harrassing we gave Nevison, everyone was deeply interested in the results of the experiment to determine who was acclimatized and who was dehydrated, although one's opinion of the validity of the test depended upon one's rank in the standings.

Shigar was the last place where cavalry officer Rizvi could go riding so he and several other sahibs left the police station to borrow a couple of horses from the mir of Shigar. Suddenly there was a clatter of horsehooves in the street as Rizvi and Schoening, who was bent far forward in the saddle with his elbows flapping, went galloping past in a wild charge toward

55

the polo field. I was not too concerned about Pete's safety, since his pony was so small he could have stepped off it at any time—until the animal returned much later with Bob Swift sitting quietly astride it.

The direct route from Shigar to the last village of Askole and then to the Baltoro Glacier is through the Skoro La, a 16,700-foot pass through the Mango Gusor range between the two villages. However, this route is blocked with snow until August and we had to march all the way around the chain and ascend the Shigar Valley to where the Basha and Braldu rivers flow together to form the Shigar River and then up the Braldu Valley to the Baltoro Glacier.

The next morning we arose at four-thirty and had the porters on the march by seven. These early starts not only avoided much of the heat of the day, but also usually allowed us to arrive at our destination in the early afternoon, which gave us plenty of time to establish camp, check in the loads, and hold a sick call for the local inhabitants. While our companions went ahead, Pete and I waited until the last porters had left, and then inspected the area before leaving. For the first few miles out of Shigar the path is lined with stately poplar trees and goes through cultivated fields of wheat. Soon Pete and I caught up with the porters, who were resting in the shade of the trees. As we passed, the men touched their foreheads and said, "Salaam alaikum," and we returned the greeting by saluting and answering, "Alaikum salaam," which means "Peace be with you," and not, as Rizvi once told me in jest, "May you rest in peace." After many of these exchanges Pete and I passed the head of the column and entered the desert.

The Shigar and Braldu valleys are desolate wastes of sand and rock, the brown monotony of which is only occasionally disrupted by the trees and terraced fields of a village nestled into the slopes of the mountains, irrigated by water that is carried from nearby streams over ancient irrigation trenches. Between these oases the only vegetation consists of a few thorny thickets of roses and barberries, clumps of wormwood, and a few gnarled junipers. The land is so barren that even the goats, which are a large part of the local economy, find it difficult to survive. Marching along over the alluvial sands between Shigar and Koshumal we found one poor animal ten feet up in a juniper tree, trying to nibble a few meager leaves.

It is sixteen miles from Shigar to Koshumal, the longest stage of our approach march. Despite the continuing overcast sky, it became hotter as the day progressed, and Pete and I passed the interminable hours by discussing a proposed expedition to Mount Everest in which he was interested. Also, we regaled each other with stories about how we could eat absolutely anything. At two in the afternoon Pete and I stopped in a village three miles short of Koshumal to purchase some apricot nuts. There, sitting in the shade with the local lambardar, the village chieftain, was Rizvi. "How would you like some tea?" he asked. Twice before during the day we had accepted similar invitations and had been given cups of delicious green tea, so, hot and thirsty, we again eagerly accepted. This time, however, the lambardar's son brought out a brackish mixture of thoroughly boiled tea, ghee, salt, and other ingredients that remained unknown. "But this isn't regular tea, Tas," I protested. "Oh, no. From here on all we'll have is Balti tea," he smilingly replied. I took a whiff and warned Pete not to smell it. Making a mental note to avoid all further invitations for tea, I watched with horror as Schoening gulped down the contents of his cup. Now everyone was looking at me. The United States' reputation in Baltistan seemed to depend upon my drinking that tea. "How did you do it, Pete?" I whispered. "Simple. I followed your advice and didn't smell it," he whispered back.

I remembered how General G. O. Bruce, leader of the 1922 British Everest Expedition, had adroitly extricated himself from a similar situation involving yak butter tea by informing his lama host that he was on a pilgrimage and had to forego the things he enjoyed most, which unfortunately had included buttered tea. Lacking both the gall and the skill to use that ruse successfully, I kept placing the cup to my lips but was unable to take the fatal step. It was just about time for us to leave and my cup was still conspicuously full, when suddenly our porter train came into the village and the men began to disperse among the trees. At the end of the column was Ghulam Razul, who came and sat down beside me, wiping the sweat off his brow. Before the lambardar could say anything, I quickly raised the cup to my lips again, pronounced its contents delicious, and asked Razul if he would like some. "Gee, sah'b," he politely answered; and with a show of deep reluctance I gave him my cup, hoping that I was putting on a convincing demonstration that my love for Balti tea was exceeded only by my consideration for our hardworking sirdar. As we hiked out of town I expressed my admiration for Schoening's iron stomach. "I wish I hadn't done it. I don't feel so well now," he said modestly.

Pete, Tas, and I arrived at Koshumal and joined our comrades, who were lying about in a green pasture on the outskirts of the village. A group of local Baltis gathered around to stare at us. There were quite a few children and suddenly one shy little boy emerged from behind a tall man who was standing in front of us and presented a small bouquet of blue and yellow flowers to Schoening. Pete gave him a piece of candy in return and then we were deluged with small boys carrying flowers. Many of the local people put these blossoms on their caps to add a touch of color to their drab clothes, so we stuck our little presents in the bands of our ten-gallon hats, to the delight of all the onlookers.

It started to sprinkle so we decided to pitch our big base camp tent. This was a semicylindrical model that Schoening had obtained for only eighty dollars. We had been greatly impressed with Pete's business acumen until the tent was removed from its container. It was an experimental design, which required semicircular top poles at both the front and rear of the tent, and a long bar to serve as an overhead beam. After spending forty-five minutes jabbing various pole ends together, we finally got them matched up and the tent pitched. At first there were no side ropes guying it down and the slightest breeze threatened to lift our sail off the ground. There was a hole four inches in diameter for a stovepipe in the center of the roof, which also allowed prospective purchasers to view the interior after the tent had been set up. Every night we stuffed a parka or a towel up into this hole and the last man to stake out a position in the tent by laying down his air mattress had to sleep under it. That night it rained, which increased the competition for the corner positions in the weeks to follow.

The sky remained overcast the next day as we continued our march over the sandy waste of the Shigar Valley. Except for Pete, who still had all the paper rupees, all of us carried small twenty-five pound packs. Everyone was stiff and sore, and we plodded along slowly but steadily. Occasionally someone would try to sing, but soon his feeble effort would stop. Upon reaching the mouth of the Braldu River we turned north and began following the left bank of the river. The Braldu Valley is narrower, and its sides more precipitous than those of the Shigar Valley. Soon the trail disappeared as small channels of the river flowed up against the wall of the gorge. There were three channels to cross but the first one was the worst because when we entered it we were warm, dry, and happy. Swift went barefoot while I wore my light shoes, which protected my feet against the rocky bottom. Upon reaching the opposite side I had to rip them off since they retained cold water. Starting across the last channel we noticed the porters, who were not delayed by having to stop to take off boots, plunging into the first one.

Now it began to rain. I did not bother to slip my pants back on, and just put a parka over my shirt. Bob Swift remained barefoot and his raw, open blisters bobbed up and down in front of me as we slogged along through muddy fields, looking as miserable as we felt. Then we realized how ridiculous we looked and began to laugh. Swift cracked, "Don't worry, general. We'll catch up with them at Little Big Horn." The porters who began to overtake us with their short shuffling steps were amused by our appearance.

Still walking along the left sandbank of the Braldu River, Swift and I came to a little village where Schoening and Nevison were waiting for us. Several miles ahead on the opposite side of the river was the village of Dasso where the 1953 party to K2 had to cross on *zahks*. These frail craft, which are made of goatskins or cowskins, can carry only five men with loads at one time and it had taken eight hours to ferry the expedition across the river. Pete said, "If we can just ford the Braldu, it will save us an

Sun, sand, and blisters. Balti porters on the approach march.

entire day. A Balti came running down the trail just now yelling, 'Zahk, Zahk,' which means that Andy, Tas, and Mac up ahead can't get across and have sent for a raft, so we had better try it here." With that the four of us went down to the shore of the main channel, leaving the porters sitting along the side of an irrigation canal. Schoening waded into the river and began working his way across the swift torrent. The water rose over his knees, but he made it across safely, put down his pack, and returned. "We can put up a fixed line and get them all over," he said. We yelled to Razul and the constable to bring the porters over to the river, and soon they began to gather along the bank. The men were hesitant about entering the river until Pete, who had changed his mind about the necessity of a fixed line, grabbed the hands of a couple of them and started across. With the reluctance of lemmings diving into the sea, the porters formed up into groups of four and five men and then plunged into the water. Men who continued to vacillate were led across by the HAPs. A few porters who were extremely unhappy were shoved into the river by Razul and the constable, but once they got started they were all right. The current was swift and the smooth rocks on the bottom afforded slippery footing. The constable rode across piggyback on Rahim Khan's shoulders and everyone waited in eager anticipation for the big splash, which never came. After the main channel there was a shorter but deeper crossing; however, the bottom was sandy and there was little current. The cold water had a numbing effect on our blisters and we hiked rapidly up the trail on the right bank of the Braldu to the village of Dasso.

Sitting on the bank of the river directly across from the village, Kauffman, Rizvi, and McCormack suddenly received one of the most discouraging views in the sport of mountaineering. They could see the entire caravan still several miles away, marching up the river, but on the opposite side! Refusing to retreat down to where the main party had crossed, they stripped off their pants and plunged into the chest-deep water. With the aid of a couple of local Baltis who specialized in river crossings they got across safely. When they met the rest of the expedition on the outskirts of Dasso, they were still in their underwear.

Every day when we stopped in a new village, large numbers of sick Baltis gathered around our camp seeking medical treatment. Sometimes they were brought in by the village lambardar, but often they came individually for help. The people of Baltistan are afflicted with many diseases, but trachoma, tuberculosis, parasitism, and goiter are especially prevalent. They live in abject poverty, but their pathetic condition would be tremendously improved by the application of even the most fundamental of public health principles. The irrigation ditches are used for both drinking water and sewage disposal. Even if there were a stream of fresh water outside a village, it would be impossible to convince the inhabitants that they should walk out to it rather than use a nearby stagnant pond that is more convenient.

No sooner was the big tent up in Dasso than Tom Nevison began his afternoon sick call. Treatment was difficult enough, but diagnosis was almost impossible. All of Nevison's questions and all of the patients' answers had to be translated, twice. Nevison would ask a question in English, Rizvi would translate it into Urdu, and the police constable would translate it from Urdu to Balti for the patient to understand. The answer repeated the process in reverse. Nevison became extremely adept at rapidly pinning down specific symptoms to a given organ of the body with a brief series of limiting questions that could be answered by a simple "yes" or "no." More than once, after Tom began to beam with satisfaction after a particularly brilliant interrogation had finally located the source of trouble, the patient explained that he was fine; it was his wife who was sick but was too shy to come for help.

As he treated each person Nevison dictated notes to another sahib, who recorded the case history of each patient. This was difficult because most Baltis do not know their age and it is impossible to guess. Often Tom would say, "A man. About thirty. Trachoma in the right eye. Application of ophthalmic ointment." And on they came. Babies with bloated stomachs, old women with cancer, young girls with worms. Many times Tom could help them. Many times he could not. The incurable cases were the easiest to treat medically. All Nevison could do was to give them some aspirin to deaden their pain temporarily, or an Alka-Seltzer, which always delighted them because of its fizz. Even in some of the instances when he could cure a patient, Nevison would remain pessimistic. "He is all right now," Tom would say, after giving some Balti a massive dose of antibiotic, "but he will just go back living under these same conditions and get reinfected." Sometimes he would effect a temporary relief and warn the patient to go to the hospital at Skardu if he wanted to save his life. But on the march out we always found these patients in their same villages, only in worse condition.

One of Nevison's remedies was always permanently effective. Just before leaving Cambridge, Massachusetts, Tom had taken a quick two-hour course in tooth extraction from a friend who is a dentist, and in Dasso he got his first opportunity to demonstrate his new skill. The lambardar brought over a sick man with a lower molar that had rotted down to the gums. While one of the HAPs held the Balti's head to keep it from moving, Tom managed to get a grip on the offending tooth with the forceps, and after a considerable struggle he pulled it out. The patient grimaced with pain but never uttered a sound. Nevison performed several other extractions during the trip and none of the patients ever said anything. One man was so delighted with the results that he wanted another rotten molar pulled and Nevison obliged. The Baltis are a tough and long-suffering people.

After dinner, thirty of the porters gathered in a little semicircle under a nearby apricot tree and began to sing. The haunting falsetto of their voices matched the bleakness of our surroundings. We liked it and gave them a small drum to play. As some of the sahibs sat down cross-legged beside them, a Balti with Mongolian features who was wearing a Tibetan hat jumped up and started to dance while the rest of the men chanted, clapped their hands, and swayed rhythmically. The dancer moved faster and faster, his arms gyrating wildly, as the tempo of the clapping and the drumbeat increased. When he sat down, another Balti sprang up. The dancing became more and more frenzied until all the participants were exhausted. Then the porters drifted off into the village and we went to bed.

6

TO ASKOLE

We awoke to the 5:00 A.M. news broadcast from Radio Moscow, the only station we could consistently receive. Occasionally we got the BBC or Radio Australia, and once we heard the stirring strains of "Columbia, the Gem of the Ocean." On that occasion, we had waited expectantly. Then the announcer had said, "This is the Voice of America in Tangiers. The following broadcast will be in Swahili." But this was an isolated instance and always, twenty-four hours a day, there was Radio Moscow, loud, clear, and in many languages. At first, we just ignored it and guessed whether the news was good or bad by the infallible system of always taking the opposite point of view. Then, after hearing clever distortions day after day and realizing that most Americans are not aware of the unrelenting campaign of hate that is being waged against them, we slowly began to boil. Andy Kauffman had brought a Free Hungarian flag, which no one took very seriously. However, as our frustration increased due to our inability to counteract the vast outpouring of lies that greeted us every time we turned on the shortwave receiver, that flag became our personal symbol of defiance. We became grimly determined to plant it on the summit of Hidden Peak, thousands of feet higher than any Communist flag had flown on any mountain.

Beyond Dasso the trail went over the sand flats of the Braldu River. Schoening and I hiked along, the porters caught up with us, and soon we were in the midst of the caravan. Although the Baltis walked with a fast, short-stepped shuffle, they stopped every few minutes and propped their resting-sticks under their loads to relieve the pressure of the ropes upon their shoulders, so the average speed of the caravan was fairly slow. One of the older Balti porters, who carried a medical box and the typewriter, would grin enthusiastically and say "Shabash," Balti for "Well done," whenever he trotted by. Then he would stop to rest and we would pass him. Soon he would go trotting by again, still grinning. We repeated this cycle over and over.

The valley became a narrow gorge. The Braldu River turned sharply to the left or north, and our path climbed over a shoulder 1,000 feet high. The track became so steep and rough that horses could not use it. Across the river a village nestled into the mountainside and long thin scars of trails crisscrossed the brown slopes that surrounded it. At the head of the valley we could see the village of Chokpo where the Braldu turns east up another gorge toward Askole. The sun broke through a hole in the low clouds, bathing our vicinity in light, while the rest of the country remained in the purple shade. The weather had remained like this since we left Skardu and, while in the lower valleys we welcomed the relief from the desert heat, the constant overcast worried us. If the skies did not clear and allow the late winter snow on the Baltoro Glacier to melt, the expedition was going to be in serious trouble.

For several miles we walked along a terrace whose lichen-covered rocks reminded me of the big, boulder-strewn peneplains of the Colorado Rockies. At the end of this plateau, the trail entered a narrow ravine ten feet wide at the top, and spiraled down the sides of the washout for several hundred feet through perpendicular cliffs of crumbling rock until it reached an open slope and descended to the river. While our porters shuffled down the gully, Schoening and I took movies of the scene. We continued up the valley to some cultivated fields where the trail disappeared, and we walked along the tops of the irrigation ditches. After crossing a two-plank bridge over a tributary stream, Schoening and I arrived in the village of Chokpo and found the rest of the party relaxing under some apricot trees while children gathered on the bluffs above to stare at these strange creatures.

The porters arrived and deposited their loads. According to the political agent's regulations, they were entitled to receive three cigarettes a day from Skardu to Askole and five cigarettes a day from Askole onward. As we did not learn of this requirement until reaching Skardu, our supply was too small, and we had to withhold the ration until we reached Chokpo. Now Ghulam Razul and the other HAPs distributed cigarettes and matches to the expectant porters.

When Swift and I set up the camera to take movies of the afternoon's sick call, Rizvi promptly disappeared looking for a suitable patient. He returned with a calf tucked underneath one arm. Nevison gravely examined the animal with a tongue depressor and a stethoscope. "It's healthy," he said as the calf kicked free and scampered away. Then the deluge of serious patients began.

That night we had goat again for dinner. Although we had brought approach march rations, we ate local food whenever possible. Ostensibly this was to increase our food reserves for the siege of the mountain; actually it was because our meat supply consisted primarily of ox tongue. When this discovery had been made our emotions ranged from vague uneasiness to outright dismay, depending on how much each sahib craved ox tongue. We did have other varieties of meat—corned beef and lamb tongue; also, there was a large quantity of oxtail soup, which evoked the bitter comment from Bob Swift, "We have the tongue and the tail; where's the rest of the animal?" Moreover, the food list indicated that ox tongue was the only kind of meat in the high-altitude rations. Later, when the expedition was over, I learned what had happened. Because of the Muslim ban on pork, we had ordered canned roast beef; however, that was not readily available in England, and our food suppliers had to substitute corned beef and ox tongue quickly in order to meet the shipping deadline.

The next day, Sunday, May 25, was Malaria Pill Day, according to Tom Nevison, who added the pills to the daily dose of vitamin tablets that he distributed in individual plastic bottles to each sahib. Every night he collected the containers and refilled them. In this manner Nevison could make sure that no one forgot to take his pills.

Beyond Chokpo, there were two possible routes. We could follow the right side of the Braldu and climb over a 2,000-foot shoulder to the village of Chongo; or we could stay low in the gorge, cross the river to the village of Hotu, then recross the river to Askole. As the trail to Chongo was narrow and slippery and the constable reported that there were plank bridges over the river, we chose the latter route.

To Askole

We left Chokpo promptly at seven. While the rest of the sahibs went ahead with the movie camera, Schoening and I remained with the porters. Once again we skirted the steep sides of the gorge by walking along the sandy edge of the Braldu. After several hours of marching, Pete and I caught up with Nevison and Kauffman near some deep rock crevices that contained rushing water.

Later, we came to a steep sandy slope that was scarred by rock slides. It rose for several thousand feet straight out of the river, so we began to traverse it just above the water. Everyone was following in the tracks made by the man ahead of him when Pete shouted, "Look out!" A rock the size of an egg whizzed past my head and imbedded itself in the sand near my right foot. It was impossible to take cover so we just kept plodding. The Baltis realized the hazards of the place. Despite their habit of resting their shoulders every few minutes, they continued shuffling for over a mile and a half until the bottom of the gorge flattened out and the danger was behind us.

Finally we reached our bridge over the Braldu—two poles laid parallel two feet apart over the rushing current and connected by twigs, with flat rocks upon them to serve as stepping-stones. We tramped across this fragile structure and climbed through terraced fields of wheat and barley to the squalid village of Hotu.

We pitched camp in the corner of a filthy yard enclosed by a high mud wall. The porters arrived, deposited their loads, and melted into the village. This was one of the mysteries of the trip. No matter how small the village, our army of porters would always disappear within moments after arriving at the day's destination, and we would not see them again until it was time to depart the following morning.

We always took great precautions with our drinking water. First, the local water was run through a filter, which Nevison had made from a pressure cooker, to remove physical impurities. Then it was boiled for twenty minutes. Although the HAPs made a show of humoring us in this vital matter, it was obvious that they regarded this procedure as a great waste of time. In Hotu, Bob Swift decided to inspect the water supply himself. He returned very unhappy and reported, "It's a stagnant pool covered with green scum and is used for drinking, washing, and watering the livestock." We increased our supervision over the kitchen. Also, we never inspected our water supply again. It was bad for morale.

After dinner, we speculated about the rumor that the second bridge over the Braldu was gone. Rizvi was certain that we would find a bridge in the morning. "What makes you so sure?" someone asked. "Oh, the police constable told the villagers that if they didn't have the bridge up before dawn, he would levy a five-rupee fine on every man, woman, and child in town," Rizvi replied.

It rained all night. The next morning we followed the trail out of Hotu for three miles around the mountainside and then descended to the Braldu. There were no signs that there had ever been a bridge across the river. Amid much splashing and cries of "Shabash," we led the porters into the swift frigid water. As in the ford below Dasso, the river had split into two channels with the second one being the narrower and deeper. Halfway across I heard a man next to me shout, "Tik, sah'b?" meaning "Okay?" It was our old Balti with the medical box and the typewriter. The water was over his waist, but he plunged forward still wearing that incessant grin.

When we reached the far side of the river, the other members of the party left to visit some hot springs near the village of Chongo while I accompanied the porters to Askole. We climbed up the steep riverbank, studded with loose rocks. One porter dislodged a boulder that barely missed the man beneath him, and cries of alarm echoed up from the rear of the column. The caravan reached the top of the terrace and headed toward Askole.

Askole, at 10,000 feet, is the last village on the way to the Baltoro Glacier. It is a compact cluster of two-story mud and stone huts that huddle under green poplar and willow trees. During the winter the families live upstairs in their houses while their livestock is stabled on the ground floor. Extensive wheat fields surround the village; however, herds of goats are the principal support of the inhabitants. Every expedition has had to stop

Only three more rivers to cross. Pete Schoening leads the porters across the Braldu River.

here to obtain more supplies and porters for the final week's march into the mountains. The lambardar proudly exhibited a letter of recommendation given to one of his predecessors by the Duke of Abruzzi in 1909. We pitched our camp in a field on the outskirts of the village in a field enclosed by brier hedges and curious bystanders.

That afternoon we paid the porters who wanted to quit the expedition. It was a complicated operation. When we were in Rawalpindi, Rizvi and I, obsessed with the necessity of being able to make correct change in paying porter wages, had ordered 3,000 rupees in coins as well as 18,000 rupees in notes of various denominations. Upon going to the bank to obtain the money, we stared in disbelief as the clerks hauled out one heavy sack after another and dumped them at our feet. The rupee, which is worth slightly more than twenty cents, is divided into sixteen parts called annas, and in the bags that were stacked before us there were anna bits, two-anna bits, quarter rupees, and half rupees. We reduced by one-third the number of sacks containing anna bits, but there still remained over 120 pounds of change, more than two porter loads. In Skardu we scattered the bags throughout various approach march boxes, and as Nevison had already made a lightning-flash stencil to mark containers holding communications equipment, we branded all boxes containing money with two lightning flashes. During the six-day march, all the sahibs had kept a close watch on the numerous "double lightning" loads. By the time we arrived in Askole the enormity of our miscalculation was apparent. There would be only a few paydays during the entire trip; one small sack of change would be adequate for all our needs. Because of the logistics problem beyond Askole, weight had to be reduced to a minimum. There was only one way we could get rid of the coins. "The porters will be paid in change," said Schoening firmly.

All the "double lightning" boxes were dragged into the tent and Kauffman, McCormack, Swift, and Nevison began to count the coins and put them into rupee stacks. The pay line was established outside the closed entrance. The constable called each porter's name. Razul gave the man his cigarettes and cut the metal tag from his shirt. Rizvi calculated the amount of wages due and directed the man to the makeshift table where Schoening and I sat. As the Balti approached, Pete or I would yell out the number of rupees needed, usually twenty-four, the full wages for the march from Skardu. Like a cook in a small cafe, someone inside the tent would echo, "Twenty-four rupees coming up," and a tin plate containing twenty-four stacks of coins would be thrust out of the door. After gesturing to the porter to cup his hands, Pete and I would dump the change into them. Often a man's tiny hands could not hold all his wages, especially if he were being paid in anna bits, and he would lift up his shirttail to hold the coins. Once I could not repress a chuckle at the absurdity of the situation and a

A different drummer. Balti porters singing and dancing during the approach march.

caustic voice came out of the tent: "If you think it's so funny, you can come back here and start counting; we could use help."

Earlier, Pete and I had given the first few men some five-rupee notes to start the line moving. We had almost finished paying the porters when suddenly there was a loud commotion in the adjacent yard. Many Baltis were shouting angrily and shoving each other about. They were finally starting to riot! "Rizvi," I shouted. "What's happening?" "It's nothing," he replied. "One of the porters just waved a five-rupee note and asked for change, and all the other men are screaming, 'Take mine!'"

We spent Tuesday, May 27, obtaining additional supplies and porters. Beyond Askole all rations needed by the porters for the approach and return marches had to be carried by the expedition. How much would we need? Each porter was entitled to receive thirty ounces of atta a day, which, with a few other items, brought his daily ration to over two pounds. As the trip up the Baltoro Glacier would take from eight to ten days, plus five days to return, each man required approximately thirty pounds of atta. Moreover, the porters carrying food for the porters carrying loads required more porters to carry their food, who, in turn, required still more porters to carry their food. Then there were the variable factors. Each day a number of loads of atta would be consumed and their carriers discharged. The number of men released each day would decrease, however, as the distance they were from Askole increased. Furthermore, extra porters would have to be retained at Payu to carry firewood up the glacier for the men to cook chupattis. After several hours of concentrated study, three of the mathematical geniuses in the party came up with three different answers to the problem, so we just guessed that one man carrying atta for every two men carrying loads, or 3,600 pounds of flour, would be adequate.

The political agent had instructed the lambardar to have the necessary atta ready for us and Rizvi and Schoening went to the local granary to obtain it. The flour was carefully weighed by the chief granary officer and put into goatskin bags, lent to us upon the agreement that we would pay ten rupees for every bag lost or damaged beyond repair. That afternoon sixty goatskins of atta were delivered to our camp and the lambardar sent his son Ali to receive payment. Even after paying the porters there was still too much change, and Schoening decided that the rest of it would be used to pay the 1,200 rupees we owed for the flour. I took Ali inside the tent, gave him a coin sack, and began throwing money into it. As I passed the 300-rupee count and the bag could barely be lifted off the ground, the boy began to object to every fresh stack of coins. Finally I could not control my laughter any longer and went outside. "I'll pay him," said Pete, disappearing inside the tent. Soon the Balti's vehement protests were followed by Schoening answering, "Just 100 rupees more and we will pay you the rest in bills. Half in change. Half in bills. Tik?" Schoening kept his word. We gave Ali six 100-rupee notes, which probably could not be changed that side of Skardu. It was fortunate that we were leaving town the following morning.

Back at the village of Chokpo Schoening had noticed that one of the HAPs, Issac, had been insulting to Ghulam Razul. Then upon getting up to carry out Razul's instructions, he had hurled his cup of coffee to the ground. On an expedition where each member's life depends upon the actions of his comrades, such insubordination cannot be tolerated, and after thoroughly discussing the matter with Rizvi, Schoening reluctantly decided to dismiss Issac, although Razul stated that he could keep the HAP under control. Besides, we had found another man in Askole, Qasim, who had not come to Skardu but who had received excellent recommendations from the 1954 Italian expedition to K2. Being let go was heartbreaking for Issac because it meant not only a loss of income but, even more important, a loss of status. One minute he was a high-altitude porter dressed in climbing clothes and the next he was the same as the other Baltis. We did not have an extra set of climbing clothes, but Schoening gave him a set of khakis, which minimized his reduction in rank. Later we found out that men are never fired in Baltistan; other men are hired to take their places. We paid Issac his wages plus a tip and hoped he would be able to obtain a position with either the Italian party or the Japanese expedition, which was coming in June to attempt Chogolisa.

The constable and assistant constable drew up a roster of 160 wallahs who would carry loads from Askole onward. ("Wallah," meaning "fellow" in Balti, is used in connection with a job or place, as a *zahk* wallah or an Askole wallah.) We hoped to avoid a porter strike by balancing the number of men from Askole with the men from Skardu. The men from

The Staff of Life. Making chupattis, the basic staple of the Balti diet.

Skardu are not so husky as the Askole wallahs and their thin clothing and light sandals do not compare with the coarse wool clothing and the mukluks of the mountain men. However, in contrast to the Askole men, who are a sophisticated, quiet, sullen group, the Baltis from the lower valleys are outgoing and enthusiastic. If only they had the protective clothing! Eventually half of our porters were men who had accompanied us from Skardu and the rest were recruited at Askole. The constable had to leave us to return to Shigar, his main post, but the assistant would continue on to Base Camp. Rizvi assured us that the assistant was an experienced man because he was a veteran of many porter strikes. "If he's so good, why didn't he prevent all those strikes he was in?" snapped Pete. By three in the afternoon most of the work had been completed. The loads had been reorganized, repacked, and a new inventory made of their contents.

We awoke before dawn the next morning to the cry of the local muezzin. The melodic chant calling the faithful to prayer made us realize that we were halfway around the world in a strange and isolated land. Then from behind us came another bell-like cry. It sounded as if a shepherd out with his flock of goats was repeating the call from the top of some nearby mountain, but it was undoubtedly only an echo of the original cry. For a moment, time seemed to stand still and we were separated from the rest of the world not

70

only by distance but also by centuries. Suddenly we remembered that there were 160 loads to distribute before our day's march could begin.

The reassignment of loads began promptly at seven. First, the men from Skardu who were continuing were allowed to locate their old boxes to which their goat-hair ropes were still attached. Several of these men showed up without proper sandals, and we reluctantly had to release them. Then the new porters were allowed in, with Swift and Rizvi stationed at the main entrance to the yard to check off the men's names against our new roster. Kauffman and Razul issued the metal tags and McCormack, Schoening, Nevison, and I attempted to escort the porters to their assigned loads. It began as an orderly process, but the Baltis filtered past the checkpoints and soon everyone was part of a large, yelling, heaving mass of humanity, as the porters, not realizing how carefully we had weighed the loads, fought each other to get the lightest ones. The remainder of the 3,000 feet of cord that had been brought to assist the men in tying up their loads disappeared rapidly. Later we learned that cord is almost more valuable to a Balti than money.

The roll call began, and then the familiar long line of stooped brown-clad men with rectangular boxes on their backs began to file out of the yard. Schoening and I waited until the last porter had departed. Ali Lambardar, wearing a bright yellow cap and leading a goat by a string, arrived to accompany us. Although he was being paid full wages for merely leading a goat, we were happy to have him join us since he could be held responsible if anything went wrong. He spoke a few words of English and never got angry, but he looked after his own interests adequately. As soon as the last sahib had departed, the swarm of kids who had been watching from behind the brier hedges descended upon our campground and picked it clean.

As we walked down the main street of Askole, people gathered in doorways and windows to watch us go by with our boots and ice-axes. We noticed several young mothers with their babies up on the rooftops, but like most women in Baltistan they were very shy and ran when we glanced in their direction. We reached the green fields on the outskirts of the village and said good-bye to the constable, who had come down to see us safely off. Then the entire column of seven sahibs, six HAPs, and 160 porters began to march into the cold wind that blew down the Braldu Gorge.

7

THE BALTORO GLACIER

Exuberant because the last human habitation was behind us, Schoening and I began to sing. Immediately the porters joined in. The chief of the seven men carrying the heavy oxygen loads, who were from the same village, led one chant after another. When a song was finished he would smile at us and say, "Tik?" We always answered, "Tik," and the men would start singing again. A few miles beyond Askole the trail dropped down to the Braldu River bed, at the confluence of the Braldu and a small river that flows out of the side of the Biafo Glacier. After crossing this tributary, we stopped for lunch. Pete and I gave the Baltis sitting nearest us some hard candy and they, in turn, presented us with pieces of chupatti. After lunch they brought out hookahs and from the various groups of squatting men came the cry, "Matcheez, sah'b." Watching the Baltis pass their water pipes from man to man, Schoening said, "I'd sure like to try smoking one," and to the great delight of everyone present, he did.

Lunch over, we resumed marching across the alluvial fan of the Biafo River. After an hour we came to the Biafo Glacier, over two miles wide, which flows down a tributary valley from the north and almost blocks the Braldu Valley. The track disappeared and the porters picked their way over the rubble-strewn surface of the glacier. There were few crevasses but many perpendicular splits where one side had slipped down several feet. Many of the Baltis were not wearing their sheepskin boots and there were occasional splotches of blood in the track where a porter had cut his foot on a sharp rock. Eventually we came to the rocky plain on the far side of the glacier. From this point onward the valley and river we were following is called the Biaho instead of the Braldu.

At two in the afternoon, we arrived at a gigantic boulder called Korophon, the first of the traditional stopping-places for all expeditions marching into the Baltoro Muztagh. All these locations have names although they are nothing but campsites. They are supposed to be one day's march apart. However, many of these stages are very short and under favorable circumstances an expedition can cover two of them in one day. But the porters, like horses leaving the barn, moved very slowly going away from Askole. The advance group of sahibs and HAPs had already pitched two tents, and there was a four-foot-high enclosure of stones built out from the boulder, which afforded excellent shelter for most of our Baltis.

After the loads had been checked in, Rizvi and the assistant constable assembled all the porters and delivered a scathing reprimand. Apparently a can of powdered milk had disappeared, and Tas wanted to make sure that it did not happen again. Despite this incident, nothing of importance was lost during the entire approach march. One reason may have been that Rizvi told the men that all our food contained pork. The pep talk over, the Baltis scattered over the sandy countryside, gathering firewood to cook their chupattis. Hussein and Haji began preparing dinner while the sahibs took turns playing the "bagpipe." This was a polyethylene bag that Nevison had brought along to test our breathing rates at different altitudes. It had an attachment at its mouth that permitted the user to inhale normally while exhaling into the bag. While someone timed him, the victim would pace up and down, breathing into the bag until it was full. The

*At the Korophon boulder Rizvi and the assistant constable lecture
the porters about a missing can of milk.*

higher we were, the more rapid our breathing and the quicker the bag was
filled. This test, together with blood samples, helped Nevison to determine
how acclimatized we were.

At Korophon we made several unpleasant discoveries. First, one of
our three five-gallon containers of kerosene had lost one-third of its contents. Second, according to our food lists, we had only one and a half
pounds of salt. Although we had brought some rock salt for the Baltis,
there was not enough for ourselves. We could only hope that the canned
meat contained sufficient salt to meet our minimum requirements until
Dick Irvin and Gil Roberts arrived with more supplies. Later, on the
mountain, we would find unlisted boxes of salt in the high-altitude rations.

During the night there was a downpour accompanied by a high wind
that threatened to collapse our tent. Water dripped on us from a saturated
parka, which had been stuffed into the hole in the roof. At four in the
morning Schoening went outside and covered the loads with tarps. Eventually the rain stopped. When we packed up camp, the tents were wet, the
loads were wet, everything was wet. Five porters whose loads of atta had
been consumed were paid and released. Cigarettes were distributed to the
rest of the men, and finally the caravan got under way for Bardumal, the
next stage. After walking along the right bank of the Biaho River for
several miles, we came to the junction with the Dumordo River, which
flows out of a tributary valley to the north. There was a rope bridge two
miles upstream, but it would have taken hours for our small army to cross

it, so once again everyone took off his boots and pants and waded into the water. After reaching the other side, we wiped the sand and water off our feet with our socks, put our boots and pants back on, and continued the march.

A cold wind began to blow down the Biaho Valley, and after a brief stop for lunch, the porters rapidly shuffled forward over the sandy river-bed. We came to some caves in the rock, but the advance group was not there. It began to sprinkle and Schoening and I pushed ahead of the caravan. Turning a corner we saw the tent a mile ahead of us, pitched upon a sandbank that had been undercut by the river. Billowing in the wind, the tent strained against its moorings like a balloon. Pete and I increased our pace and reached the shelter of the tent just as it began to pour. Our respite was short, as the porters arrived fifteen minutes later and all the sahibs had to go outside to stack the loads. We had learned our lesson the hard way; now the boxes were piled up into tight stacks and covered with tarpaulins.

That evening as the rain pelted the tent, we discussed our situation. Not only would the Baltoro Glacier be covered with fresh snow, but also the porters could not get warm and dry even in the daytime. Moreover, although there was plenty of atta and tea, we were lacking certain items of food to which the porters were entitled by regulation. We had not learned of these requirements until it was too late to fulfill them, and if the porters called their traditional strike at Urdukas, three marches away, we could not protest their action. The only thing that we could do to remedy the situation would be to pay the men the amount of money that the missing rations represented. Everyone agreed that this was fair, but when should the announcement be made? Several sahibs wanted to wait until Urdukas so that the extra money could be used in bargaining with the men. Bob Swift argued that granting the extra money during a strike would appear as a concession, and that in order to be able to insist that the porters comply with the regulations, we too would have to live up to our part of the agreement. Therefore it was decided that an immediate announcement must be made. Rizvi called a meeting of the leaders of each village's contingent. Standing in the rain, Tas very carefully explained that we were giving each porter an additional rupee a day, not as a wage increase but solely as compensation for the insufficient food ration. The allowance was made retroactive from Askole. There were cries of "Zindabad!" ("Hoorah!") and one by one each leader stepped forward to wish us success on the mountain. We could hear the Baltis singing until late into the cold, wet night. Perhaps it would have been more effective to have waited until Urdukas before making the announcement; however, we immediately felt better for having tried to be fair with our porters.

The following morning, May 30, it was still overcast. Worried about a possible delay on the Baltoro Glacier due to the unseasonable conditions,

Mirage or mountains? The Trango Towers rise through the mist above the Baltoro Glacier.

we instructed five atta-bearing porters who were being released to bring up more loads of flour from Askole and leave them at Payu, the next stage, for the returning porters. This would enable us to wait an extra day on the glacier for more favorable weather before having to release the men. As the caravan left Bardumal, the valley was infiltrated by gray clouds that concealed the sides and ends of the mysterious purple gorge. Ahead of us mountains with outlines as soft as a mirage seemed to float through the mist ready to vanish if one could touch them. The Biaho River cut up against the wall on our left, and we had to climb up and across a cliff on narrow ledges seventy-five feet above the water. It was amazing how well the porters maintained their footing wearing their slippery mukluks and carrying awkward loads. Every few minutes they would stop and prop their resting-sticks under the boxes. Stop and go, stop and go, the column contracted and expanded like a giant caterpillar as the men crossed alternating passages of difficult and easy ground. Then we descended back to the riverbed and hiked along the sand flats. The track that we would have to follow on the march out, when the river would be high, wound its tortuous way across the cliffs high above us. After ascending a ridge that ended at the river, we could see for the first time the historic Baltoro Glacier. Covered with black rock and darker than the sides of the surrounding mountains, it occupied the entire valley ahead of us. The Biaho River flowed out in full force from underneath its snout.

We arrived at a beautiful clump of willow and rose trees on the lower slopes of Payu Peak, one of the guardians to the entrance of the Baltoro, and pitched our tent upon a flat platform beside a stream that rippled down through the long grass. The Baltis spread out in groups of ten to twelve men and built improvised shelters. The porters began gathering wood, not only for the evening meal but also for the rest of the trip, since Liligo and Urdukas, the next two stages, had been denuded by prior expeditions. Payu was our loveliest campsite during the entire approach march, but we temporarily ignored the magnificent scenery in order to reorganize and consolidate the loads. Meanwhile the HAPs slaughtered the goat and prepared him for dinner. We had become somewhat attached to the animal and were unhappy to see him killed. However, the goat had his revenge. Three days of marching had made him tougher than the sahibs' teeth.

That night it snowed. The fresh mantle of snow made the near view of wet men, wet loads, and wet tents as dismal as it made the distant view of spires, rising into the mist, beautiful. "If the weather doesn't get better fast, we've had it. All the porters will quit," said Rizvi. But after this last storm the long-threatening skies slowly began to clear and we managed to get the caravan under way by nine in the morning.

Several miles beyond Payu the track dropped down the side of the hill to the snout of the Baltoro Glacier, where the porters stopped to rest. Quietly all the Baltis gathered together in one large group. Then, standing up, they began to chant and the isolated stillness was pierced by the rising and falling cries of 150 men. Sitting off to one side Pete Schoening and I remained motionless, as even to take a photograph seemed inappropriate. For five minutes their lonely wail blended into our harsh environment. No one moved until the last sound had faded from the surrounding walls; then the men slowly returned to their loads. Later when we questioned the assistant constable about this incident he said the men were not praying but merely following a local custom. This may have been true; however, the ceremony was extremely impressive to have nothing behind it except tradition.

The end of the Baltoro Glacier is between 300 and 500 feet high and we had to climb a steep scree gully along the right side of the snout and then over the loose debris of the glacier itself in order to reach the top. From here we began to march diagonally to our right across the glacier toward Liligo. There were no signs of a track, but the porters—led by Qasim, our HAP from Askole—seemed to know the easiest route across the slippery rubble-covered ice. As the sun warmed the glacier, rocks began to tumble constantly down into the green water of numerous surface pools. Up and down, in and out, we slowly picked our way over and around ridges of sharp stones. Some of the Baltis still insisted on walking barefoot and one porter received a nasty cut above his ankle.

We were surrounded by the innumerable groups of fantastic granite towers that line both sides of the lower Baltoro Glacier. Any one of these massifs would be the most impressive mountain range in the United States. Still untouched, these incredible pinnacles will provide new challenges for coming generations of mountaineers long after the present Himalayan problems have become classic ascents. The mountains of the Central Himalaya and Nepal are beautiful, but the mountains of the Karakoram are powerful and majestic. They inspire awe, not rapture. These peaks pierce through years of formal education and association with high mountains to evoke an echo of primitive fears buried beneath centuries of civilization. Gazing up at sheer walls shrouded by gray clouds, we no longer laughed at the thought of our superstitious ancestors who believed that demons and devils inhabit the high places of the earth. The line, if any, between us and our chanting Baltis was extremely thin. But such moods came over us only during the brief rest stops because thought and emotion are blunted almost as effectively by physical activity as by sleep.

At four o'clock we reached Liligo, a flat sandy opening between the glacier and the right wall of the valley. The sahibs constructed a shelter out of porter boxes and tarpaulins that protected 25 men, but the remaining 125 porters had to build small shelters out of stones. After dinner, members of the expedition went over to a nearby cliff and tried to make a low-level traverse across the wall about six feet above the ground. There was one extremely delicate move, and one sahib after another fell off. Bob Swift almost got across but his right hand could not grip the rock too well with a plaster cast on it. Eventually Pete Schoening made it. By then some of the porters had become intrigued with our pastime and decided to attempt the pitch. One barefoot Balti after another climbed up the rock and fell off as they kept trying to jump across the gap. Finally one man, demonstrating perfect balance technique, successfully made the traverse while his elated comrades cheered. If only he were one of our high-altitude porters!

The first of June. A new month, and still we had not reached Base Camp. The caravan started for Urdukas by six-thirty in the morning. While the rest of the sahibs went ahead, Pete Schoening and I, together with Rahim Khan, remained behind for several hours to film the magnificent panorama that spread past us from horizon to horizon. To the left, or west, was Payu Peak with its spur of gigantic pinnacles. Then there were the Trango Towers, the Lobsang Towers, and, rising behind another mass of pinnacles, the Muztagh Tower. In the far distance to the east we could see Gasherbrum IV rising above Concordia, with the hazy outline of Broad Peak's massive bulk just north of it. There was not a cloud in the sky nor the slightest breath of wind. The weather had turned good just when we needed it most. If all went well the expedition would reach Concordia in two more days, for in the Karakoram, unlike lesser ranges, distance is measured in days, not hours.

Several hours later, Schoening and I caught up with porters who were on the right lateral moraine of the glacier. The caravan followed this moraine for several miles and then angled obliquely toward Urdukas, a green slope of grass and bushes 300 feet above the Baltoro, directly opposite the Lobsang Towers.

The final climb from the glacier to our campsite was the scene of an amusing incident. Every night during the march to Askole, Abdul Rahim tried to meet the sahibs just outside camp and take their packs. Except for Pete Schoening, who was carrying fifty pounds of rupees, all of us had light packs. However, after Askole, most of the sahibs carried forty pounds or more to get into physical condition. At Urdukas, Abdul decided to resume his gracious custom and, meeting Pete and me halfway up the final slope into camp, he insisted on taking our loads. After arguing for a minute or so, we reluctantly consented and tossed him our packs, which, combined, weighed over ninety pounds. Picking them up, the astonished HAP realized that he had received more than he had bargained for, but he gamely struggled up the loose sandy slope with the packs. It was a long time before Abdul offered to take two loads from the sahibs again.

Urdukas is a historic place. Our tents were pitched in the identical site that our predecessors up the Baltoro had used. On a nearby rock were the initials of the Austrian Alpine Club and the inscription, "The end of the world," in German. Around us were numerous caves under large boulders that had protected Balti shepherds and hunters for years.

The porters checked in their loads while Bob Swift and Tom McCormack passed out cigarettes to them. Twenty-five goatskins of atta were distributed to the men or cached in the rocks for the Baltis to use on their return trip. The carriers of these loads, most of whom were from Skardu and had inadequate clothing, were paid their wages. We began reorganizing the remaining loads and the HAPs started dinner. Then we noticed that some of the Askole wallahs were gathering on the hillside behind our tent. Soon most of them were sitting down in long rows and arguing with the assistant constable, while the men from the other villages watched from a discreet distance.

The parting advice of K2 veteran Bob Bates to Tom Nevison had been, "Look out for a strike at Urdukas." Now the only question was how much were the men going to protest. The seven sahibs, the assistant constable, and Ghulam Razul stood behind the tent and exchanged stony glances with the porters. "What do they want?" asked Pete. "They want a day's rest, with pay, to cook the chupattis needed for the remainder of the march, and extra men to carry the food," said Rizvi, translating into English the assistant constable's translation into Urdu of what the porters had said in Balti.

"Why can't they cook the chupattis tonight?" demanded Pete.

"They say that they haven't enough time."

"They would have had enough time if they had spent it working instead of sitting around," snapped Schoening.

Some of the Baltis were more vociferous than the others, and we made a mental note of them. Finally we decided that the request for extra porters to carry the chupattis was legitimate; otherwise each man would be carrying over seventy-five pounds if his rations were added to his load of expedition equipment. "But we are leaving at nine-thirty in the morning and any man who isn't ready to go at that time will be left behind. Tell them that, Tas," said Pete.

There were more protests. Then Rizvi dramatically declared: "I am a Syed, a descendant of The Prophet, and I swear that you will be fairly treated by the expedition. Any man who causes trouble will be sent to Skardu for punishment. I wish to hear nothing further about this matter." There are many Syeds in Muslim countries; in fact, Issac, the HAP we had dismissed at Askole, was one. However, the manner in which Rizvi made the announcement greatly impressed the Baltis. Stunned, the Askole wallahs silently rose to their feet and dispersed. Our troubles were not over. We had to rehire some of the ill-clad porters that had just been released, to carry the chupattis. They began to grumble.

"Abdul Rahim," Rizvi barked.

"Gee, sah'b."

"If the men from your village continue to cause trouble you will be fired."

The HAP talked to his relatives and friends and the crisis was over. One by one, the other sahibs congratulated Rizvi on his masterful handling of the situation. "If the weather remains good we will continue. If not. . ." and he shrugged his shoulders.

Early the next morning wisps of smoke rose from numerous fires as the Baltis made their chupattis. The skies remained clear, but we were uncertain how effective our ultimatum had been. First a small handful of men came to pick up their loads, then more and more porters appeared, and finally there was a wild scramble for the boxes as each man became afraid that he would be left without a load.

During this chaos two mail runners who had just come up the glacier arrived and handed me a telegram, which stated that our request for special weather broadcasts should be routed through the American embassy in Karachi. Andy Kauffman and I immediately drafted a note to the embassy requesting assistance; however, it would take days for the message to get back to Skardu. At least for awhile we would not be disturbed by unfavorable weather reports. After giving the runners a second note for Dick Irvin and Gil Roberts requesting more kerosene and salt, we dispatched them back to the political agent. By now the porters were beginning to move out, except for one man who had been late and whose load had been reassigned. We paid the unhappy Balti his wages and followed the caravan out of camp. Out of curiosity I glanced at my watch. It was nine-thirty.

We walked past the mouth of the Yermanendu Glacier and then cut out to the center of the Baltoro and followed along a large moraine. Once we had to drop down into a gully formed by a surface stream and up the opposite side. Weaving through the mounds of loose debris we encountered some short barriers of bare ice from ten to fifteen feet high. The sahibs cut steps up these obstacles and the porters followed. Some of the Baltis were still walking barefoot with their mukluks suspended from their loads, a tough way to save leather. Masherbrum to the south was an extremely impressive sight, and Nevison and McCormack stopped to set up the various expedition cameras on tripods to photograph it.

At lunchtime, Schoening and I were very happy to see most of the porters stand up when Rizvi arrived. It bode well that they held him in such esteem. During lunch Rizvi pointed out the height on Masherbrum that he had reached on the opposite side the preceding year, while Schoening, who once claimed that he had seen a route up the north side in 1953, admitted that he no longer saw a way up that stupendous wall. The porters made a green paste by grinding some weeds on the rocks and dipped their chupattis into it. They invited us to try some—perhaps "dared" would be a better word—and we did. It tasted like wild onion.

After each Balti had had his turn in smoking the community hookahs, we again got underway. The porters marched for only a half-hour before they halted and put down their loads. "What's happening?" demanded Schoening. "They say that this is the standard stage," replied Rizvi. "Apparently Desio stopped here in 1954." "Desio!" Pete and I both exclaimed simultaneously, for we knew that Ardito Desio, leader of the 1954 Italian expedition that had climbed K2, and his party had been wading through two feet of soft snow in a blizzard when they were forced to stop. "Remind the porters that my 1953 party and many other expeditions have camped miles ahead," said Schoening sharply. Their bluff had failed; the Baltis grudgingly shouldered their loads and we continued on.

That afternoon we passed the first of the famous "Ice Ships" of the Baltoro, tall seracs over 100 feet high that resemble ships under full sail. There were three of them in a row and Schoening and Rizvi climbed partway up the side of the middle one in order to provide an object for comparison in photographs.

The expedition began to encounter an increasing number of snow patches and we started to worry about the conditions ahead. At four o'clock the caravan arrived at a depression in the moraine where the advance group of Andy Kauffman, Bob Swift, Tom McCormack, and Tom Nevison were preparing a tent platform. The porters went to work immediately to make shelters out of stones and equipment boxes. We gave some of the groups tarpaulins, but the others just had to huddle out in the open

Through the ice ships toward Gasherbrum IV. The expedition approaches Concordia.

under light blankets. That night we distributed the thirty-five-cent snow goggles that Andy Kauffman had obtained in France. These cheap goggles had shiny metal rims that instantly appealed to the Baltis, who filled the air with cries of "Zindabad!" Furthermore, they proved so effective and comfortable that even the sahibs began to use them frequently, although we had several other types that were much more expensive.

The next day, June 3, only 200 yards out of camp, we reached the edge of the winter's snow that still covered the glacier. At first the surface was hard, but as another beautiful hot day dawned over the Karakoram, it began to soften. All the sahibs got out in front of the caravan to tramp down a path. By noon we had gone only three miles. We kept on slogging. The snow was so rotten that even the oxygen wallahs who were at the end of the 130-man column occasionally broke through the beaten track up to their knees and had to struggle out again. The sky became overcast but it still remained hot. By four in the afternoon we had covered another two miles and were three miles short of our goal, Concordia, when it began to snow. The porters dragged along one step at a time. In the middle of nowhere we stopped and started to establish camp.

On June 4, we awoke to a gray sky that threatened to turn into a blizzard at any moment. But the snow was frozen hard. Just before leaving, we told the porters that it would be the last day for most of them if, by nightfall, the expedition arrived to within a reasonable distance of the site for Base Camp. The porters began to hike rapidly over the hard-surfaced snow. They seldom stopped, and by ten in the morning they had reached Concordia. Looking up the Godwin Austen Glacier toward K2, we could see only a part of its summit through the clouds. The wind chilled us and occasionally a few flakes of snow fell, but these minor inconveniences were welcomed so long as the snow remained firm. After an hour lunch stop the caravan began to march southeast along the upper Baltoro Glacier, which joins the Godwin Austen and other glaciers at Concordia to form the Baltoro. With mountains rising up on all sides of us it was difficult to realize that we were at an altitude of 15,500 feet, 1,000 feet higher than Mount Whitney, the loftiest elevation in the United States outside of Alaska. The sun began to shine, softening the snow, but we were still able to move rapidly.

Marching up the central moraine of the glacier, we encountered a large snowbridge over a wide and deep crevasse that the advance route-finding party had crossed. Some of the porters went over the bridge, but the rest of the Baltis balked. Schoening, Rizvi, and I walked over the bridge and then, in response to our shouts of encouragement, the remaining porters crossed, only to sit down again in the snow. Ghulam Razul yelled at them to move on and even cuffed one nearby recalcitrant, but the Baltis refused to budge. Then Rizvi threatened them, and, grumbling under their breath, the porters slowly picked themselves up and continued on. At four we arrived at a point about three miles from a ridge that descends from Gasherbrum VI and around which the upper Baltoro Glacier turns east toward Hidden Peak and is called the Abruzzi Glacier. It was too late to push on, so we stopped and pitched camp, miles short of our objective.

The porters who volunteered to remain and relay supplies to Base Camp were lined up and their clothing was carefully inspected. Tom Nevison checked the physical condition of the candidates and then we selected twenty of the best Askole wallahs under the leadership of Ali Lambardar for the task. After the last of the other porters was paid and the last complaint settled, we relinquished the big tent to the twenty Askole men who were remaining with us. The other Baltis spent the night in the open near camp and early the following morning, before the rest of us woke up, they departed on their return journey.

8

WHERE'S
BASE CAMP?

The morning of the fifth of June was foggy and we were unable to distinguish any landmarks. Moreover, we were slightly uncertain as to exactly where Hidden Peak was, except that we knew our mountain must be located somewhere around the corner of the ridge of Gasherbrum VI. At breakfast it was decided that Pete Schoening, Andy Kauffman, and Rahim Khan, our strongest HAP, should take one tent and push forward to locate a base camp site on the Abruzzi Glacier while everyone else began relaying supplies. After agreeing to attempt radio contact at 6:00 P.M., the reconnaissance party disappeared into the mist.

At nine the first relay shouldered 60-pound loads and departed. They went two miles up the moraine, established a dump, and returned. Tom Nevison and I remained behind to reorganize the supply boxes and at eleven, when we left camp with 40-pound loads, it began to snow. On the hike to the dump, we passed the porters and HAPs who were returning, and on our trip back we passed them again as they made their second run. The snowfall increased, and during lunch Nevison and I debated whether we should make a second trip to the dump or retire to our tents. The 80 pounds that we would carry seemed insignificant compared with the remaining 3,000 that had to be moved, but every little bit helped so we made another run and again passed the porters as they returned to camp. Each relay of porters and HAPs could carry approximately 25 of the 100 loads of expedition supplies that had to be taken to Base Camp. Therefore, it was extremely important that at least three runs be made to the dump, which would permit the remaining 25 loads to be carried all the way up to the Abruzzi Glacier the following day. However, as Nevison and I returned from the dump the second time there was no sign of the porters making the critical third relay. We were going to lose an entire day, which was inexcusable, for the porters were taking three hours to make the round trip, something that Tom and I did first in two hours and then in an hour and forty minutes. Earlier in the afternoon Rizvi had attempted to make the Baltis do a third run but they had adamantly refused.

Upon returning to camp I summoned Ghulam Razul and angrily instructed him to tell the porters that the doctor sahib and I, who had been sitting behind desks for the past year, were making the run to the dump in half the time of men who supposedly had carried loads all their lives. They were loafing and we knew it. As it was five o'clock and getting dark, I did not expect any results from my outburst, but suddenly there was an angry murmur inside the base camp tent and the Askole wallahs came pouring out of it. It has been said that Baltis have little pride, but my insults stung the porters more than Rizvi's threats. Furious, they wrapped their ropes around the loads and set off through the falling snow to make the third relay. Overjoyed at this unexpected development, Nevison and I strapped a couple of boxes to our packs and fell into the middle of the column. The porters were determined to prove how good they were and pushed forward without a single pause. Occasionally one of them would shout, "Chelo! Chelo!" (Balti for "Go! Go!"). Up at the front of the line someone said, "Urdukas tomorrow," and all the Baltis laughed. We just ignored this implied threat.

It was 6:00 P.M. when we reached the dump, and Tom Nevison, who had brought along a walkie-talkie, tried to establish radio contact with the reconnaissance party, but all efforts to reach them failed. After putting away the radio, Tom and I hurried to catch up with the porters and everyone arrived in our temporary camp by six-thirty. After passing out four extra cigarettes to each porter, we sat around inside the kitchen tent and greedily devoured the excellent dinner that Bob Swift had prepared. In the next tent the Baltis were singing. Not only had they vindicated their honor but they also had some extra cigarettes to show for it. Now all the remaining equipment could be carried straight through to Base Camp the following day, provided, of course, that we learned where the camp was to be located.

Meanwhile Pete Schoening, Andy Kauffman, and Rahim Khan were encountering some difficulties. The central moraine of the upper Baltoro Glacier, which the expedition had followed from Concordia and upon which we were then camped, turns toward the east along with the upper Baltoro and continues up the center of the Abruzzi Glacier. In short, it is a continuous highway right up to the base of Hidden Peak. The reconnaissance party was unable to discover this because of the poor visibility, and we remained unaware of its presence until the Italians marched up it nine days later. Unable to see more than 200 yards, Pete and Andy barely discerned a broad snow highway that seemed to lead up through the jumbled icefall where the Baltoro Glacier turns the corner to become the Abruzzi Glacier. Zigzagging back and forth, they proceeded up this. The snow was soft and frequently they fell up to their waists in concealed holes. Finally they reached the top of the icefall. However, they were still uncertain about their exact location until they got a brief glimpse of a dark slope off to their left or north. Correctly assuming that it was the side of Gasherbrum VI and that there probably would be a reasonable route between the mountain and the glacier, Schoening and Kauffman headed toward it. After several hours of groping their way across crevasses and around seracs, they reached the edge of the glacier just above the icefall at three-thirty in the afternoon. They were still unable to see any distance, but Pete and Andy could tell that Base Camp could be situated farther up the Abruzzi Glacier and far enough away from the side of Gasherbrum VI to be safe from avalanches. Originally, Schoening and Kauffman had hoped to be able to radio this information to us in the main party, then continue their reconnaissance the next day. Later, when the scheduled 6:00 P.M. radio contact failed, they realized that they would have to return.

It continued to snow all night, and the next morning, June 6, when those of us in the main party shouldered the remaining loads and broke camp, we still were enveloped by fog. Walking ahead of the column I suddenly saw three figures loom up in the mist. It was the reconnaissance party. They had descended the corner of the Abruzzi Glacier by following a gully between the cliff and the icefall and then were able to find a reasonable route through some crevasses back to our moraine in the middle of the upper Baltoro. This new route was a great improvement over their original way. However, the porters would have to be roped while crossing the crevassed section between the moraine and the side of the glacier, and we wondered what kind of psychological effect this would have on the Baltis.

The entire expedition gathered at the dump and the sahibs held a quick conference. It was decided that Nevison, Rizvi, and I would remain and establish a camp at the dump for the porters and HAPs while everyone else continued on to the site of Base Camp. Tom McCormack would escort the porters and HAPs back to the dump camp while Bob Swift, Andy Kauffman, and Pete Schoening would stay at Base Camp in order to start reconnoitering Hidden Peak. Despite the knowledge gained from the 1936 French expedition, we were practically on our own insofar as selecting a route up the mountain was concerned, and a thorough reconnaissance was imperative. By conducting such a reconnaissance during the three days that would be spent relaying the expedition's supplies from the dump into Base Camp, we would be able to proceed according to schedule. The conference over, we quickly reorganized the loads once more so that the most important and heaviest boxes would be carried up first, since conditions remained so miserable we were afraid the twenty Askole wallahs might quit at any moment, leaving only thirteen sahibs and HAPs to move tons of equipment.

As Nevison, Rizvi, and I started to establish a camp, the rest of the party departed. Occasionally we caught glimpses of them weaving their way through the crevasses. After much effort the three of us managed to pitch both the big base camp tent for the porters and the rectangular kitchen tent, as well as a pyramid tent for the HAPs and two high-altitude tents for the sahibs. At noon a sudden storm, as furious as it was short, flattened the kitchen tent with Nevison, Rizvi, and me inside, eating lunch. As we struggled with the wildly flapping canvas I noticed that the base camp tent, twenty yards distant, was starting to collapse. Dashing through the snow I reached it but was too late to prevent one curved tent pole from being bent completely out of shape.

When the storm finally died down and the sun came out, our new camp was wrecked. Methodically Nevison, Rizvi, and I tried to restore it. The kitchen tent was repitched and thoroughly guyed down. Then Tom Nevison began repairing the damaged pole of the base camp tent. The problem was not merely bending a spare pole into the proper shape, for the original one had a hole in it for the roof pole and we had no way of making a new hole. There were some poles to hold up an awning and Nevison took one of these (we never used the awning) and, using two kerosene containers as an improvised vise, bent it into the proper shape. Then he fastened it to the original one with wire and tape so that the new substitute furnished the proper shape while the old pole still had the necessary hole for the roof beam. Although it looked extremely fragile, this brilliant improvisation lasted for the duration of the trip. We repitched the base camp tent in a more sheltered place on the moraine and waited for the first relay to return. At five-thirty they dragged into camp. Tom McCormack, who was leading, mechanically lifted one foot at a time, and the porters following in his tracks were not doing much better. The HAPs just collapsed on the ground beside the dump and gulped down the tea that we had prepared for them.

Our morale that night sagged slightly. As the base camp ration boxes were extremely heavy, all of them had been carried up in the first relay, resulting in no meat at the dump camp, except for the high-altitude boxes, which could not be touched. Dinner consisted of soup, a few cans of warmed vegetables, and chupattis. The porters had run out of ghee so we offered them some cans of New Zealand butter, of which there was an enormous supply. The Baltis refused to accept the butter until they were assured that it was a bonus and that their rupee subsistence allowance would not be cut off. They used it to cook pirattas, which are chupattis cooked in ghee, but they never did like it. Apparently the truly excellent butter was too bland for their jaded taste. Also, Ali Lambardar wanted an ice-axe. He did not have the slightest idea how to use one, but the six HAPs had axes and he felt that his social position required it. With grave misgivings I lent him my spare Bhend. Anything to keep the Baltis happy; besides, I was beginning to like Ali, although Rizvi assured me that this was only because I could not understand all the horrible things he was saying about us.

June 7 was another cold misty day. Hussein wakened Rizvi and me by the civilized technique of passing cups of hot chocolate into our tent. I looked at my watch. The lateness of the hour and the warmth in my stomach gave me the courage to crawl out of the sleeping bag and stumble over to the kitchen tent, where I struggled into my boots and had breakfast. Rizvi soon joined me. It was decided that McCormack and Nevison should rest and then occupy Base Camp the next day, as only one or two sahibs were needed to accompany the porters.

When it was time to leave, there was the usual chaos as the Askole wallahs swarmed over the dump trying to select the lightest loads. My carefully calculated priority system was being ruined and I let out a yell. Rizvi and Razul shooed the porters off, then called their names one by one so I could lead the unhappy men to the proper boxes. I wanted the HAPs, who would have plenty of heavy carrying to do on the mountain, and Ali, to have lighter loads, but the boxes got mixed and they had to carry a full sixty pounds anyway. Strapping on forty-pound boxes, Rizvi and I led the column of men out of camp. It was nine when we finally left, which was a very late start, and I made a feeble resolution that this performance would not be repeated.

After a half-mile we reached the point where the route left the moraine and crossed a crevassed area to reach the east side of the upper Baltoro Glacier. The twenty porters, six HAPs, Rizvi, and I tied into four 120-foot nylon climbing ropes about ten feet apart. If anyone fell into a crevasse he would probably pull down an entire rope; however, it made the Baltis feel more secure. Visibility was limited but the tracks made the day before were still in fair condition, although they had disappeared in places. Schoening and Kauffman had put in willow wands to mark the route. Several times I had to cut bucket steps into some short ice slopes and hope that the Baltis with their smooth-soled mukluks could stick in them. It began to hail. Even so, the porters wanted to halt and rest every few minutes. Our signals were quite simple. Whenever they wanted to stop to put their resting-sticks under the loads, they would shout "Shabash!" The first time that they did this I thought they were yelling the usual mutual encouragement and I plunged ahead, only to be brought up short by the rope. Turning around, I saw six Baltis sitting down behind me. When the porters were ready to go they would say, "Tik, sah'b," and sometimes I could stimulate progress with an inquisitive "Tik?" And as the hail came down we went "shabashing" and "tikking" through the crevasses, over the snow ridges, and down into the troughs. We came to some small seracs, three feet high, which in the mist resembled miniature Christmas trees. After an hour we reached the far side of the glacier and took off the ropes. The hail changed to snow, and I was afraid that we might get caught in a blizzard, but the Baltis wanted to stop and celebrate another safe crossing. Ghulam Razul led the singing and clapping of hands while several of the men got up and danced. This put all the porters in a good humor, although it seemed like an exhausting way to rest. Everyone got soaked to the skin, but the thought of the fifty loads still remaining at the dump encouraged Rizvi and me to smile, sing, and clap our hands also.

Finally the Baltis became too tired to dance any longer, so we picked up the loads and continued on between the mountainside and the glacier. Just this side of the corner of the buttress there was a flat dry area and the men insisted on stopping for lunch. The only thing wrong with the place was that rocks that had fallen from the rotten cliffs disappearing into the mists above us studded the ground like cannonballs on a Civil War battlefield. The Baltis liked the spot, and I was afraid to suggest that we move on since they might get the impression that their work was dangerous and quit. No rocks fell during the days we kept using the place, so the debris on the ground had probably accumulated over a long period of years. Rizvi arrived after a few minutes' delay and I could not resist needling him.

"And as the hail came down we went 'shabashing' and 'tikking' through the crevasses..." to establish base camp.

"What kept you?" I asked. "Some trains have to be pushed from the rear," he replied.

After lunch we descended 40 feet into a scree gully between the cliff and the glacier and followed it around the corner. Large icicles fell off the side of the glacier as we climbed 300 feet up to the head of the gully, which was higher than the top of the Abruzzi Glacier's icefall. Base Camp, now only a short distance away, could not be seen through the storm. We were sitting down for our last rest when Ali suddenly got a nosebleed. Blood spattered his clothes while his anxious fellow-villagers crowded around him. Now the porters will quit for sure, I thought, handing him some Kleenex I had with me. I kept trying to explain that he should lie down and put his head back, but it was of no avail because he always sat up too soon. The Baltis started to become morose. Ali then tried to stop the bleeding by stuffing the Kleenex up his nostril. This did not help. Besides, every time the blood began to coagulate he blew his nose violently and the snow turned crimson again. The silly nosebleed rapidly assumed the proportions of a major crisis. "Tas," I pleaded. "Please make him put his head back until the bleeding stops." Rizvi did, and after a tense ten minutes Ali raised

90

his head, nothing happened, and we were on our way again.

Base Camp consisted of a collection of boxes. There was not even a tent, as Schoening, Kauffman, and Swift had gone ahead and pushed their reconnaissance despite the bad weather. Rizvi and I broke into a box of base camp rations to get some meat to take back to the dump camp. I have never heard of prior Himalayan expeditions carrying food back the day after it has been relayed to a higher camp. However, they never had the benefit of my wonderful load priority system. Also, there was some chewing gum in the box, which I distributed to the porters. We were getting ready to leave when suddenly there was a commotion on the far side of the camp. "What's happening, Tas?" I asked. Rizvi conferred with Razul and then casually replied, "A porter slipped and almost fell into a crevasse, but he's all right."

Marching in lock step, roped up ten feet apart, we blindly followed our tracks through fog across the upper Baltoro Glacier back to the dump camp. That evening Rizvi joined the HAPs for a dinner of lentils and curry instead of sharing a can of ox tongue with Nevison, McCormack, and me. He became ill and was temporarily out of action.

On June 8 McCormack and Nevison, who were going to occupy Base Camp, escorted the porters, while I went with them to take movies. The sky was clear and the impressive Muztagh Tower gleamed in the distance. Once we could see exactly where we were, there seemed to be an atmosphere of unreality about us. For years I had looked with wonder at Vittorio Sella's famous photograph of the Muztagh Tower and now that mountain formed the background for my friends. It was impossible to believe that we were actually in the Karakoram. Only the softening snow broke the enchanted spell cast by the mountains. The return trip was going to be rough. If only the porters would move more rapidly and save time. But it was impossible to explain to the Baltis the necessity of speed, especially on such a warm, lovely day.

Upon reaching the side of the glacier, Nevison and McCormack pushed on to Base Camp while the rest of the caravan stopped and had lunch. Later as we turned the corner and climbed up the scree gully beside the icefall, waves of heat, reflected by the glaring surface of the Abruzzi Glacier, shimmered in the hot sun. Beads of sweat saturated our eyebrows and slid down our faces, stinging our eyes and fogging our goggles. We came over the rise and there it was—Hidden Peak.

It was like seeing the Grand Canyon for the first time. The shape was familiar but the size was beyond belief. In front of us and 10,000 feet above our heads, at the top of a gigantic pyramid that rises directly out of the South Gasherbrum and Abruzzi glaciers, was the summit. Just below it, a glacier tumbled down the mountain underneath the tremendous hanging ice cliffs of the west face. To the left, the bare rock of the northwest ridge swept up the final pyramid. To the right the French buttress climbed into the sky and culminated in the point called Hidden South (23,200 feet) before connecting with the high snow plateau that extends for miles toward the southeast at an elevation of over 23,000 feet. Beyond the French spur, almost out of the scene, the arête tried by André Roch in 1934 rose for thousands of feet before it, too, joined the plateau, five miles from the summit. For years we had mentally climbed Hidden Peak. We had located many camps on many routes and had devised innumerable strategies, but staring up at the massive bulk of rock, snow, and ice that now confronted us, all one could say was, "We're going to climb that thing! How?"

When the Baltis and I arrived at Base Camp, McCormack and Nevison had already pitched their tent. The porters wanted to break up for firewood the crates protecting the oxygen bottles. However, we could not afford to take chances with the oxygen equipment and refused to let them do it.

The return trip across the upper Baltoro Glacier to the dump camp was as miserable as I had anticipated. We sank in at every step, while the hot sun seared our faces. A precious tube of zinc oxide that Nevison had given me was rapidly exhausted as the Baltis wanted some when they saw me applying it to my lips. Arriving back at camp I was very glad to see that Rizvi was feeling much better. Dinner that night was a gruel made out of atta and sugar. Perhaps it was a sign of progress that all the food was up at Base Camp.

Meanwhile Pete Schoening, Andy Kauffman, and Bob Swift had finished reconnoitering the western side of Hidden Peak and the South Gasherbrum Glacier, which leads into the cirque of the Gasherbrums. On June 6, after accompanying the first relay of supplies to the base camp site, they went back to the tent that Kauffman and Schoening had left near the top of the Abruzzi icefall during the first reconnaissance. There they spent the night. The next morning, June 7, undeterred by the overcast, they folded their tent and hiked up the lateral moraine of the Abruzzi Glacier until they reached its junction with the South Gasherbrum Glacier. Although they could barely see the sides of Gasherbrum VI and Hidden Peak, they turned north and started up the center of the icefall of the South Gasherbrum Glacier. The area was honeycombed with crevasses covered by thin slabs of snow, which they kept breaking through, sometimes up to their shoulders. Having to pull themselves out of these holes while wearing heavy packs was exhausting labor. Moreover, they were in a whiteout, which made it impossible to tell whether they were walking up or down, much less be able to distinguish crevasses. In that flat light they could have walked into the side of a serac before being aware of its presence. Finally, at noon, Pete, Andy, and Bob decided to pitch camp at 18,500 feet in the middle of the icefall. They were unable to find an area sufficiently free of crevasses to allow them to put up the tent safely, so they made a platform

"We came over the rise and there it was." Hidden Peak, 26,470
feet, from the Abruzzi Glacier.

by chopping off the slanting top of a serac fifty feet high and put the tent
on it. Here they spent the rest of the day writing in their logs, reading *The
Oxford Book of English Verse*, and wondering when their tent platform
would collapse into the depth below.

When the reconnaissance party awoke the next morning it was clear
and cold—so cold, in fact, that they made three attempts to leave the tent
before finally getting under way. However, they were able to get a good
view of the huge peaks that surrounded them. On the west side of the cirque
were Gasherbrum VI and Gasherbrum V. Ahead of them to the north was
the incredible Gasherbrum IV (only 20 meters lower than the magic
number of 8,000), which the Italians were going to attempt. To the right of
the high col east of Gasherbrum IV was Gasherbrum III, also above 26,000
feet. Then the larger pyramid of Gasherbrum II, the Eight Thousander
climbed by the Austrians in 1956, rose high above the head of the South
Gasherbrum Glacier. Pete, Andy, and Bob continued their climb up between huge creaking seracs through the center of the icefall. After two
hours they reached the top of the icefall and ran into a series of large longi-
tudinal crevasses that appeared bottomless. There were constant
"karuumphs" that seemed to echo for hundreds of feet in opposite directions, and the entire surface that they were standing on would shake.

Backtracking slightly they cut over to the west and followed a trough that went underneath the west face of Hidden Peak. Again they came to a labyrinth of crevasses. Once, all three men fell into separate crevasses at the same time. It appeared that the entire area might fall into the depths, so they retreated back through a corridor of seracs, and after crawling through a keyhole in an ice wall, they emerged on the other side near their tent. They halted briefly for lunch and packed up their personal gear. Then they left the tent behind and started down the South Gasherbrum Glacier. Plunging through many more concealed crevasses, the reconnaissance party arrived at four-thirty in Base Camp, where Tom McCormack and Tom Nevison greeted them.

It had been a strenuous two days but Schoening, Kauffman, and Swift had accomplished their objective. Not only had they investigated the west glacier of Hidden Peak, but they also had discovered another possible route up the northwest ridge that led directly from the South Gasherbrum Glacier to the summit. The lower slopes of the ridge appeared quite easy, and while the final 2,500 feet was over rock, it was not too steeply inclined.

On June 9, Rizvi and I led the last relay of supplies from the dump camp on the upper Baltoro Glacier to Base Camp. All the tents were struck, except the big one the Baltis were using, and we started across the glacier. It was a warm day and we sank into the snow. I was very happy that it was the last run. So were the porters. When we reached the side of the glacier they began their customary singing and dancing with unusual vigor. We had brought the drum along and the Askole wallahs beat it furiously before handing it to Rizvi. Then as Tas pounded out a rhythm they shouted and laughed. Balti after Balti went into a frenzied dance and stopped only upon becoming completely exhausted. This was the last time. Today they would be paid. Tomorrow they would leave the sterile world of ice and rock and return to their brown hills.

Several hours later the caravan reached Base Camp. The other sahibs were waiting for us. We gave each man his wages plus a little *baksheesh*, a tip. Then, after a brief discussion, Ali Lambardar surrendered my ice-axe, and the porters departed, escorted by Ghulam Razul and Rahim Khan, who were to bring up the big tent the following morning.

With mixed feelings we watched the Baltis disappear from sight. We had had to prod and threaten to keep them moving, and it was a great relief to be no longer dependent upon their vicissitudes. But thanks to those stubborn men who walked barefoot over sharp stones and ice, we were at the base of Hidden Peak. Despite our worst fears, the porters had not caused us any delay.

With the departure of the porters the last of the unfamiliar uncertainties were behind us. From this point on we would be doing what we had done for years—climbing a mountain. What lay ahead were only the usual

obstacles of rock, snow, ice, altitude, and weather, albeit on an unprecedented scale. Or at least that is what we kept inwardly reassuring ourselves
in the presence of the large inanimate object that now was in our sight as
well as in our minds during all our conscious hours. We had reached our
Eight Thousander. All we had to do was climb it.

Tom Nevison: "Where now?"

9

A DECISION
IS MADE

Base Camp was situated at 17,000 feet on the lateral moraine of the Abruzzi Glacier about halfway between the second and third avalanche chutes on the south side of Gasherbrum VI, east of the corner buttress. The surroundings were magnificent. Across the glacier, avalanches regularly poured down the ice cliffs of Baltoro Kangri. To the southwest the white pyramid of Chogolisa rose into the sky. We could never fully enjoy its beauty, for every time we looked at the east face, its tremendous ice flutings slowly turning purple in the growing shadows of the afternoon, we were reminded that it had been only a year since Hermann Buhl, one of the finest mountaineers in the world, had fallen through its cornice. Hidden Peak was directly ahead of us to the northeast, and miles away was Sia Kangri at the head of the Abruzzi Glacier.

The few large open crevasses in the moraine did not disturb us. However, patches of winter snow concealed many deep narrow cracks that slowly began to widen. One of them was underneath a tent. While everyone readily accepted the innumerable crevasses that had to be crossed in the main section of the glacier, most of us resented these intrusions in our backyard.

There was a small pool in a depression in the moraine thirty yards to the east of camp. Although it was always frozen in the morning, it thawed during the afternoon. One had to stand on the ice at the edge in order to dip a pot into the open water in the center of the pool. Often the ice broke. If by chance one's boots had been dry, this was indeed a tragedy. The water bearer had to carry the pots back to camp without spilling the contents every time he fell waist-deep in the soft snow. It required a little practice, and the person who fetched the water always received from his thirsty comrades such generous platitudes as, "I guess you really aren't such a bad guy after all." They hoped that he would be foolish enough to make a second trip. He never was.

At first Base Camp was just a few high-altitude tents and a pile of boxes. But ever since man emerged from caves he has longed to live in houses and on June 9, while waiting for Rizvi and me to arrive with the final relay of supplies, Schoening, Swift, Nevison, Kauffman, and McCormack responded to this primitive urge and began to make a hut out of the supply boxes. They leveled off the uneven rocky surface of the moraine and by the time Tas and I reached camp, they had erected the walls. The roof beams were made from the boards of the oxygen crates and then were covered with ponchos and tarpaulins.

Earlier, back at Payu, Tom Nevison had cut down a ten-foot pole to hold a wire antenna for the shortwave receiver. All the way up the Baltoro Glacier the pole had to be carried in a vertical position to prevent it from catching on the sides of moraines, seracs, and other obstacles. Now Tom strung it with wires and proudly erected it beside the entrance to the hut while Rizvi and Kauffman tied Pakistani and American pennants to it about halfway up.

In the center of the shack a large crate and several smaller ones served as a table and chairs. Just inside the entrance was the cylindrical cardboard drum that contained the film. The boxes in one of the walls formed open

Mountain of memory. Chogolisa from Base Camp. Hermann Buhl died the year before in a fall through its cornice.

shelves on which we stacked our equipment and the base camp rations. The bottom shelves contained nylon ropes, stoves, pitons, extra crampons, and many other odds and ends including the typewriter, while the food was put in the higher boxes. When the job was finished, the interior of the hut resembled a cross between a mountaineering supply store and a grocery.

After this rearrangement we realized that there was enough oatmeal, canned butter, and powdered coffee to last through the winter. The meat supply, also, would last indefinitely. According to Rizvi the British Masherbrum Expedition had considered ox tongue a delicacy, and they were most unhappy when their HAPs consumed the entire supply at one sitting. Now these same HAPs decided that meat prevented them from acclimatizing. We could not even give the ox tongue away.

June 10 was one of those rare days in which we could reach out and almost touch the tops of the surrounding mountains. Such weather should be reserved for climbing, not for inspecting equipment. Methodically we began to organize everything so that in the days to come men and supplies could move efficiently up the mountain without being delayed by the lack of some critical item that had been overlooked. String underwear, wool underwear, wool pants, wool shirts, down pants, down jackets, wind suits, balaclava helmets, silk gloves, wool gloves, leather overmitts, down overmitts, snow goggles, climbing boots, reindeer boots, gaiters, crampons, and ice-axes were spread over the sun-warmed rocks in such profusion that it was difficult to move without stepping on something. There was the usual bewildering variety of climbing hats. Swift and Schoening continued to wear their cowboy hats. McCormack and Kauffman sported Tyrolean models, I had a fishing cap, and Nevison had the most original headgear of all, an old flying helmet, which made his appearance resemble a barnstorming pilot of the early thirties.

Rizvi was happy to discover that his reindeer boots fitted perfectly. However, Swift could wear only one pair of socks inside his. Moreover, all the gaiters were the same size. Only McCormack could squeeze a pair over his reindeer boots. Everyone began to worry. Do our crampons fit! They fitted perfectly and our morale went up again.

After carefully checking each article, everyone stacked his personal equipment into three piles. First, there were the clothing and equipment that we would not use again until the march out. This included khaki clothing, wallets, and items of a similar nature. The second pile contained the articles that we were going to need on the lower slopes of the mountain. The third pile of equipment included those special items, such as reindeer boots, down pants, down mittens, and wind pants, that would not be used except above Camp III. The last group also included extra pairs of clean socks and anything else the climber would be happy to have during the final phase of the climb. Each pile of gear was put into a large polyethylene bag, which was labeled. The bags containing the march-out clothing were placed into boxes, which were sealed. Then each man put his high-altitude bag into his personal box with his name on it. Thus, if for any reason a man on the mountain could not come down but needed his high-altitude equipment, anyone who was at Base Camp could easily locate it and send it up.

We had a wonderful time playing with our toys, especially with the reindeer boots, which resembled furry kittens. Our individual ice-axes, which had been specially made for each man, had our names engraved on the pick. While this personal touch was new to us, Kauffman said that it is a common practice for mountaineers in the Alps to have their names put on their axes to prevent accidental switching in dark, crowded alpine huts. It seems that the axe that is left behind in such mistakes is usually inferior to the one that is taken.

McCormack and Kauffman had the nicest toys of all. They had to check the pressure in the twenty-eight oxygen bottles. This was a crucial moment, for Marmet had warned us that we could expect partial loss from twenty-five percent of our bottles. Mac and Andy tried to pretend that it was a dull chore, but their beaming faces betrayed them. Only one bottle

"We could almost reach out and touch the tops of the surrounding mountains." The Mitre, 19,718 feet, at Concordia.

was low in pressure. Then they checked the oxygen regulators. All the regulators functioned perfectly, but the manometers on the five instruments that had been made for our expedition were defective. Only the manometer on the sixth regulator, an old instrument from the 1956 Swiss Everest Expedition that Marmet had lent us for a spare, gave accurate readings. Kauffman wrote the amount of each regulator's discrepancy on a piece of adhesive tape and fastened it to the offending instrument. Then he spread the tubes, masks, bladders, and helmets over the ground. Suddenly he began rummaging through the container. "What's the matter, Andy?" I asked. "The metal clips needed to attach the mask to the helmet are somewhere," he muttered, and McCormack and I joined him in sifting through the excelsior that was scattered about. Normally we would not have bothered to tear up everything looking for them, but Marmet is such a perfectionist that we felt the clips had to be somewhere. After searching for them for a half-hour we finally gave up and used safety pins, which worked satisfactorily. Later, when the expedition was over and I mentioned this incident to Jürg, he said, "You know, that was the only item of equipment that I didn't check personally."

Tom Nevison put batteries into our three walkie-talkies and began to test them. He promptly discovered that all the radios were not tuned to the same wavelength. One set could talk only to the second and receive from the third so that only two radios were really effective. Undaunted, Nevison and Schoening stepped off a hundred paces and began to transmit to each other. With an audible noise a tube in Nevison's set blew. Nevison got the second radio. "Can you read me? Can you read me?" floated back and forth. Everyone else in the vicinity could easily "read" both of them, as they yelled into the microphones in order to be understood. "Hey, Pete. If you'll take the receiver away from your ear you can hear him better," someone shouted.

The only nonessential article that the expedition had brought was a boomerang. Bob Swift's logical argument of "What will we do if we encounter some kangaroos on the upper Baltoro Glacier?" was irrefutable. Two days earlier Tom Nevison had torn the plaster cast from Swift's right arm with a pair of pliers. Now Bob celebrated by giving the boomerang a few tosses. A glacier places a severe penalty on poor technique, and Bob usually got the weapon to return to within a reasonable distance of its starting-point. Then McCormack became intrigued with the thing and after receiving a few brief words of instruction, he leaned back and gave the boomerang a mighty throw. It flew straight as an arrow. "Look out for the crevasses," someone called as McCormack began trudging down the moraine.

At noon Rahim Khan and Ghulam Razul arrived from the dump on the upper Baltoro Glacier with the base camp tent. The HAPs immediately cleaned and aired it before we pitched it beside the hut.

After lunch we gathered in the sun while Nevison explained the medical equipment. Besides the big fishing box that Nevison used as his main medical kit, there were first aid kits for each camp and personal first aid kits for each man. Also Nevison had prepared a special "pneumonia kit" for each camp, which consisted of four injection units with over 300,000 units of penicillin in each one. In addition, we planned to stock every new camp with at least six bottles of oxygen before occupying it. Through a combination of the antibiotics in the first aid kits, the penicillin injection units, and the oxygen apparatus, we hoped the danger of pneumonia would be reduced to a minimum.

Next Kauffman instructed everyone in the use of the oxygen equipment while I took movies of the scene. As we were the first American expedition ever to take oxygen for climbing purposes, we had only a vague idea of the detailed technical theory behind the equipment. However, we had the finest oxygen apparatus in the world, and Marmet had done an excellent job of teaching us how to use it. After watching Andy demonstrate the equipment, everyone took turns putting on the mask and adjusting the apparatus. Within an hour all the other sahibs knew how to adjust the rate of flow, how to check and clear stoppages, and how to make emergency repairs.

By midafternoon everything had been organized for the climb and, with the exception of the butane-gas stoves that Andy was going to demonstrate after dinner, everyone had been briefed in the use of all the equipment. There remained one major problem. Which way were we going to tackle the mountain towering over us?

Only a fool takes chances. A mountaineer takes calculated risks. He may miscalculate and miscalculate badly, but that does not relieve him from the responsibility of evaluating everything he knows about the difficulties and dangers involved in all possible courses of action before arriving at a decision. The more experience a mountaineer has, the more accurate are his estimates of difficulty and danger. Carefully considering all factors, he must balance the danger involved against the chance of success. Then he must decide whether the goal justifies the risk that will be involved. This is a personal decision that every mountaineer must resolve according to his personal philosophy of mountaineering and life. The more important the objective, the higher the risk a person is willing to assume in order to achieve it. Even so, if a mountaineer accepts those risks, he is still bound to do everything within his power to minimize the dangers involved in his course of action. It is impossible to be one hundred percent safe. Merely to be alive is to be in danger. He should not be afraid to accept the challenge of the unknown, but he should not proceed carelessly. Incompetence, not enterprise, is the sin.

There were five possible routes up Hidden Peak. Looking up at the mountain they were from left to right, or northwest to southwest: The northwest ridge, the western glacier underneath the summit pyramid, the south spur that leads to the subsidiary peak of Hidden South and then to the southeast snow plateau, a glacier just beyond the south spur, and finally the ridge reconnoitered by André Roch, which also leads to the snow plateau.

Choosing a route in the Himalaya is a process of elimination rather than selection. The art of route-finding is separating the impossible from the improbable and the improbable from the merely difficult. The latter is the route. The south spur route over Hidden South was eliminated first. Everyone agreed that it was the worst of the five possibilities. It consisted of down-slanting rock slabs leading up to a snow slope under Hidden South. It would be necessary to traverse Hidden South and drop at least 500 feet down the steep far side in order to establish one or more camps on the snow plateau. No one was very enthusiastic about having this obstacle behind the advance parties. Moreover, this was the route that the French had tried to force in 1936. Although they had had a team of magnificent climbers, and had displayed great tenacity and courage in establishing four camps on the spur, they had been turned back by bad weather at an altitude of only 22,000 feet.

Now the process of elimination became more difficult. The western glacier was extremely tempting. It was the most direct route to the summit and connected with the snow plateau just south of the final pyramid. The route was over snow and ice, although there was some question as to the difficulty of finding a way through the icefalls on the glacier. Unfortunately, the lower section of the glacier was directly underneath the hanging ice cliffs of the west face of the summit pyramid. While there did not seem to be many signs of avalanches, these cliffs could fall at any time and if they did, the resulting avalanche would sweep the entire route. We agreed that some mountaineers might accept the risk; however, we felt that the possibility of the entire expedition's getting wiped out made this otherwise attractive route unjustifiable.

We had not yet seen the small glacier behind the French spur that joined the Abruzzi Glacier. It had been explored in 1936 by Marcel Ichac, who called it the Glacier du Milieu. He had told Kauffman that there were some large crevasses at its head, and then a steep snow slope led up to the southeast plateau. This route joined the plateau near the same point that the Roch ridge did, so we did not consider it too seriously, as the ridge appeared safer.

Thus, our choice was narrowed to either the northwest ridge or the Roch arête. To reach the northwest ridge we would have to have two camps on the South Gasherbrum Glacier. The first of these camps had already been established by the reconnaissance party. Then at least three more camps would have to be placed on the lower part of the ridge up to 24,000 feet. While the final rock section of the ridge leading to the summit was less than thirty degrees, it was impossible to determine whether a camp could be placed on it.

The Roch ridge rises from the Abruzzi Glacier and joins the southeast plateau at an altitude of 22,500 feet. From there it is about five miles over gentle snow slopes to the base of the final pyramid, which did not appear very difficult on that side. The ridge itself was about five miles up the Abruzzi Glacier from Base Camp. Camp I would have to be established there and then several camps would have to be placed upon the ridge. Finally two camps or more would be required out on the high snow plateau. The ridge itself did not appear very difficult and we knew that André Roch, without using crampons, had climbed to 20,000 feet on it in only three hours.

Crowding around the crate that served as the table inside our shack we debated the merits of the two routes. It was the only violent argument during the entire trip. With the success and safety of the expedition at stake, the dispute became as furious as only an argument can when its participants are convinced that they are right. I was absolutely against the northwest ridge, and Bob Swift felt exactly the same way about the Roch spur. The other members of the expedition were in between, although they tended to favor the northwest ridge, primarily because it was the shortest route to the summit. There were many minor arguments against both routes, which we hurled at each other. The South Gasherbrum Glacier would have so many holes in it that we would constantly have to escort the HAPs. There were cornices on the Roch ridge that might stop us completely. However, these were used merely for tactical harassment. The main battle was whether we preferred 2,500 feet of rock climbing or five miles of snow plodding to the summit.

I had read many Himalayan accounts and the disadvantages of climbing on rock on very high mountains had become indelibly impressed in my mind. After years of trying to climb Everest over the down-slanting slabs of the north face, mountaineers had finally climbed the mountain several times by a snow route from the south side. In fact, with the significant exception of K2, all the Eight Thousanders that have been ascended were climbed by what are essentially snow routes. Snow can require tremendous physical effort, but rock climbing demands balance and thought. Moreover, at 26,000 feet, it takes only a few feet of difficulty to stop assault teams. At lower elevations, anything can be climbed if one has the time and energy to place sufficient pitons and bolts, but at high altitude the situation is completely different. My prejudice against rock was reinforced by the experience of the American expedition to Makalu in 1954. They had attempted the rocky southeast ridge and had to turn back at 23,500 feet. The next year the French chose a snow route and got the entire party on the summit. Above all, our predecessors on Hidden Peak had selected a rock route and had failed. However, it had to be admitted that the northwest ridge looked feasible. Up to 24,000 feet it was quite reasonable and in the event of bad weather we could easily retreat. Only the summit assault teams would be taking any risk. Furthermore, looking at the upper section through binoculars, there did not appear to be any large sections of the ridge that would cause trouble, although one could not see small details from that distance.

Bob Swift had done some of the most difficult rock climbs in Yosemite Valley. In 1956 he and Dick Irvin had been caught by the monsoon on the long, exposed northwest ridge of Rakaposhi and were lucky to escape alive. He was unalterably opposed to a long snow plateau the condition of which was unknown. It could be undermined with crevasses that would stop us completely. In all probability the snow would be soft, and we would have great difficulty in breaking trail, if we could move at all. Most important, if we were caught on the snow plateau by the monsoon, we would probably be trapped. For distance, the southeast plateau on Hidden Peak resembles the infamous Silver Saddle on Nanga Parbat, and everyone remembered the fate of Willy Merkl, Willo Welsenbach, and seven other climbers and sherpas who died on that mountain in 1934. The monsoon had caught that ill-fated German expedition at their highest camp, and one by one, climbers and sherpas had collapsed and died as they tried to fight their way down the mountain through mounting drifts of soft snow.

However, our oxygen equipment gave us added strength and mobility. If the conditions were good, we should be able to climb the mountain in a couple of days from the junction of the Roch ridge and the plateau, the long distance notwithstanding. We would not have to move out onto the plateau until the weather turned good and the danger of being trapped would be reduced to a minimum. Besides, in the Nanga Parbat disaster, Erwin Schneider and Peter Aschenbrenner had escaped because they moved rapidly, and we had greater mobility than they had.

Pete Schoening said that both routes would go and added that he thought the northwest ridge would be easier than the Abruzzi ridge on K2. The Abruzzi ridge! Suddenly I realized what was happening. K2 has the same significance to American mountaineers as Everest has to the British and Nanga Parbat has to the Germans. It has been the object of most of the major American efforts in the Himalaya. When American mountaineers think about climbing in the Himalaya they think in terms of K2. The Abruzzi ridge is the only feasible route up that mountain and it is rock. This, combined with the fact that, with the exception of a few climbers around Seattle, American mountaineers are basically rock climbers, explained why Americans have always been willing to attempt rock routes in the Himalaya. Pete had summed it up with his one comment, "It's easier than the Abruzzi ridge." And the Abruzzi ridge is still one of the most difficult routes on any Eight Thousander.

Finally Pete Schoening put the following proposition to the group. "Assuming that the Roch arête is easy, how many are in favor of it?" I raised my hand. I was alone.

However, we had not reconnoitered the Glacier du Milieu and the Roch ridge, and everyone agreed that we would be very foolish to make a final decision without at least looking at them. Accordingly we decided that the next morning Schoening, Kauffman, and I would go over to the base of the ridge. There we would establish camp and make radio contact at 4:00 P.M. to inform the group at Base Camp what we had discovered. Meanwhile the rest of the sahibs and the HAPs would make the first relay of supplies to Camp I, which had been established on the South Gasherbrum Glacier. This would give us a start on the northwest ridge. The chances that the party would select the Roch arête were slim, but if the route was as easy as André Roch claimed, perhaps I could sway Pete and Andy. Also, some of the other sahibs might change their minds after stepping into a few hidden crevasses going up the South Gasherbrum Glacier. It was a hope anyway.

That evening after dinner Kauffman demonstrated how the butane-gas stoves worked. One of the major problems of high-altitude mountaineering is dehydration. The only way the mountaineer can obtain water is by melting snow. Not only does this consume a large amount of fuel, but most gasoline- and kerosene-burning stoves also tend to be temperamental. They have to be primed and often they are difficult to start. One has to be very careful not to set the tent on fire by allowing the stove to flare up or get knocked over. All in all, it requires considerable mental effort to use them safely at high altitude. Andy pulled out a blue, squat, flat-bottomed bottle, screwed a burner into its top, and struck a match. At first he had some trouble because the burner was new and had to be broken in, but soon the stove always lit with a controlled flame on the first match. The rest of us watched this demonstration with great interest. The days of safety valves blowing up in a geyser of fire were over. Whenever we became thirsty, we could just fill a *dekshis* with snow, put it on the stove, and strike a match.

Kauffman had also brought along a lantern attachment that would screw into the butane-gas bottles. This was a wonderful device, which had several iron rods surrounding the glass chimney over the mantle. But how did it work? The lantern was passed from man to man like a Chinese puzzle and everyone got an opportunity to marvel at the ingenuity of French industry. It was a complete enigma. "I wasn't paying too much attention when Raymond Leininger was showing this to me," confessed Kauffman. We knew how to operate and repair the oxygen equipment; surely we could figure out how the lantern worked. "No, no, not that way. Put the wires like this. Now let's try it. There it goes. See, I told you so." The lantern lighted up briefly and then went out, as a little wisp of smoke curled out of the chimney. "Idiot, you're burning the mantle. Let me try it," and another sahib would demonstrate his technique. This was more fun than checking oxygen regulators. The evening passed quite rapidly. Finally we figured out how the lantern worked. It proved to be very simple, and fortunately we had several spare mantles. It was dark so we used the lantern to go to bed.

At six the next morning the other sahibs were just stumbling out of the base camp tent to get their daily ration of oatmeal when Schoening, Kauffman, and I left to go over to the base of the Roch ridge. We went up the side of the glacier for about a quarter of a mile and then decided to cut over to the medial moraine. Between us and the moraine there was a maze of small seracs, frozen surface pools, water troughs, and crevasses. "This is about as good a place to cross as any," said Pete. "May as well try it," Andy and I replied resignedly. We had to weave our way around many small holes, but the snow was hard and forty-five minutes later we were through. From then on, the surface of the Abruzzi Glacier was relatively smooth, and we just walked up the glacier toward Sia Kangri. Soon we could look up the South Gasherbrum Glacier into the cirque of the Gasherbrums. Gasherbrum IV appeared extremely steep, and we were glad that the Italians were going to attempt to climb it instead of us. The only possible route on it seemed to be the ridge that rises out of the col between it and Gasherbrum III.

It was another cloudless day and the snow began to soften slightly, but it was still early in the morning and we continued to move rapidly. The gradient was so gentle that we did not realize how much altitude we were gaining until we looked back at Base Camp. After passing the French buttress we reached the mouth of the Glacier du Milieu and were able to get a good look at it. There was fresh debris on the upper part of the glacier and numerous avalanche tracks marred the steep snow slopes beyond it. The slope that forms the southeast side of Hidden South looked especially unpleasant. The three of us agreed that if we were willing to accept the kind of risk involved in the Glacier du Milieu, we should try the western glacier and come out right underneath the summit pyramid instead of miles away.

Beyond the Glacier du Milieu is the Roch ridge. Actually it is a rib that connects the southeast plateau with the Abruzzi Glacier. The side that borders the Glacier du Milieu is a precipitous rocky wall, but the side facing the Abruzzi Glacer rises for 3,500 feet in an unbroken concave snow slope that terminates in a dome of snow and ice. The left border of this slope is a rock and snow buttress. The lower part of the buttress drops off to the Abruzzi Glacier in rock cliffs hundreds of feet high while the upper part forms the left shoulder for the crest of the snow slope. This crest is a narrow corniced arête that runs from the top of the buttress up to the dome. From the dome, at about 22,000 feet, the ridge gains only about 500 feet as it extends for over a half-mile to join the plateau at a point five miles from the summit of Hidden Peak.

Pete, Andy, and I climbed about 300 feet up the snow slope at the right edge of the rock buttress to the top of some rocks where a small couloir between us and the main snow slope afforded some protection against any small avalanches that might come down. It was now nine-thirty in the morning and we collapsed on our packs. Guzzling from the canteen, Andy and I watched Pete start to chop out a tent platform. "If you'll just wait a minute, we'll help you," I gasped as Schoening flailed the slope. Soon our guilty consciences began to overbalance our fatigue and we stumbled over to help Pete. Fortunately most of the work had been done, but Andy and I were able to make a show of the old team spirit.

We pitched the tent, which completely filled the platform that had been made. The location was spectacular; the altitude was 18,800 feet, and I had a headache. Andy did not feel very well either, as this was the one day of the trip that he was actually ill. After we had melted snow for a gallon of water and had lunch, we were sitting in front of the tent admiring the scenery when suddenly there was a loud rumble. Avalanches had been constantly falling off the mountains around us, but this was different.

Looking up at Sia Kangri, we could see that the summit cornice had broken off. As it fell it triggered off the snow masses clinging to the mile-high wall in front of us and with a tremendous roar the entire face avalanched. It hit the Abruzzi Glacier and began to roll down it, preceded by a gigantic cloud of snow that rushed at us. Although we were several miles away from the base of the cliff, we began to secure our tent, but the cloud of snow drifted by us in a relatively gentle breeze. When the dust finally settled we could see that the debris had come down the glacier for about a mile. It was the largest avalanche any of us had ever seen.

During the afternoon I began to persuade Kauffman and Schoening that the Roch ridge was the best route. I turned to Andy. "We walked over here without any trouble, didn't we?"

"Yes," said Andy.

"You saw the slopes above us?"

"Yes."

"It's just walking as far as we can see. At least for the next 2,000 feet, isn't it?"

"Yes," said Andy. "It does look pretty good, but what did André Roch say? Roch is one of the best snow and ice climbers in the Alps. If he said the route is all right, then I'm in favor of it."

"André said it was all right," I reassured him.

Pete Schoening was more difficult. Everything was fine to Schoening. He gladly would climb either route, but the northwest ridge seemed to be a little more direct. "I want to have another look at the slope above us," he said. He and I left the tent and climbed up about 150 feet. The snow was soft and we were sinking in at every step. After ten minutes I yelled up to him, "Look, Pete, it's like this for the next 2,000 feet." "You're right," he replied and we returned to the tent. "I guess that this is the best way," he said. "I'll tell the boys at Base Camp to come on over."

After the sahibs who remained at Base Camp had finished their pot of cold oatmeal, they arranged the loads for the carry to Camp I on the South Gasherbrum Glacier. McCormack, Rizvi, and Nevison became suspicious as to what lay ahead when Swift spent an hour thoroughly instructing the HAPs in the technique of safe glacier travel. Finally at eight they set out. The South Gasherbrum Glacier was deteriorating, and during the entire trip everyone kept pulling his legs out of crevasses. They dumped fifteen boxes of high-altitude rations at the camp and then struggled down. The snow had softened. They enlarged all their previous holes and greatly increased our knowledge of that glacier by making many new holes. They

"A walk in the sky." The route up the Roch ridge and along the plateau to the summit.

ANDRÉ ROCH

returned to Base Camp at three o'clock and made a large pot of lemonade.

We could see the general location of Base Camp from our reconnaissance camp at the foot of the Roch ridge, and at exactly 4:00 P.M. expedition time we received a mirror flash. The day before, in order to establish the time of radio contact, Nevison and I had dramatically synchronized our watches although the true time remained unknown. In the course of an expedition it is inevitable that everyone will set his watch by someone else's and expedition time is always based upon the person's watch that is still running after others have run down. If it had not been for the short-wave receiver, we could have established a good betting-pool as to the correct time when we finally returned to civilization. The mirror flash proved that we had a direct line of sight contact for our radios, and while I flashed a reply with our signal mirror, Schoening began to transmit, "This is Schoening at recon. camp calling Base Camp. Come in Base Camp." Nothing happened. He repeated the call. A combination of squawks and groans came out of the walkie-talkie. Suddenly we heard Nevison's voice, loud and clear, saying, "Base Camp to recon. party. Got your transmission but can't read you. Over." Pete pushed the mike button again and said, "This is the route. Repeat. This is the route." Nevison's reply sounded like feeding time at a tropical birdhouse. We tried it again at 4:15, then at 4:30. Through the static we gathered that Nevison wanted us to return to Base Camp to talk things over. Further contacts, preceded by mirror flashes, were attempted at 4:45 and 5:00 before we finally gave up. It was our last radio transmission for the duration of the trip.

My wristwatch alarm went off at 4:30 A.M. Schoening began to prepare breakfast while Kauffman and I slowly struggled into our boots. At six we emerged from the tent into the cold morning air and strapped on our crampons. Andy started off but Pete, who was carrying the pack, soon took over the lead. We followed the main snow slope for 300 feet to skirt the cliff band that rose above the glacier. Then, to avoid the danger of avalanches, we turned up the right side of the buttress and climbed to its crest. This side was also a snow slope; however, it was studded with large rock outcrops that divided it into numerous gullies in its lower section. When we reached the crest of the ridge, we roped up and traversed some rock outcrops. The ridge became corniced on the left or north side and connected to a wide snow slope. Climbing up this slope one step at a time, we broke through the crust and sank calf-deep into unconsolidated powder snow that lay over an icy base. We became increasingly unhappy as the angle of the slope increased and the layer of powder snow thinned. There was no danger of a large avalanche. However, we were no longer over the right side of the buttress with its gentle runout, and if the top surface slid, we would be carried over the cliffs that dropped onto the Abruzzi Glacier.

Suddenly Schoening, who was leading, cried, "This slope is creeping!"

Pete was a short distance from the top of the slope and the only question in our minds was: Which way off—up or down? "Let's go down," yelled Andy and we rapidly descended. Sitting down at its base, we ate some chocolate bars and discussed the situation. Pete explained that he had some difficulty removing his ice-axe, and he could not place it back into the same hole. With the confidence that comes from a position of relative safety, we decided that the slope would be safe if fixed lines could be attached to it. We assured ourselves that we were just suffering from a little touch of nerves because of all the avalanches that were constantly coming down the mountains around us.

We descended the side of the buttress and upon passing the last of the rock outcrops, we took off the rope and our crampons. Pete went into a standing glissade and shot down the slope. Andy and I were commenting on his excellent style when he hit a patch of soft snow, flipped into the air, came down, flipped again, hit in a sprawl of arms and legs, went into a self-arrest, and stopped. "I don't recommend it," he yelled, picking himself up. Kauffman and I heeled down.

We arrived back at the tent at nine-thirty and melted pot after pot of snow to quench the thirst that had resulted from our labored breathing in the dry air. We were tired, but we had to return to Base Camp, and the longer we postponed it the worse the snow would become. We left at eleven and sank in at every step. It was too late. Schoening took over the lead from Kauffman and stolidly broke trail. We decided to cut across the crevassed area between the central moraine and the side of the glacier farther east than our previous crossing. This was a mistake. We plunged up to our waists into concealed holes and it required a gasping effort to drag ourselves out. A mist enveloped us, which reduced the stifling heat a trifle, but we could no longer see Gasherbrum VI and lost our bearings. Schoening never seemed to slow down. I began to wonder what was wrong with me and was considering giving up the sport when I turned around and looked at Kauffman. One glance at his agonized face and I realized what the trouble was. We were tied to a steam engine. Schoening kept bucking ahead and when Andy and I requested that we stop to rest, the expression on his face was bewilderment, not disgust. During the entire trip Pete made a deliberate effort to set a slow steady pace, and he could never understand why his companions always seemed to be on the verge of collapse. We found the tracks that had been made by the other sahibs on their run up the South Gasherbrum Glacier and followed them into Base Camp. Just outside camp Abdul Rahim and Hussein met us and took our packs. We stumbled into the cool hut and drank the lemonade that Nevison and Swift had prepared for us.

That afternoon in the base camp tent we had our final argument over the route. Schoening called for a vote. Rizvi stated that the HAPs did not like the South Gasherbrum Glacier, and he now favored the Roch ridge. Nevison, thinking out loud, expressed his fundamental doubts about both routes, then concluded that since it would be easier to evacuate a sick man off the Roch ridge, he favored that route. Swift still favored the northwest ridge and McCormack seconded him. Kauffman said that he was slightly in favor of the Roch ridge. I was still emphatically in favor of the Roch ridge. Four people were vaguely in favor of the Roch ridge and two were definitely against it. Schoening summed everything up by saying that both routes could be climbed and while he personally was inclined to pick the northwest ridge, the consensus of the expedition was that we should try the Roch ridge. That was it. Tomorrow everyone would haul loads over to the base of the arête.

During the past few days I had been absolutely confident that the Roch ridge was the best route. Now that the expedition had selected it, I suddenly began to have my doubts. I came out of the tent and looked at the northwest ridge. It really did look simple. Then I looked over at the Roch ridge. It would go. It had to go.

Camp II view.

10

CAMP II

S choening believed in the efficacy of slogans to stimulate party morale. At six-thirty in the morning when we started to make the first relay to Camp I, Pete shouldered a sixty-pound load and cried, "Bearcat!" All the other sahibs looked at him as if he had lost his mind. It was a try. Shortly after leaving Base Camp, we arrived at the cutoff over to the medial moraine. The day before, the HAPs had hauled some food boxes to this point, and we stopped while they

113

strapped them to their loads. All the sahibs were tied into one rope, and I suggested that we split up. I even volunteered to lead a second rope. It was not a magnanimous offer on my part. I was still feeling the effects of yesterday's effort and wanted to get off Schoening's rope at all cost.

The second trip through the crevasses between the side of the glacier and the moraine was easier than the first. It seemed improbable that we would find a better way, so we placed willow wands to mark the route. After crossing the crevassed section, we made good time over the hard snow. We passed an avalanche fan from a couloir in the rock buttress at the base of our ridge and established the dump for Camp I at about 18,500 feet on the Abruzzi Glacier. It was an excellent site, flat and free from avalanche danger. Even if the entire slope above avalanched, the camp would be safe.

Tomorrow Pete Schoening and Tom Nevison were to locate a site for Camp II and consolidate the route by attaching fixed rope. This would enable another team to establish that camp the following day. When the rest of us left to return to Base Camp, Pete and Tom began relaying their loads, including 2,000 feet of manila rope, to the small reconnaissance camp 300 feet up the ridge.

It was a pleasant stroll back until we hit the crevassed section. The snow had softened and we kept plunging into holes. First one leg went in and then the other. Since I was leading, I was resigned to my fate, but Swift, at the rear of the line, kept breaking through the crust in places that the rest of us had walked over. Bob was the heaviest member of the expedition and suffered severely because of it. When Swift broke trail, it was really broken. When someone else broke trail, Swift had to rebreak it anyway. This constant stepping into crevasses was more frustrating than dangerous. Once when on a small pressure ridge, I fell through to my waist and my friends started laughing. The crevasse was open at the end and they could see my legs wiggling. Even after we reached the side of the glacier, we kept putting our feet into small concealed holes, barking our shins.

We spent the rest of the afternoon in Base Camp sipping lemonade and studying the Roch arête with binoculars. Kauffman, McCormack, and I with Abdul Rahim and Qasim were supposed to establish Camp II and push the route up the dome where we would place Camp III. There was only one problem. Where were we going to put Camp II? The angle of the ridge was not extremely steep but it was unrelenting. There was not a flat space on it large enough to hold a tent. The only possibility seemed to be a short horizontal stretch, perhaps thirty feet long, behind a rock buttress 2,500 feet above the Abruzzi Glacier. It was not very good but everything else looked worse.

Then we studied the route beyond the rock buttress. This would be the most difficult section of the climb. Andy kept peering through the binoculars at the dome and saying, "It's all windslab. Look at the glossy surface. There, you can see tracks from other slides. It will avalanche and kill us all!" It looked unpleasant but it was all right. Besides, Kauffman has made gloomy predictions for years and no one believes them, least of all Andy. Once we were on the ridge, he would be in the vanguard as usual.

Bob Swift's blisters were still in bad shape and now he caught a mild infection. As his efforts would be more important later, the rest of us insisted that he spend the following day in Base Camp taking some movies that were badly needed.

Since they had to return to Base Camp, Tas and his team of four HAPs left at dawn, June 14, for Camp I. The rest of us left at the civilized hour of seven. We were about two miles from Camp I when we spotted Schoening and Nevison on the slope below the reconnaissance tent, descending very rapidly. They could not have put in the fixed rope already. What was wrong? At nine-thirty we met them as they started to return to Base Camp. Nothing was wrong. They had left their tent at three-thirty in the morning and reached our previous high point an hour later. Then Schoening had tied into the end of the manila rope and, while Nevison belayed him, had climbed up the slope that had scared us. When Pete reached the top of the slope, he drove in an ice piton and attached the rope. Twenty feet farther he put in a four-foot aluminum rappel picket as a second anchoring point. Nevison cut the rope from the coil and attached it to another rappel picket. Then he joined Schoening. They repeated this efficient process over and over. By eight-thirty they had put in over 2,000 feet of rope in a continuous line and had climbed to within forty feet of the bottom of the rock buttress before they were forced to quit. They had run out of manila rope. It was a fine performance. Furthermore, to my great delight, Nevison seemed to be in good shape instead of having the "fish out of water" appearance so normal for Schoening's companions on such a jaunt. "Did you see what was behind the buttress?" asked Andy. "No, we didn't," said Pete. "But I'm pretty sure you can get a camp in there. We'll start making relays up to Camp II day after tomorrow. Good luck." With that we parted.

While Tas and his four HAPs wandered back to the fleshpots of Base Camp, Andy, Mac, and I pitched two high-altitude tents and one small pyramid model. Andy, who was the official flag bearer, tied our various pennants to the tent poles, which added a bit of color to our surroundings. The reconnaissance camp had served its purpose, so we sent Abdul and Qasim to retrieve the tent.

The early start is one of the most horrible aspects of mountaineering. If all the solemn oaths—made with stars as their witnesses—were kept, the sport of mountaineering would vanish within a fortnight. However, the alternative of plowing through soft snow or dodging avalanches is infinitely worse. The secret for getting away early is to prepare everything the night before. Then all you have to do in the morning is to put on the pack and start trudging. By the time you become aware of what is happening, it is too late to turn back. So in the hot afternoon sun, we swallowed aspirin and organized our loads.

We left at five in the morning. The snow was frozen and we did not put on the rope. After walking through the well-marked route in a small crevasse area outside camp, we climbed to the site of the former reconnaissance tent. There we added more coils of manila rope to our forty- to fifty-pound loads. As there was no avalanche danger, we climbed up the gully that had been our route of descent during the reconnaissance. Qasim had forgotten to bring his crampons, and his rubber-soled boots were slippery. The most talented of the HAPs, with pride to match, he said nothing and kept climbing. Once when McCormack bent over to tighten a crampon strap, an ice hammer slipped out of his pack and went down the slope. We did not bother to retrieve it but gestured to Qasim and Abdul to pick it up on their return to Camp I.

For the first thousand feet we made steady progress. Then we began to sink in. When we reached the first fixed line, we were hot and very tired. We grabbed the rope with both hands and slowly dragged ourselves upward, one step at a time. The first slope was the worst. It was too steep to allow us to sit down comfortably. Besides, we were always a little afraid of it, so we kept on plugging, constantly glancing up to see how far away the top was. The rucksack felt as if it would crush me into the slope. Just to reach the top and collapse on it became an obsession. Only forty feet and I can take it off, I thought. Thirty feet. Twenty feet. An all-out effort now. Ten feet. I sank into the snow and watched McCormack, bent double under his load, on the rope below. Why the sight of your companions in similar distress in reassuring, I will never know. Perhaps one wants to feel that one's misery is normal for such a situation. On the Abruzzi Glacier four specks were heading for Base Camp. The rest of the party had made the relay to Camp I and now Schoening, Nevison, Haji, and Rahim Khan were returning. Rizvi and Swift, who were to make the first relay to Camp II, pitched the big white tent at Camp I.

The rest was over and I grabbed the fixed rope again. Qasim and Abdul Rahim were just ahead of me. Kauffman was 200 yards up the slope. It did not look very far away, but it would take forty-five minutes to reach the spot. We plowed a track through the soft snow. The fixed rope was invaluable. We seemed to be pulling ourselves up the mountain by our arms, with the uphill leg just furnishing the starting kick. Then the rope ended. Kauffman had left his pack behind while he climbed the last 100 feet to the top of the rock buttress. One by one the rest of us dragged ourselves across

Porters walk through irrigated fields near the village of Hotu on their way up the Braldu Valley. Mango Gusor (20,632 feet) is in the background. Except for such fields, Baltistan is scorched earth and rock.

The main party before leaving the Skardu Rest House. Front, from left: Andy Kauffman, Tom Nevison, Bob Swift. Rear: Tom McCormack, Pete Schoening, Nick Clinch, Tas Rizvi. Mohd Akram is not shown.

The camp at Payu after a snow storm. Payu was the loveliest campsite of the entire approach march.

Tom McCormack, Bob Swift, and Tas Rizvi pass out cigarettes to the Baltis as they leave Payu camp. The porters are carrying wood to cook chupattis.

The expedition trudges over the snow-covered Baltoro Glacier toward
Concordia. Gasherbrum IV is in distance.

The overnight camp on the Baltoro Glacier just before Concordia.
Gasherbrum IV, first climbed by the Italians, is in background.

Chogolisa (25,110 feet) climbed by the Japanese later in the summer.
Hermann Buhl was killed here the year before in a fall through a
cornice.

Dump camp on the upper Baltoro Glacier, with the Mitre, left, and the Muztagh Tower in the background. The big white tent housed the Askole men who were relaying loads to Base Camp.

The Base Camp shack built out of porter boxes, oxygen crates, and tarpaulins. It was a cross between a mountaineering supply store and a grocery.

Hidden Peak (26,470 feet) above the Abruzzi Glacier. The summit on the left, Hidden South in the middle, and the Roch ridge used by the expedition on the far right.

Sia Kangri (23,500 feet) at the head of the Abruzzi Glacier. Large avalanches came down its snowy faces.

The Roch ridge seen from the Abruzzi Glacier on the way to Camp I. The route went up the ridge on the other side of the rocks.

Looking down at Camp I from the lower part of the Roch ridge. The route up the Abruzzi Glacier from Base Camp to Camp I is in the distance. This run became known as the "pneumonia patrol."

Camp I at the height of the supply build-up, with the flags of various countries flying from the tents.

Mohd Akram at Camp III (22,000 feet). Chogolisa (25,110 feet) to the left and Masherbrum (25,660 feet) to the right. The lower Abruzzi Glacier with Base Camp is in right foreground.

Right, *relaying supplies between Camps III and IV. Camp III is at the end of the ridge. The massive bulk of Baltoro Kangri (23,761 feet) is in the rear.*

The summit of Hidden Peak from Camp IV, over 4,000 feet higher and miles of soft snow away. The route went up the plateau between Hidden South and Urdok Peak.

Camp IV (22,500 feet). The oxygen bottles still have their protective covers. Behind camp is the end of the ridge, down which the party rappelled.

Tom Nevison and Pete Schoening prepare the oxygen equipment on one pack
to be used by the climber breaking trail in the soft snow of the plateau.

From left, Gasherbrums IV, III, and II, two summits of Broad Peak, and K2
from the summit of Hidden Peak. The summit of Gasherbrum III blends into
the summit of Broad Peak. All of these mountains are above 26,000 feet.

On the summit of Hidden Peak, July 5, 1958, Andy Kauffman holds the American flag and the Pakistani flag made by the schoolchildren of Skardu.

Andy Kauffman, with his blistered face, back in Camp I after the summit climb.

The expedition poses in front of Hidden Peak at Base Camp after the climb. Front, from left: Bob Swift, Tom Nevison, Dick Irvin. Rear: Mohd Akram, Gil Roberts, Tas Rizvi, Pete Schoening, Nick Clinch, Andy Kauffman, Tom McCormack.

Pete Schoening after the climb

Pete Schoening stands at Concordia and looks at K2 (28,250 feet), the objective of three previous American expeditions and the site where, in 1953, he held five falling men at 25,000 feet.

the snow slope and sat down on some down-slanting ledges. It was one in the afternoon. It had taken us seven hours to make this drag and we still had 300 feet of rock climbing ahead. "There had better be a campsite behind the buttress; there is nothing here," said McCormack. "No good, sah'b, no good," repeated Abdul Rahim over and over, indicating that it was too far. He was right. It was too far. But there was no place to stop.

Kauffman had tied a nylon climbing rope to a loose rock to serve as a fixed line on the lower section of the buttress. "Be careful when you use it," he warned. "If you put any weight on it, it'll come off." Kauffman descended the last 100 feet from the top of the buttress and tossed down a belay rope. I frantically tried to unsnarl a coil of manila rope to be used as a hauling line while McCormack took the end of it and struggled up to join Kauffman. Andy then climbed back to the top of the buttress and the fun really began. The snow slope bypassed the buttress, but it was in terrible condition so everything had to be hauled up the rock.

We were exhausted and now our efforts required mental concentration. Andy belayed McCormack while he tackled the first difficult pitch. Mac fought it for fifteen minutes before he took off his pack. Then he started up again. Meanwhile Qasim climbed up to McCormack's ledge. A shower of rocks came down. Abdul Rahim went up and stationed himself thirty feet below Qasim. There were more falling rocks. Then I went up. The slabs were slick and covered with loose debris and I forgave Qasim and Abdul for their barrage. Finally McCormack reached Kauffman. "Go over there and pitch camp," said Andy, pointing to the spot that we had selected from Base Camp. "Where?" exclaimed McCormack, staring at the knife edge of snow that was our "flat area." "Don't ask me where," snapped Andy. "Schoening says there's a campsite. Make one!" McCormack went over to the ridge and began to hack out a tent platform. Ice chips rained upon the three of us below.

Kauffman established a hauling line between Qasim and himself. By gestures he got Qasim to tie one of our high-altitude tents to the line and he pulled it up. It was a fairly successful effort—it jammed only once. I took Abdul Rahim's pack and yelled at Qasim, who tossed down a rope and hauled the load to his stance. Next he tied it to Kauffman's hauling line.

This simple operation took eons and was accompanied by much shouting between Andy and me at the top of our voices. We also took turns shouting at Qasim, who was performing magnificently, although he could not understand a word we were saying. I climbed up to Qasim and motioned for him to descend. It was four-thirty, and he and Abdul would have to hurry to reach Camp I before dark. I belayed Qasim down to the nylon climbing rope that Kauffman had attached and gestured to him to take that rope for his descent. With great relief we watched the two HAPs retreat rapidly down the fixed lines toward Camp I. They were safe. Then we turned to our immediate problem.

As I tackled the first short chimney, a cascade of snow and ice came down. McCormack was really chopping out that platform. A few shouts in his direction and the ice chips ceased to drop down my neck. Now I saw what had stopped McCormack. The climbing was not very difficult, but in my tired condition I could not get up with the pack on. Kauffman tried to haul it up. It cleared the first chimney and then jammed. We freed the line. It jammed again. Andy and I sandwiched our instructions between mutual unpleasantries about each other's ability and ancestry. McCormack resumed work on the platform and the ice came down again. We had to have a place to sleep, so this trivial annoyance was now ignored. Kauffman hauled my pack up; then he suddenly shouted, 'There goes a tent! No! Wait! It stopped! I think I can retrieve it." "Hope so," I yelled up. "We haven't even paid for it yet." He managed to reach down, grab the $150 tent, and fasten it to his anchor rope.

It was starting to get dark. I climbed up to Kauffman, who was anchored ten feet below the top of the buttress. "We've got to get those loads," I gasped. "If you can give me a belay perhaps I can carry some of them up," he answered. I climbed to the top of the buttress, straddled it, and anchored to a loose rock. After straightening out the ropes, I discovered that I could rig up a fixed line as well as give Andy a belay. And so it was. Kauffman descended for the first load. "Are you sure you have a good belay?" he called. "I'm bombproof. You're doing fine. Come on up," I answered. Slowly he staggered up. McCormack came over and took the pack to the tent platform. Andy descended again. "UP ROPE, UP ROPE," echoed from below and then Kauffman's pale face appeared over the edge of the rock. McCormack began wrestling with the high-altitude tent. Andy descended for the third time and dumped the contents of two food boxes into his rucksack. "I'll have to leave the fixed rope behind and get it in the morning," he yelled.

"Forget it!" I answered.

"Climbing."

"Climb."

Andy reached the first ledge and took a rest. McCormack had the tent pitched and began putting our air mattresses and sleeping bags inside. Andy started up the last stretch. "Watch me, I'm getting a little tired. I may want tension," he said apologetically. There was the scrape of hard rubber on rock, then Andy heaved into view. He stood quietly for several minutes, balanced by the belay rope, and panted.

Kauffman and I joined McCormack inside the tent. "What time is it?" asked Andy. I glanced at my watch. "Six o'clock," I replied. "Thirteen hours! Who said that six hours is a normal day's work in the Himalaya?" said Andy as he started the butane-gas stove. "How high are we?" asked

McCormack. I dug out the altimeter that I had borrowed at the last minute. The dial indicated 6,005 meters. "That can't be right. We're higher than the Conway Saddle over there," said McCormack. I looked again. It was the six-thousand-meter altimeter that had been put in a box labeled eight thousand meters. That was the end of our altitude surveys. Camp II was about 21,000 feet high.

The tent completely filled the platform that McCormack had so laboriously cut out. Kauffman and McCormack faced the main entrance while I, in the middle, had my head toward the rear of the tent. McCormack asked me to dispose of a can, and when I opened the flap I stared down at the Abruzzi Glacier, 2,500 feet below. I just dropped the can and it shot down the slope, first rolling, then ricocheting from the rock outcrops, and finally falling parabolically out of sight toward the glacier. Our garbage disposal facilities were excellent.

The three of us spent a restless night. During the entire trip I noticed that I was bothered by insomnia the first night at a higher elevation, but after that I slept fairly well. We were somewhat cramped, but our lack of environment discouraged us from wiggling too violently. Someone moved slightly. Someone else whispered, "Hey, take it easy." The movement stopped. The offender asked, "Mac, are you sure you have this thing well anchored?" "I think so," came the reply. Then we tried to go back to sleep.

While at Base Camp, we had planned to get an early start and take the final ridge by storm, but when six o'clock came, it was too cold and we were too tired for any early morning high-altitude heroics. McCormack poured some water from a thermos bottle into a *dekshis* and began heating it to make hot chocolate. Andy gave the traditional signal for the morning ritual of getting dressed. "I think my boots are down at your end of the tent," he said. There seemed to be an amazing amount of junk in my end of the tent. I held up a soggy boot. "Is this it?"

"No, that's McCormack's," he replied.

"I can't seem to find them. Wait. Here they are underneath Mac's air mattress."

I gave the boots to Andy. McCormack distributed hot chocolate in plastic cups. "Excellent, Mac," said Andy. "You have natural talent," I added. McCormack accepted these compliments with becoming modesty. Besides, he realized that in the Himalaya any dish that is hot and consists primarily of water brings ringing praise for its talented creator. In fact the only way to get criticized is to spill a pot of hot liquid over your companion's sleeping bag.

McCormack had coughed steadily all night, so we decided that he should spend the day straightening camp. Kauffman and I attached a fixed line to the top of the rock buttress and threw it down the adjacent snow slope. This enabled us to avoid the rock. Then Andy descended to the coils of manila rope that we had left behind. He untangled them and extended

119

the fixed line down to the previous high point, which had been established by Schoening and Nevison. Meanwhile, we could see Bob Swift and Qasim rapidly climbing up the slopes below. Rizvi, Razul, Abdul Rahim, and Hussein were right behind them. The buildup into Camp II had really begun. If we did not start moving out, we were going to be run down by the support team. At ten, Qasim suddenly appeared at the head of the fixed rope. Everyone else had dumped his load at the base of the buttress, but not this remarkable HAP. Despite his tremendous exertions the day before, he had carried his load the entire distance to Camp II. "How are you, Qasim?" we asked, taking his pack. "Tik, sah'b," he replied happily.

Embarrassed by Qasim's arrival, Andy and I left McCormack to entertain our guest and belatedly started up the ridge. I kicked steps through soft snow to the base of a second rock buttress that terminated in the arête leading to the dome. The snow slope bypassed this obstacle on the right, but it was mushy and unstable so I picked my way up some glazed slabs directly ahead of us. After 100 feet of climbing on eggshells, I reached a loose rock, which served as a belay stance. Kauffman joined me, dropped the pack, and led through. The final section of the buttress was steep and there were several possible routes. Finally Kauffman said, "I'm taking off my crampons and climbing directly up the wall." A few minutes later he was at the top of the buttress. "Come ahead!" he yelled. I picked up the pack and Kauffman's crampons and started up. To save time I did not take off my crampons and after a considerable struggle I joined Kauffman.

It was quite a spot. Three hundred feet below us, the tent at Camp II looked like a buzzard's roost that had been abandoned because it was too cramped. Beyond it in almost a straight line was Camp I on the Abruzzi Glacier. To the north we could see almost the entire snow plateau leading to the summit pyramid five miles away. It was more encouraging to look at the nearby south ridge, for we were as high as the French Camp IV. Then we studied the route ahead. A narrow arête with small double cornices and several rock barriers stretched for 150 yards to the base of a snow slope leading to the dome. On the right was the headwall of the slope, which dropped 3,000 feet to the Abruzzi Glacier. "It would be a quick way to descend to Camp I in case of a storm," said Kauffman, "but it would be a wild ride," he added quickly. I agreed with him, but I was not about to try it. There was no possibility of sliding down the left side of the ridge. It was a rock wall that dropped directly to the Glacier du Milieu.

Andy started to lead across the arête. He tightroped for thirty feet along the crest, traversed a five-foot-high snow tower on its left side, and then gave me a belay. When I reached the tower I demolished it and climbed over the top. This took some time but it made the route safer. Then Andy started up the right side of a twenty-foot step in the ridge. The snow was extremely rotten and finally he quit as his steps kept going down

"Hours of boredom." Carrying loads up to Camp II. Qasim, as usual, in the forefront.

the mountainside. We retreated to the top of the buttress, attached fixed line, and descended to Camp II. We had gained and consolidated 300 feet. At this rate it would take a year to reach the summit. We resolved that tomorrow we would get an early start and put an end to this nonsense.

Arriving at the tent, we found that McCormack was feeling weak. Kauffman gave him some tetracycline tablets, then turned to me and said, "You snore too loudly. Better start chopping out another tent platform." I did not protest the eviction for it was too crowded in that tent anyway. There was ice underlying the snow, and it took me an hour to make a platform wide enough to hold half a tent. When I tried to pitch it, the inside poles skittered around on the ice while the outside ones hung over the slope. For a few minutes I held the poles and wondered what to do, because if I let go, the outside poles would fall down the mountain. "Tie them together at the top," suggested Andy, which I did. Then I anchored the end ropes to a rappel picket and a shovel and fastened the ropes on the uphill side to an ice-axe. The downhill part of the tent just sagged over the slope. As the tent occupied the only level ground, I had difficulty walking around it. However, the interior was very comfortable. For the first time in my life, I could sit up inside a tent by merely hanging my legs over the edge.

After a leisurely dinner with Kauffman and McCormack, I filled my thermos bottle with coffee, and safeguarding myself with an ice-axe, climbed the few feet to my tent. The sun was going down. Pink clouds floated across the sky, obscuring the summit of Masherbrum, which dominated the scene. Down below, the Abruzzi Glacier with its moraines and crevasses appeared like the spine of a living animal. The Swiss flag had freed itself from the rest of the pennants that Kauffman had brought and flapped in the wind. It was a beautiful scene. Unfortunately it meant that the weather was changing.

It snowed all night and the next day. Activity at Camps I and II ceased. But a little snow never stopped the relaying of supplies from Base Camp. On June 17, Schoening, Nevison, Rahim Khan, and Haji got their usual predawn start and made their third straight run to Camp I with sixty-pound loads. Upon returning, they met Walter Bonatti and Toni Gobbi with 120 porters, the vanguard of the Italian expedition, coming up the central moraine. Many of the porters had been with us and there was a loud reunion. The Italians had given the Baltis snow goggles that had a leather shield for the nose, but they preferred our simple ones with shiny rims, so Pete Schoening and Tom Nevison promptly traded theirs.

Just then Akram arrived and there was a second loud reunion. Akram's personal porter was paid and Rahim Khan and Haji carried his equipment to Base Camp. The rest of the afternoon Nevison and Schoening sat inside the dripping hut and listened to Akram's experiences. He had marched in with the Italians, who were having a few problems. Fosco Maraini was down at Concordia with 300 loads while another 45 loads still remained at Urdukas. Moreover, half of their high-altitude porters had quit, taking the clothing that had been given to them. Everyone was overjoyed to see Akram, and with his arrival the main party of the expedition was at full strength.

At Camp II, life was not dull. As the snow piled up on the tent I began to wonder if the cotton cords would break, sending the tent and its contents down the slope. The wind kept lifting the floor of the tent, and I put my camera and boots on it to hold it down. McCormack's condition slowly became worse and Kauffman increased his diet of pills. At noon I was inspired to leave my tent by the magic words, "Dinner's ready." I joined McCormack and Kauffman and devoured more than my share of their delicious dinner. I do not recall what it was, but I distinctly remember that it was tastily prepared. Then I cleared the tents and filled the cooking pots with snow, the usual duties of the person who was dressed to be outside. Returning to my tent I suddenly had an inspiration. I never had trusted the ice-axe that was supporting the uphill side of my tent and now I tied the guy ropes to the end of the fixed line, which was anchored to the top of the second rock buttress. Happy, I crawled inside my sleeping bag, ignoring the obvious fact that the weak link in the chain was the cotton guy ropes, not the firmly driven ice-axe.

It continued to snow all night. At five the next morning, June 18, I heard Andy yelling, "McCormack is getting worse. We must go down."

We struggled into our boots and roped up. Six inches of powder snow covered the slopes. There was danger of surface slides and I was thankful that the fixed ropes were in. Kauffman went first, McCormack was in the middle, and I was last. We grabbed the fixed line with both hands and slid down in a shower of snow. It was misty and we could not see more than a few feet ahead. Then the first fixed rope ran out and we relearned a cardinal rule. Fixed ropes should always be linked together. The next fixed line was buried underneath the snow and we could not find it. "It's got to be here somewhere," said Kauffman, pawing around. I descended a little farther searching for the rope and then, upon looking back, I said, "You must be near the top of it there. I recognize the location." By now we were digging through the snow like three starving mongrels looking for a bone on a midwinter day. We had to find that rope, not only for protection against surface slides but also for guidance in the fog. Returning to Camp II was out of the question; McCormack had to descend to avoid getting pneumonia. Suddenly Andy shouted, "I have it." Brief cheers. I led off on the wallow down the slope.

It was impossible to rappel because we sank too deeply into the soft snow, so we leaned against the fixed rope and kicked steps. We kept expecting the slope to slide at any minute, but it never did. We reached the bottom of the fixed line and glissaded down the lower gullies, taking the layer of powder snow with us. Upon reaching the main slope we unroped. My left knee bothered me and I limped behind my comrades. Just outside Camp I we put on the rope again to cross some crevasses. Abdul Rahim and Hussein met us and took our loads. Then we stumbled into the big tent to join Swift and Rizvi. "Bad news. Razul fell into a crevasse and sprained his knee badly. He can hardly walk," said Rizvi.

That same morning Schoening, Nevison, Rahim Khan, and Haji left Base Camp to make their fourth relay. As he was going to remain in Camp I, Nevison put a few extra items into his pack, including the shortwave receiver. Although it was snowing, the temperature was warm, even before sunrise. Immediately they sank into the snow. Farther on, they plunged hip-deep into a water table just underneath the surface of the glacier. Several times they tried to distribute their weight over the surface crust by crawling on their hands and knees. This did not help. The blowing snow covered their previous tracks and obscured the trail markers. About two miles short of Camp I, Schoening realized that they were going too slowly to make a round trip, so he and Haji cached their loads and retreated. Nevison and Rahim Khan slowly continued.

While returning, Schoening and Haji stopped at the Italians' base camp, which they had established on the central moraine of the Abruzzi Glacier. June 18 was Toni Gobbi's birthday, and Pete joined Walter Bonatti in toasting Gobbi's health with tomato juice and singing "Happy Birthday." Schoening told them about our South Gasherbrum Glacier camp, which was stocked with 200 pounds of food. With our camps on opposite routes to the summit, the Italians must have thought that we were attempting the first pincer movement in the history of mountaineering. Since our abandoned camp was on the Italians' route to Gasherbrum IV and their base camp was on our route to Camp I, Schoening traded them our 200 pounds of food on the South Gasherbrum Glacier for an equal amount from the Italians' supply. Also Gobbi and Bonatti offered to bring down our tent and equipment while Pete promised to give them a list of the contents of our high-altitude ration boxes. Schoening had a wonderful time and it was late when he and Haji left the Italians to return to Base Camp.

About an hour after McCormack, Kauffman, and I had reached Camp I, Nevison unexpectedly appeared at the entrance of the tent. "Next summer I'm going to the shore," he said, throwing his seventy-pound rucksack on the floor. Nevison flopped down beside it on a sleeping bag. He slowly opened his pack and threw a small dark green polyethylene sack to the center of the tent. "Mail. Akram brought it in," he said. Five pairs of hands grabbed at the sack simultaneously. Kauffman and Rizvi had several letters. Bob Swift had one from his parents. I had a large stack of mail about expedition business. This was very important because we wanted to know if it would be safe to return to civilization when the trip was over. Then there was McCormack's mail. The other members of the expedition were either married or hardened bachelors, but not McCormack. He had letters from three different girls in as many countries. After the rest of us had consumed our dull offerings, we turned on McCormack and began to make him feel the full burden of comradeship. "But they really aren't very interesting," he protested. "Now, Mac. Remember your responsibilities toward maintaining the morale of the party," we said. Finally, overwhelmed by our insistent reminders of his obligation to the "team," he capitulated. McCormack was right. The letters were not very interesting.

After lunch we were sitting quietly inside the tent, reading, sorting equipment, and listening to the radio when McCormack casually asked Nevison, "Say, what does coughing up blood mean?" "What!" exclaimed Nevison, as the rest of us turned and stared at McCormack. "Well," drawled Tom, quickly recovering his professional nonchalance, "you probably have a little touch of pneumonia. Stay on antibiotics and take it easy for a few days. Don't do any work. Just remain low and rest." Then Swift made a large pot of lemonade and as we drank it, we discussed the situation. Nevison reported that Akram had said the monsoon had hit Bombay so hard that the great port had been closed for several days. There was much speculating as to how far away Bombay was, which way the monsoon traveled, and how fast it moved. It was still snowing outside but the weather made climbing only unpleasant, not impossible. We decided that tomorrow Swift, Nevison, and Kauffman would reoccupy Camp II and then start to work on the ridge beyond. Everyone else would relay loads. We could not afford to waste a single day. Somewhere the monsoon was coming toward us and we had a long way to go.

11

THE PNEUMONIA
PATROL

The next morning, June 19, was warm and foggy. We ate a leisurely breakfast and assembled our loads in slow motion. By ten we had accumulated enough energy to drift out of camp. Swift, Nevison, and Kauffman moved out first. Then Hussein, Qasim, Abdul Rahim, and Rahim Khan each picked up two twenty-pound food boxes and departed. Rizvi and I brought up the rear.

A foot of new snow covered the slope. We did not bother to rope up. The primary danger was avalanches, and the rope would tend only to drag us under. Two hundred feet up the slope the first group, composed of Swift, Nevison, and Kauffman, zigzagged back and forth plowing a deep track through the snow. As they did so, they cut the layer of powder snow loose and it slid down, refilling the tracks below so that Rizvi and I had to replow them. Avalanches falling unseen off Baltoro Kangri boomed loudly. Rizvi and I fell farther and farther behind. The first group and then the HAPs disappeared into the mist. They were moving very slowly. But I was even slower. It took me an hour to gain 200 vertical feet in one couloir. Somewhere off to the right there was the hiss of surface slides. The layer of soft snow became deeper. It required great effort to climb 10 feet and I sat down constantly. By now I had ceased to recite song lyrics or Lewis Carroll nonsense rhymes over and over; I just picked a temporary objective and counted each step until I finally quit 20 feet short of it. Then I picked another temporary objective. Rizvi set his food box down 300 feet above me and descended, coughing violently. Now I had a new objective. I would eat lunch sitting on Rizvi's box, where the seat of my pants would not get cold and wet. It was a marvelous goal. Gone was the summit, gone was Camp II; all that mattered was Rizvi's box. How wonderful it was going to be to sit on that nice, dry, flat, firm box. I reached it and collapsed. As I ate my chocolate bar and dried cheese, the clouds parted temporarily and I saw the HAPs starting up the fixed ropes. Lunch filled me with renewed vigor. I would not quit until I reached the bottom of the fixed ropes, halfway between Camps I and II. And on it went. Climbing in the Himalaya has been described as hours of boredom punctuated by moments of stark terror, but not even the thought that the entire slope might avalanche relieved the monotony of carrying loads up it. We were too tired to care.

I reached the bottom of the fixed rope, dumped out my load of two oxygen bottles, and marked the location with a willow wand. After waiting an hour for the HAPs to return, I realized that I had to leave as it would take me a long time to limp back to Camp I. I left a nylon climbing rope tied to the fixed line in case the HAPs wanted to use it to keep together in the fog, and started down. I cut to the left too soon and found myself in an unfamiliar gully. The snow balled up on the crampons and I had to knock off the large sticky clumps with my ice-axe after each step. I was picking my way down step by step when I became aware of shadowy presences behind me. It was the HAPs. They were roped up with Qasim in the lead. They politely offered to let me tie into their rope, but since they were perfectly safe and I could not keep up with them without hurting my knees, I declined. "Tik, sah'b?" asked Abdul Rahim anxiously. "Tik," I answered, and waved them on. They rapidly faded away into the bottomless mist, their line of dark deep footsteps giving me a point of reference in the whiteout. I followed their tracks, never thinking more than several steps ahead. Abdul Rahim met me a hundred yards from Camp I and took my empty pack. I sat limply on a box outside the base camp tent while Qasim and Abdul removed my crampons and gaiters. For once I was not even embarrassed by this attention. I was grateful for anything that would save me energy.

The HAPs had not reached Camp II. They had cached their loads at the base of the rock buttress and returned. Only Kauffman, Nevison, and Swift, who did not have to make a round trip, pushed on. A freezing wind knifed into them as they pulled themselves up the fixed lines. Kauffman reached Camp II first. He filled a *dekshis* with snow and began to melt the snow to make soup. Under Andy's paternal eye the snow slowly turned into water and began to get hot. Nevison and Swift arrived, tried to brush the snow from their wind suits, and crawled into the tent. "Boy, are my feet cold! I can wear only one pair of socks inside these things," said Swift, removing his boots. His toes were colorless. "We've got to warm them up immediately. Here, put them in this," said Nevison, handing Swift the pot of water. "What are you doing to my soup!" exclaimed Andy, who had been caught off-guard by Nevison's maneuver. "Warming my toes," replied Swift, wiggling them in the hot water. Kauffman began filling another *dekshis* with snow. "Dinner is going to be delayed," he said.

The same day Schoening and Haji arrived at Camp I with two loads of oxygen. After drinking the tea that McCormack had prepared for them, Schoening decided to leave Haji and return to Base Camp with Ghulam Razul, who was still suffering from his knee injury. While returning, Schoening and Razul stopped at the Italian camp to deliver a food list and were invited to lunch by the hospitable Italians. They were plied with soup, spaghetti, fresh meat from an ibex that Cassin had shot, and some delicious cheese for dessert, but even so they remained loyal to our expedition. After thanking their generous hosts, they started the last two miles back to Base Camp. Razul could hardly walk and Schoening had to tramp down a path fourteen to eighteen inches wide so Razul could drag the injured leg behind him. After great effort they reached Base Camp and Akram and Schoening applied hot towels to the injured knee. Then Razul took a sleeping pill and went to bed.

That evening Akram sat outside the tent while Schoening typed a letter to his wife. Suddenly Akram exclaimed, "Come here, quick! There's an animal!"

"Where?" said Pete, pushing the typewriter away and walking to the entrance.

"He's gone. I think you scared him away," Akram replied. "He had a long tail and looked like a cat. Probably a snow leopard."

"This high on the glacier? Now you're positive it wasn't an abominable snowman?" said Pete, returning to the typewriter. He began anew on his letter. Akram said, "He's here again." Pete tiptoed to the entrance but the animal was gone. They began looking for tracks in the snow and discovered the paw imprints of a member of the cat family. The prints measured two and a half inches in length. "Guess there's more wildlife around here than we thought," said Schoening. Then he and Akram went to bed.

On June 20, Kauffman and Nevison crawled out of their tent at Camp II into a cold gray sky. It took them a while to fasten their crampons and tie into the rope with numb fingers; then they grabbed the fixed line and pulled themselves up to the top of the second rock buttress 300 feet above camp. Nevison anchored to a rock and Kauffman started to lead across the narrow, double-corniced ridge. "Snow's in worse shape than last time," said Andy as a step hissed down the slope. "It'll go all right, but I'm afraid that it'll be too dangerous for laden porters, even after we get the fixed rope in," said Nevison. Kauffman agreed. Just then they spotted Bob Swift at Camp II. They shouted their conclusions down to Swift and asked him to relay the news to Camp I. Swift left immediately. He cut over to the main snow slope, which we had always avoided for fear of avalanches, and began to glissade rapidly down it.

Down at Camp I the five HAPs, escorted by Rizvi, who still coughed violently, left to make the relay to Camp II. The HAPs were doing a superb job. Sahibs came and sahibs went, but the HAPs continued to carry the expedition up the mountain on their broad backs. Although he was feeling much better, McCormack was still weak and my knees were so sore I could barely move. Sitting outside the tent, McCormack and I saw Swift descending with gigantic strides. Something had gone wrong, but we did not know what it was.

Then two figures appeared on the Abruzzi Glacier. McCormack began making a large pot of lemonade. Thirty minutes later Schoening and Akram came into camp. "How was it?" I asked. "Fine," said Schoening, putting down his heavy load. "We just kept a steady pace all the way." I went over to Akram, who was lying crumpled beside his pack. "It's sure good to see you again," I said, taking his load. He looked up, smiled faintly, and said, "We stopped only once in the last three miles." "Don't worry, you're doing fine. You're not acclimatized and besides no one can keep up with Pete," I said. This made Akram feel better and we all went inside the tent.

We were drinking McCormack's lemonade when Swift arrived. Out of breath with his record-breaking descent, he turned to Schoening and said, "I saw you approaching Camp I and I had to catch you before you returned." He then described the situation on the ridge. "We think you should have a look at it," he concluded. It was now eleven.

Schoening was unhappy but he said, "Okay, I'll pack my things and go to Camp II today. Who will go to Base Camp with Akram?" Akram had carried oxygen bottles and as there were no extra sleeping bags, he could not remain at Camp I. Also, someone had to attend Ghulam Razul.

We looked at each other. It would be a knee-sinking struggle all the way. Both Swift and I wanted to make a relay to Camp II the next day and McCormack was under orders to rest. McCormack broke the silence. "I'll go back with Akram. I'm supposed to be recovering at low altitude anyway."

A half-hour later Schoening swung on his rucksack and said, "While we're pushing the route through tomorrow, have two HAPs come up with personal gear to stay at Camp II so they can start relaying up the dome." With that he started off. It was a long, long haul to Camp II, the snow was soft, and Pete moved very slowly. He had another grueling day ahead and he was conserving every ounce of strength. Watching him painfully drag himself up the slope, I knew that the ridge would go. If it could be climbed Schoening would climb it. And the ridge could be climbed. Yet it was also a sad sight. Because of our limited manpower, our principal reserve was Schoening's tremendous energy, and everyone except Pete wanted to save it for the critical summit assault rather than have it dissipated during the early stages of the climb. Now, only a little way beyond Camp II, we were forced to rely upon his strength and skill to break the bottleneck.

As Schoening plodded upward, the fragments of the day's relay to Camp II drifted past him. First he met Rizvi, who had developed a bad knee and had to turn back at the bottom of the fixed lines. At the top of the first fixed line he came upon Haji lying exhausted beside his load. Then he passed the other four HAPs, who had deposited their loads at the base of the rock buttress and were descending. Finally he arrived at Camp II and was warmly greeted by Kauffman and Nevison. While they prepared dinner, Schoening chopped out the rest of the platform that I had started. Now there were two tents fully pitched at Camp II. The place was becoming almost habitable.

McCormack and Akram postponed their departure for Base Camp until four in the afternoon in the hope that the snow would begin to harden. When the appointed hour arrived, they bravely started out. They broke through the crust with the first step and continued to sink up to their thighs as they gradually disappeared out of sight down the glacier.

On June 21 I woke up to the purr of the butane-gas stove. Swift was sitting up in his sleeping bag preparing breakfast. Frankly, I am a terrible cook and after climbing for years with Dick Irvin, who is a wizard with a stove, I have become spoiled. Fortunately, whenever Swift was in camp he assumed this chore and prepared the morning oatmeal amid the snores of his lazy companions, who always tried to get an extra ten minutes of sleep before crawling out into the cruel world. This morning was no exception. After being fortified by a cup of hot chocolate, I donned my boots and wind suit and went outside. "How is it out there?" Swift called. "Unpleasant. The clouds are down low and it's snowing lightly," I replied. Then I went over to the HAPs' tent and opened the flap. "Salaam," I said with forced cheeriness. There were a few grumbled "Salaams" in return as the HAPs started their breakfast. Haji was not feeling too well but he wanted to make the relay. The other HAPs felt fine. The previous night Rizvi had told Qasim and Rahim Khan that they were to stay at Camp II. They were delighted. The higher they climbed, the more pay they got.

At six, the five HAPs and I left Camp I. As I intended to pick up my previous load of oxygen bottles, I was carrying only a few pounds of hot chocolate for the group at Camp II. Qasim and Rahim Khan carried their personal equipment and the other HAPs had two food boxes each. It was cold and we were able to crampon rapidly up the frozen slope. My rest day had worked wonders and I was happy to discover that my knees did not bother me unless I made an extremely high step. We covered in minutes what had previously taken hours. The wind increased and it began to snow harder. After several hours we reached the bottom of the fixed rope and I picked up the bottles of oxygen.

I was afraid that I might hold the HAPs back and offered to allow them to go first, but they were very deferential and politely requested that I lead. I was very touched by this and started up the fixed line. Despite the cold the snow here was unconsolidated, and I had to break trail through knee-deep powder. An hour later I began to have my doubts as to the real reason for the HAPs' respectfulness as I watched them rapidly ascend the steps I had so laboriously kicked. I was strongly tempted to let them take over the lead, as they appeared far fresher than I felt, but the thought that by doing this I was expiating my sin of loafing the day before kept me plugging away at the slope.

At the top of the first section of the fixed line were four food boxes. The distance from Camp I to Camp II was so great that few of us, sahibs or HAPs, ever made a complete round trip in one day. As a result loads were scattered about the mountain like debris washed up on a beach, each box marking someone's high point. Looking up, I could see three figures on the ridge above Camp II. They were only halfway across the critical section and were caught in the full force of the wind. There would be no break-through to the dome today. This meant there was no need for Qasim and Rahim Khan at Camp II. In fact, they would just be consuming scarce food. Through gestures, I instructed the two HAPs to deposit their personal gear and pick up the four food boxes instead. By doing this we would get the last of the scattered loads off the slope. Even if we did not reach Camp II we could put the boxes at the main dump below the rock buttress. Qasim and Rahim Khan were puzzled about this, and when they realized that they would have to carry their personal gear back to Camp I, I could see in their faces that they wished the sahibs would make up their minds as to what was supposed to be done. They strapped the boxes to their packboards and we continued.

The storm turned into a blizzard. Above, Schoening, Kauffman, and

Nevison were beating a hasty retreat to Camp II. Behind them the snow came off the ridge in a solid white sheet. Like refugees from a nightmare they grabbed the fixed line and were blown out over the slope by the wind. One by one they dropped down the rope so fast that it looked like a series of controlled falls rather than rappels. Now the HAPs and I were climbing directly into the wind. The snow froze to our wind suits and goggles on impact. We reached the dump, which was the high-water mark of the previous relays. It was useless to try to continue. From here the loads could easily be retrieved from Camp II. The HAPs came up. "Bas, bas, enough, enough," I yelled at them and everyone dropped his load. We secured the dump so surface avalanches would not carry it away. As I wanted to contact the party at Camp II, I gestured for the HAPs to descend without me. I hurriedly put on my balaclava helmet and down overmitts and watched the HAPs disappear down the slope. There was a lull in the wind and I started up the fixed line toward Camp II. I climbed several hundred feet. Then the intensity of the storm increased. This was getting to be hopeless. I turned and started to descend. Over the wind I heard a shout and saw someone coming down the fixed line. It was Schoening. We met halfway between the dump and Camp II.

"You shouldn't be alone in this weather," he said.

"It's okay, I've got the fixed rope. I told the HAPs to go on down because I noticed you had to retreat off the ridge. How's it going?"

"It'll go. We quit because of the wind. At one point while I was belaying Andy, my toes got so cold I had to take off my boots and stick my feet inside the pack."

"How difficult's the ridge?"

"When we get the fixed rope in, there won't be any difficulty. The snow's in bad shape, and we're having to demolish the cornices and walk along the top. Once I had to place a piton and do a little rock climbing to avoid the snow. We'll be able to push it through tomorrow. You'd better send four HAPs up so they can start relaying to Camp III."

"Okay. Tas and I have to make a run down to Base Camp tomorrow to pick up some more oxygen, but Swift is going to escort the HAPs. I'll probably come up the day after. Oh, yes, I thought you might be getting a little sick of tea." I reached into my pack and handed Schoening the cans of hot chocolate. "Also, here are a couple of oxygen regulators. Guess that's it. Good luck on the dome."

Schoening put the chocolate and the regulators inside his pack. "Take it easy on the way down," he said. He slowly began to haul himself up the fixed line. His wind suit was covered with snow. He looked tired, I thought. Then I descended as fast as I could to escape the cold wind.

At the bottom of the fixed line I cut to the left where it was sheltered. Once I was out of the wind I became extremely hot and took off my wind suit and down jacket. Soon it stopped snowing. I continued down to Camp I and arrived at noon.

When I entered the tent McCormack and Akram were sitting inside. They had brought four badly needed bottles of oxygen from Base Camp.

"I thought you were supposed to be resting," I said.

"We just decided to visit you, that's all," said McCormack.

"Did you visit the Italian base camp?" I asked, knowing full well that they had.

"Don't go near it! It'll ruin your morale!"

McCormack launched into a long description of the marvels of the Italian base camp. I glanced around at our squalid surroundings. All the sahibs were crowded into one tent, and sleeping bags, boots, air mattresses, radios, torn pocketbooks, scraps of paper, spoons, dirty clothes, match boxes, first aid kits, and other miscellaneous items littered the floor in one big mass of mushy material. Swift was pouring lemonade from a battered *dekshis* into a cracked plastic cup. In a rear corner sat our one pressure cooker, still serving its original purpose, as the hiding place for our paper rupees. Outside the tent, open food boxes and excelsior were scattered about. Beyond were two open pits with shovels beside them that the HAPs used to get snow for water and dispose of garbage. "And they have a separate mess tent with big gas stoves, and a table, and folding chairs. They even have a small cupboard for their dishes," continued McCormack, looking at me with mock reproach. "I'm sorry, fellows, but we're lucky even to be here," I said.

McCormack had one piece of bad news. Carlo Mauri, one of the Italians' strongest climbers, had been badly burned on the arm when a pressure cooker exploded. We were very unhappy to hear this.

After lunch McCormack and Akram left for Base Camp. What a rest cure! A weary, monotonous ten-mile run suitable for convalescents. The pneumonia patrol. Because of their illnesses the chances of McCormack and Akram participating in the final assault were small. They had been told to rest. But oxygen bottles had to be carried to Camp I, so they carried them. There was none of the exhilaration of pioneering the route, none of the satisfaction of making a high carry; just a sense of duty in doing a dirty, indispensable chore. As they faded out of sight, I thought of the members of other expeditions who got a paragraph in the accounts while the dramatic feats of the assault teams filled page after page: Couzy moving the base camp on Annapurna, Westmacott keeping the Khumbu icefall on Everest open, and countless others. Those not in the assault teams are the forgotten legion of the Himalaya, remembered only by their comrades.

Although Haji had not been feeling well for the last few days, he never complained. That night he became very sick and could not eat dinner. "When I go up to Camp II, I'll have Nevison come down and look at

They also serve who only carry loads. A relay leaves Camp I.

him," said Swift. "I think that's best," I replied. "I'll feel much better with Nevison here to take care of him." Then Rizvi and I went over to the HAPs' tent to make sure that Abdul Rahim, Qasim, Rahim Khan, and Hussein would be ready to stay at Camp II the following day.

Early June 22, Schoening and Kauffman left Camp II determined to finish the route to the top of the dome, while Nevison, who had developed a throat infection, packed his personal gear and descended to Camp I. Spurred by accumulated frustration, Pete and Andy whacked at the ridge with their ice-axes. "I'm afraid we don't have enough manila rope," said Schoening. "We'll just fix the worst places now and fill in the gaps later." In two hours they reached the end of the 150-yard bottleneck. The ridge broadened and they traversed left across a steep snow slope for 200 feet before climbing back to the ridge. Soon they reached a wide area beneath the final slopes of the dome. It was the first flat spot since Camp I. Schoening and Kauffman rested briefly and then started the final push. They cramponed for 200 feet up hard snow until it turned into blue ice. Kauffman anchored to an ice piton and gave Schoening a belay as he began cutting steps. They chopped 200 feet of steps up the fifty-degree ice slope and attached a nylon climbing rope to serve as fixed line. At noon Pete and Andy reached the top of the dome. The way to Camp III was finally open.

Meanwhile at Camp I Rizvi and I left for Base Camp as Swift prepared to escort the four HAPs to Camp II. McCormack had reported that the crevassed section between Base Camp and the medial moraine was rapidly deteriorating, and Tas and I wanted to get through this obstacle before the snow began to soften. When we started, the glacier was still in shadow and the snow was frozen. However, the line of eight-inch-deep tracks beside us was an unpleasant reminder to hurry. We passed within several hundred yards of the Italian camp. The many brightly colored tents were an impressive sight. No one seemed to be stirring so we decided to visit it on our return trip. We arrived at the beginning of the crevassed section and stopped at a pool to have a drink and put on the rope. The snow through this critical area was still hard and we were able to walk on the surface, so there was no delay. But McCormack was right. The area was in bad shape. Both the medial and lateral moraines were bare of snow and there were many new surface pools and streams. I was amazed at the change that had occurred within one week. Soon it would require a major effort to get through this section.

We arrived in Base Camp at nine-thirty and went inside the hut, where McCormack and Akram were finishing breakfast. Razul handed us cups of tea. "I'm afraid you're a little late for breakfast," said Akram, smiling.

"That's all right, we had breakfast long ago," I replied.

"At last the weather finally turned good again. How did you like the glacier?" said McCormack.

"It lived up to your description," I said.

"Incidentally, do we have any green cloth?"

"What on earth do you want green cloth for?"

"I'm making another Free Hungarian flag. We might lose Kauffman's and we must have one for the summit. Besides, his is too small anyway. I have already found some red and white cloth, and now all I need is some green." Later McCormack found some and made his flag. Radio Moscow was having its effect!

We spent an hour drinking tea and talking with McCormack and Akram. It was so nice and cool inside the hut that Tas and I were reluctant to leave. But the snow was softening and we had to start back. I was feeling eager and put three oxygen bottles, a movie camera, and some other equipment into my rucksack. Out of curiosity McCormack picked it up. "Feels pretty heavy," he said.

"Oh, it's okay."

"Let's weigh it," replied McCormack. The spring scale indicated eighty pounds. I recoiled in horror. "Just what are you trying to prove?" said McCormack, as I hastily pulled a bottle of oxygen out of the pack. Then I picked it up. It did not seem extraordinarily heavy. Later, when we began the march out, we used this same scale to weigh the porter loads, which were suspiciously light. Somehow the spring was probably weakened, to the great benefit of the economy of Askole.

Tas had the privilege of testing the snowbridges and he led off. The snow was still quite firm and we did not fall into very many holes. We reached the medial moraine and followed it into the Italian camp. I had hoped that the Italians would greet us while we were still a respectable distance away so I could pretend that we were not trying to beg food, but they did not hear us until we were almost inside their mess tent. Carlo Mauri, the doctor, and another climber were there and immediately offered us tea and cookies, which we eagerly accepted. Bonatti and Gobbi were working on the route through the South Gasherbrum Glacier. The rest of the expedition was still coming from Concordia with the last ninety loads. They would not arrive until the next day, which was unfortunate because I was looking forward to seeing Fosco Maraini again.

The Italian mess tent seemed like paradise indeed. The accommodations were exceeded only by the good company, although I suspected the Italians were becoming a little tired of having a different group of filthy strangers with ravenous appetites visit them every day. It was too bad that the Italians had not arrived earlier, for their hospitality greatly increased the popularity of the relay between Base Camp and Camp I.

We sat around the table and drank bowl after bowl of tea. After a third one I gave the Italians some battered packages of candy, which made it easier for me to accept the fourth bowl. Carlo Mauri sat very quietly across the table with his arm swathed in bandages. We talked a little in Spanish, but the doctor, who understood some English, served as the chief spokesman for our hosts. He informed us that they had seen four men climb the dome at a rapid pace, which was wonderful and puzzling news. Not only were we making progress but our ranks also were increasing! Then the doctor said, "You are very lucky. You are a party of friends climbing for fun. If you climb the mountain, fine; if you don't, nothing happens. We are a national expedition. If we climb the mountain we are heroes; if we don't . . ." (the doctor made a cutting gesture across his throat). His remark proved that the Italian party was basically the same as ours. True, they were guides and the best mountaineers in Italy whereas we were amateurs, but they were there for the same reasons we were. They loved the mountains and they loved to climb. Earlier Bonatti and Gobbi had made similar remarks to Schoening, and it was apparent that they would rather do without the public fanfare if it were possible to raise money otherwise. I had made an attempt to enlist public support also, but where I had failed the Italians succeeded. Now, in the field, their success hovered over them like a cloud while my failure enabled us to enjoy our trip. We had only to worry about our mountain. The poor Italians not only had to worry about their mountain, which was extremely difficult, but also about placating an unknowing public that expected victories from their "team" as if it were a game. We sympathized with them for we knew that if the Italians succeeded it would be an incredible feat, while if they failed it would not be due to any lack of courage or ability on the part of their magnificent party but to factors that are beyond control. We fervently hoped that they would climb Gasherbrum IV and avoid public scandal.

It was time to leave. The snow on the glacier was getting softer and Rizvi and I could not eat or drink anything more. We wished them good luck, and I assured Mauri that everything would be all right and he would do well on the mountain. Our departure was somewhat comical. When we had stopped I had just slipped out of the rope. Now without thinking I put my pack on first and discovered that I had originally pulled the loop of rope over my head and it was too small to pull over my hips when I stepped into it. As the Italians watched in amazement, I untied the rope and retied it again. The pack kept getting in the way and I fumbled around as if I had never seen a rope before. Finally I managed to get tied in, unsnarled my ice-axe from a coil of rope, and impatiently signaled Rizvi to start. He took three steps and fell waist-deep into a crevasse. For the next thirty minutes we floundered through crevasses and I could almost hear the Italians thinking, "They can't even tie into a rope or stay out of crevasses, and they're trying an Eight Thousander!"

After we got through the crevasses I took over the lead. We broke through the crust but maintained a slow steady pace. Over on the South Gasherbrum Glacier Bonatti and Gobbi were returning to the Italian base camp. They were moving very fast as if they had forgotten their lunch. At six, when Ias and I arrived at Camp I, we found Swift and Nevison sitting inside the tent.

"It's good to see you again, Tom. What's wrong with Haji?" I asked.

"He's got a little stomach trouble. I'm going to take him down to Base Camp tomorrow," said Nevison.

I turned to Swift. "Did the four HAPs get up to Camp II all right?"

"No trouble," he replied.

"Andy's coming down tomorrow and Pete says that you should go up. Pete's going to take the first relay to Camp III. When you see him, make him come down. He's been working hard the last few days. He's pretty tired," said Nevison.

"I'll do my best, but you know Pete."

"Say, is your spare axe around? I'd like to use it."

"It's right outside the tent here, but what happened to yours?"

"Pete broke his axe chopping out a tent platform and I gave him mine."

"Broke it! But that was a brand new Bhend! Are you sure he didn't hit a rock with it?"

"No, he was chopping ice. I saw him do it."

"How could he!" I was stunned. If anyone except Pete had broken the axe I would have thought that it was defective. However, I had already been introduced to the Schoening theory of step-cutting. "When you chop steps, you should chop like you really mean it," he would say, swinging the ice-axe from the shoulders like a lumberjack trying to win a tree-cutting contest against a power saw.

Sitting in the back of the tent, Nevison coughed heavily. I was impressed. He always seemed to do everything right, even getting sick. During the expedition everyone was briefly incapacitated at one time or another, but Nevison got his only ailment the day he had to descend to check his patients. By resting and fulfilling his medical duties at the same time, he did not waste a single precious day.

On June 23 McCormack and Akram carried more oxygen bottles to Camp I. Nevison, Rizvi, and Kauffman, who had just descended from Camp II, were waiting for them with the usual pot of tea. Everyone sat around the tent and discussed the situation. The buildup of supplies into Camp III was proceeding smoothly and the final push beyond that camp would begin within a week. Unfortunately the Abruzzi Glacier was rapidly deteriorating. If the surface streams kept increasing, Base Camp would soon be isolated. It was obvious to the group that Base Camp should be located on the moraine near the Italian camp. That would shorten the run to Camp I by two miles and eliminate the danger of the expedition's being cut off from its source of supplies. Furthermore, the medial moraine was the best route for the march out.

"We all agree that Base Camp should be on the moraine, but there's almost a ton of supplies still there. It'll take forever to shift it," said Kauffman.

"Say, the last part of the Italian expedition is coming up today from Concordia. Perhaps we could hire some of their porters to move Base Camp. What do you think, Akram? You marched in with them," said McCormack.

"I'm sure I can arrange with the Italian liaison officer to get the men we need," Akram replied.

Everyone agreed that this was the thing to do. "We'd better get moving so we can catch the porters before they're paid off and start returning to Askole," said Nevison. Nevison and Haji packed immediately and a half-hour later left with McCormack and Akram to go to Base Camp. When they reached the Italian camp, the last ninety loads from Concordia had just arrived and Baltis were milling around the tents. While McCormack went on with the sick Haji, Nevison and Akram tried to recruit porters. It was difficult to get volunteers, since all the Baltis wanted to get out of the mountains as quickly as possible. Finally Akram and the Italian liaison officer managed to persuade some of the porters that hauling loads for a mere two miles would be the easiest four rupees that they would ever earn in their lives, so at five Nevison and Akram arrived at Base Camp with twenty men. While Razul gave the porters some atta to make chupattis, the sahibs furiously prepared loads for the shuttle. It took hours to sort the equipment and pack it into sixty-pound loads. They failed to finish the job that night and had to get up early the next morning. After breakfast the scramble was on. "No, no, that box stays here, this box goes," said Nevison for the tenth time. When the last porter had his load, Razul raised his ice-axe, cried, "Shabash," and the grand parade was under way. Nevison and McCormack led the way and everyone reached the moraine safely. The porters dropped the boxes about 300 yards from the Italian camp. The three sahibs tried to persuade the Baltis to make another relay, but once was enough. The porters were paid and promptly disappeared down the glacier. Then everyone returned to Base Camp and spent the afternoon packing the remainder of the food and equipment. The next day, June 25, Nevison, McCormack, Akram, Razul, and Haji carried loads to the dump on the moraine. Nevison and McCormack continued to Camp I while Akram established our new base camp. A few less essential loads remained at the old site, but they gradually were brought to the moraine from time to time. The prompt action of Akram, Nevison, and McCormack in moving Base Camp averted a serious situation. Now with the supply line secured and shortened, everyone could safely be used in the critical phase of the climb—the big push beyond Camp III.

At nine-thirty in the morning on June 23, I left Camp I for a leisurely trip to Camp II. I carried all my high-altitude equipment as I had no intention of returning until after the mountain had been climbed. Swift, who was making a relay of oxygen, had left an hour earlier, and I could see him far ahead moving steadily up the slope. Also I saw Kauffman, who was coming down to rest. He was in excellent shape and it was increasingly apparent that he and Schoening should be the first summit team. We met 500 feet above Camp I.

"Nice going on the dome. You and Pete went up it so fast that the Italians who were watching were seeing double," I said.

"We weren't climbing very fast. Perhaps they had dirt in their binoculars."

"You've done a good job, so take it easy for a couple of days. The situation's under control, and we want you rested for the final drive."

"Don't worry about me, I'll rest. Just make Schoening come down."

"I'll try. See you in a few days."

I continued slowly upward. For once I did not have to think about time, and to my great surprise I almost enjoyed the climb to Camp II. At the start of the fixed ropes I met Swift, who was descending. "Good luck on the relaying. Tas and I will join you tomorrow," he said. Then he began striding downward again. For several minutes I watched Swift rapidly cover the slope with his long legs.

I was 200 feet below Camp II when Schoening spotted me and descended. Over my protests he ripped the pack from my back and carried it the remaining distance. There was a noisy reunion with the HAPs and then Schoening and I crawled inside his tent.

"I see you and the HAPs had a good Easter-egg hunt. There were only a couple of loads scattered on the slope. How's it been going?"

"Fine," said Pete, starting the butane-gas stove. "Yesterday when the HAPs arrived, all of us except Hussein went down to the dump and carried up a load. Today Hussein and Abdul Rahim have been bringing up the rest of the boxes while Rahim Khan, Qasim, and I made a relay to the top of the dome. Tomorrow you and I will take the four HAPs on another relay."

"Look, you've been working pretty hard the last few days and now that the route has been established and most of the fixed rope put in, everyone feels that you should go down and rest."

"I'm fine, really, and we have to take advantage of this good weather to get every load we can to Camp III."

"We're counting on you for the final assault. If you burn yourself out on this stuff, it reduces our chances of climbing the mountain. Bob and Tas are coming up tomorrow so we have plenty of manpower to hump loads."

"Okay. After I make the run to Camp III tomorrow I'll go right down. How's that."

"All right, but you definitely promise to go down afterward." I had failed in my mission, but it had been a lost cause from the start.

After dinner Schoening was filling a Thermos bottle with hot chocolate for breakfast in the morning. "Say, Pete, I have a question. How could you break an ice-axe?"

"I've always said ash handles are no good. Hickory is the only wood to use."

"But no one else breaks them, not unless they're old and rotten. Besides, where do you get hickory handles, anyway?"

"After I broke several ash ones, I started putting on my own shafts."

"You don't need a hickory handle. You need a steel shank!"

We settled into our sleeping bags and Schoening pulled out *The Oxford Book of English Verse*. "Charlie Houston always carried a copy with him on all his expeditions, but he lost it in the accident on K2. He was more upset over losing that book than over losing his sleeping bag. When he heard that I was coming on this trip, he gave me this copy." We took turns leafing through it. I found Coleridge's *Rime of the Ancient Mariner*, which I began to read aloud. Halfway through we realized that I must have skipped a page, and with that discovery we stopped the poetry reading and went to sleep.

12

BUILDUP

June 24 was clear and cold, a perfect day for climbing. After breakfast Schoening and I arranged the loads for the relay. Hussein wanted to carry only one food box. "Okay," said Pete. "One box, two trips." This was not exactly what Hussein had in mind and he protested. "No. One box, two trips; two boxes, one trip," said Schoening firmly. Hussein decided that he would make one trip with a full load, especially since the rest of us were not going to make a second run.

Schoening started out with Qasim and Rahim Khan while I followed with Hussein and Abdul Rahim on my rope. We climbed to the top of the rock buttress above camp and rested briefly. Then we started across the narrow ridge. Schoening and Kauffman had hacked out a route right along the crest and, except for a hundred-foot gap, strung it with fixed line anchored to pitons. Although the handline eliminated most of the difficulty, the ridge was extremely exposed and we moved with careful precision. The worst place was a small rock gendarme eight feet high. The fixed line ran at such an angle that it gave little support. There was a patch of soft snow for the left foot and then we had to step on an ice piton sticking four inches out of the rotten rock. It bent when I put my weight on it. "This is going to come out with someone," I thought as I gave the HAPs a belay over the section. Beyond this there was another rock gendarme, which had to be traversed on its right side. We had to lean out slightly to pass this obstacle. This was awkward with heavy loads. Then a short climb up bad snow brought us to an aluminum picket at the end of the narrow arête. It would have been nice to rest here, but there was not enough room to sit down.

The ridge widened and swept upward. We traversed left for 200 feet across a steep snow slope and then climbed upward to rejoin the crest. Manila line safeguarded the traverse, but the upward stretch was secured by a nylon climbing rope attached to several ice pitons. Above this we climbed a near vertical snow wall fifteen feet high. The snow was soft and the steps were extremely deep. As there was no fixed rope here, we had to thrust both our ice-axes and our left arms deep into the snow to maintain balance. We reached a ledge underneath a short ice wall, which we turned by making a delicate traverse to the left. From there we regained the ridge and climbed along it until we came to the flat area.

Hussein, Abdul Rahim, and I stopped to rest while Schoening and his two HAPs started up the dome. The three of us ate a chocolate bar and then followed. We cramponed up hard snow and reached a manila fixed line, which led upward for a hundred feet. The fixed line stopped as the snow turned into blue ice. A line of small steps went directly up a fifty-degree face. Sixty feet above me I could see the end of a nylon climbing rope that Schoening and Kauffman had attached to protect the slope. I started up, balancing myself by driving the pick of my axe into the ice. I had almost reached the beginning of the fixed line when a sudden jerk on the rope caught me in midstride and almost pulled me out of my steps. Scrabbling desperately to regain my balance, I turned around and discovered Hussein was blithely using our climbing rope as a fixed line. He was starting to haul himself up on it again when I let out a yell. I tried to maintain an outward calm to conceal my fury. "No, no, Hussein. Never use this rope. Only use the other rope. This rope bad. Other rope good. Understand?" "Gee, sah'b," he replied contritely.

We continued and soon reached the fixed nylon rope that secured the slope. As I neared the top of the ice pitch there was another violent jerk, and only the fact that I happened to have a firm grip on the fixed line when the jerk came prevented me from falling. The two nylon ropes dangling down the slope, the fixed line and our climbing rope, had confused Hussein and he had put his weight on the wrong one! After a few harsh words we resumed climbing. We followed some manila fixed line, which ended thirty feet from the top of the dome at 22,000 feet. Schoening, Qasim, and Rahim Khan had already cached their loads at the dump and were preparing to return when we arrived. I deposited my load, untied from the rope, and began to inspect our surroundings. After Camp II this seemed like a wonderful place, although we were uncertain as to just how much of the ridge could be used for pitching Camp III because of the cornice on the right side. But at least we could walk around a little without fear of falling off.

The view was impressive. We were now far above the Conway Saddle and beyond it was Saltoro Kangri, over 25,000 feet high. In the other direction, the 20,000-foot monsters that were so spectacular from the Baltoro Glacier blended into a formless mass. Just to the north was the neighboring south spur and Hidden South. One look at the steep and corniced ridge leading off its backside to the plateau made me thankful we were not on that route. Below the ridge avalanches constantly thundered down upon the Glacier du Milieu. It was fortunate we were not there either.

For the first time I could see most of the surface of the southeast snow plateau leading to the summit pyramid. There did not appear to be any technical difficulty, but it was certainly long. Everything would depend upon weather and snow conditions. I walked twenty feet along the ridge toward the plateau and sank in up to my ankle. If the snow conditions on the plateau are like this, we will be all right, I thought. Then the increasing cold reminded me that it was time to go down.

The section of the ice slope that was not protected by a fixed line was somewhat touchy. It would be extremely difficult to retreat down it safely in bad weather, and I made a mental note that we should fix it as soon as possible. The remaining climb down to the narrow arête was easy although I had to keep a close watch on Hussein, who acted as if he might step off the mountain at any minute. Without a load the tightrope act along the thin crest was a pleasure, especially since we now knew where all the holds were. We reached the rock buttress at the end of the traverse and went sliding down the fixed line into Camp II. Bob Swift had just arrived and on the slopes below we could see Rizvi coming up.

Schoening and Rahim Khan packed their personal gear to descend to Camp I. "We're running out of atta for the HAPs and Rahim Khan is going with me to bring up more," said Pete. "That's unfortunate, because I'm afraid that the nearest supply is clear down at Base Camp unless someone has brought some up to Camp I," I said. Rahim Khan was most unhappy about this development since his fellow HAPs, who were remaining at Camp II, would be earning a rupee a day extra. It was for this very reason that we had selected him for the job. We knew that he would be eager to return instead of wanting to stay low. Schoening and Rahim Khan departed just as Rizvi arrived at Camp II.

It was only three o'clock so Swift and I decided to descend and retrieve the last of the loads lying on the slope below. We were anxious to complete this task since the boxes could be buried by a storm. Besides, it offended our sense of propriety to have our supplies scattered over the mountainside. Bob and I got the loads up to Camp II just in time to look down and see Pete and Rahim Khan reach the Abruzzi Glacier and turn the corner of the buttress toward Camp I.

Swift prepared a large wet dinner, which disappeared immediately. Afterward Tas went to his tent while Bob and I crawled into our sleeping bags and discussed the situation. On their way up from Camp I, Swift and Rizvi had discovered a large coil of manila rope that had been left at the reconnaissance camp and forgotten. They had brought it up, which was indeed fortunate. In putting in the fixed line to Camp III, Schoening and Kauffman had had to make some hard choices in deciding what sections to protect and what to leave until later. These gaps had to be closed before someone got hurt. Tomorrow, in addition to carrying loads, Swift, Qasim, and I would take the coil of manila rope and play road crew.

The next morning, June 25, after the usual session of "Who's going to carry what?," and "I know darn well my crampons were hanging over my axe when I went to bed," everyone finally found his equipment and got a load strapped to his pack. At nine Swift, Qasim, and I left ahead of Tas and the second rope since we wanted to finish our engineering before they came along. The gap in the narrow arête was easy to bridge. Then we replaced the nylon climbing rope that had been attached to the steep snow slope beyond. We tied the new sections of fixed rope either to the ends of the rope already in place or to ice pitons and rappel pickets. The only problem was laying out the rope and cutting it to the proper length. We adopted the technique that had been used by Schoening and Nevison earlier. Instead of throwing a coil of rope down the slope, I climbed ahead, dragging the manila rope behind me. After I attached it to the next fixed point, Swift would cut the rope and tie it into the last section of fixed rope to make a continuous line running down the ridge. Then he and Qasim would join me and we would repeat the process at the next gap.

Swift was wearing a red wind suit and his cowboy hat. Also he had attached his mittens to his neck with a white cord to prevent accidentally losing them. As he climbed up the ridge he looked like a member of the Royal Canadian Mounted Police who was going to extreme trouble to get his man.

"...not even the thought that the entire slope might avalanche relieved the monotony of carrying loads up it."

Our technique of placing fixed line was quite efficient. However, we did not have enough rope to cover the flat area, and we could not replace the nylon rope on the ice slope, which grieved the collective penny-pinching soul of the expedition. The little manila rope that remained had to be saved for the ridge beyond Camp III.

Shortly after noon we reached the top of the dome. Behind us now was over a mile of rope, which stretched in a long line from Camp III to over 2,000 feet below Camp II. The only gap was in the flat area below the dome. If anything happened all we would have to do would be to grab the fixed line and slide. Swift, Qasim, and I deposited our loads at the rapidly growing dump. "Did we carry all that here?" I thought, proudly identifying myself with our hardworking HAPs. A cold wind whipped out of the northwest, and sitting on the ridge we were caught in its full force. Tas, Abdul Rahim, and Hussein appeared at the top of the fixed line 30 feet below. Qasim went down and took Rizvi's load. It was difficult to tell whether this gesture arose from a sense of duty, politeness, or mere one-upmanship. Bob and Tas started back for Camp II while the three HAPs and I had a little lunch and rearranged the dump. Soon the numbing effect of the wind began to overwhelm the beauty of the scene. It was time to get out of there.

Qasim, always eager, led, followed by Hussein and Abdul Rahim, while I brought up the rear with a tight rope, fervently hoping that no one would slip. When we reached the ice slope, Qasim, using the fixed line for support, pranced down the steps facing out, but the more conservative Hussein faced in and backed down. In doing so he managed to wrap the climbing rope several times around the fixed line. Also Hussein was using a safety sling, which he attached to the fixed line with a carabiner, and this, too, became fouled. Everything was fine as long as the entire mess could slip down the fixed line, but when Hussein reached the ice piton in the steepest part of the slope there was trouble. He stood there fumbling with the rope and trying to unravel the tangle. Qasim and Abdul Rahim correctly sized up the situation and began yelling instructions. Several minutes passed. Qasim, at the bottom of the slope, became increasingly impatient and proceeded to bawl out his fellow HAP in no uncertain terms. Abdul Rahim descended to Hussein and began to assist him. As I could not explain what to do or easily pass Abdul Rahim on the ice slope, I just kept a taut belay rope and silently watched the fiasco with uncharitable glee. I really should not have felt so vindictive since Hussein was conscientious and was trying to do a good job. If only the poor fellow would learn. Finally Abdul Rahim got him unwound and we continued. When we arrived at the narrow arête, the wind had died and it was warm. The additional fixed line had eliminated the last real difficulties; however, everyone still exercised great care in descending the crumbling rock with the ice piton sticking out. We still did not trust it, but everyone used it. There was no place else to step.

As we made the last rappel into Camp II we could see two men on the slopes below descending toward Camp I. I felt very good. It had been a fine climb. Old Hussein seemed like a pretty good guy after all. The relay to Camp III proved to be the best of the entire trip. Carrying loads from Base Camp to Camp I and from Camp I to Camp II left us physically exhausted. On the other hand, the later relay to Camp IV was short and each of us felt he was cheating by doing so little work. But the run to Camp III was delightful. The round trip took between four and five hours and the technical difficulty was just sufficient to make one feel that one had accomplished something. We returned to Camp II fairly fresh and with a clear conscience, two things that normally do not go together in the Himalaya.

When we arrived in Camp II we learned that the two men we saw descending were Andy Kauffman and Rahim Khan. They had climbed the entire distance to Camp II with some badly needed oxygen and butane-gas bottles. It was the first time that anyone had made a complete round trip since Qasim did it on the first relay, and it demonstrated that Kauffman was now in excellent form. They had left a note for us from Pete Schoening. Four men were to go up to Camp III and begin pushing the route over to the plateau. We decided that tomorrow Rizvi, Qasim, Abdul Rahim, and I would occupy Camp III while Swift and Hussein would act as support and then join us the day after.

At the beginning of the expedition I had entered in my notebook everyone's birthday that would occur during the course of the trip. Now I discovered that today was Rizvi's birthday. Obviously such a momentous occasion deserved a real celebration. Bob and I had a small can of fruit cocktail, which was as rare as it was prized. The only reason it had remained untouched was that we both knew about it and had not yet come to terms. We decided to make the supreme sacrifice. Bob dug up a large candle from the emergency kit while I borrowed some matches from Rizvi. Then we melted some wax and mounted the candle on the top of the can. I took it over to Rizvi's tent, but it was impossible to keep the candle lit. Finally after many tries and many matches I succeeded and shoved the can and candle through the entrance of the tent without setting it afire. Swift and I then sang "Happy Birthday." Tas was deeply touched. "Why, thank you very much. How nice of you. May I borrow your can opener?" I gave him my Swiss Army pocketknife and crawled back into the tent with Swift. "Here you go," said Tas, passing over a half-full can. Bob and I eagerly grabbed it and split the remaining contents with a teaspoon. There was just enough fruit left to make us realize what we were missing.

On June 26, I got ready to climb the dome for the last time. My high-altitude clothing and equipment were already at Camp III so I put a couple of butane-gas bottles in my pack, together with an air mattress and other light items. As I wanted to move slowly I started ahead of the rest of the group, who were still packing. I began to pull myself up the fixed line. Down below I could see four figures moving up the slope. Schoening, Kauffman, Nevison, and McCormack were coming up to occupy Camp II. At last the expedition was moving up the mountain in force. I reached the top of the rock buttress and began the traverse of the arête. Large snow plumes were blowing off the summit of Hidden Peak, Sia Kangri, and the other peaks. Was the weather going to get bad now? On the ridge I was completely exposed to the wind and by the time I reached the flat place I was quite cold. I stopped to put on my balaclava helmet and down over-mitts. Qasim and Hussein came into view. They were moving steadily and I waited for them. When they arrived I tied into their rope and began to lead up the final ice slope. The wind tore at us and my feet became numb. I tried to wiggle my toes to stimulate circulation, but this did not help. It required too much concentration to climb the ice slope safely to remember to keep moving my toes. I wondered how Swift's feet were. Then I remembered that he had put on his reindeer boots at Camp II. I wished I had my reindeer boots on. But they were safe in my high-altitude kit at Camp III.

We arrived at the dump with Swift, Rizvi, and Abdul Rahim close behind us. They, too, had been externally stimulated to set a rapid pace. The sky began to cloud over and get dark. Swift put down his load while Rizvi and Abdul Rahim untied from the rope. Then Bob coiled it and tossed the end to Hussein. "Here! Tie in. Let's go!" Hussein roped up and started down. "See you tomorrow," said Swift as he wheeled and followed the HAP's tracks. A minute later they were out of sight.

"We'd better get the tents up before it starts snowing. It's getting pretty nasty," said Rizvi. We leveled out two tent platforms end to end along the top of the ridge. Then we tried to pitch the tents. The cloth thrashed about wildly and the stakes were useless in the soft snow. Finally we got the guy ropes anchored to ice-axes and oxygen bottles. When it became time to move on we would figure out a substitute, but right then the most important thing was to get the tents up any way we could. We linked the adjacent ends together to form a tunnel that provided an inside passage between the two tents. Qasim and Abdul Rahim occupied the tent toward the plateau while Tas and I threw our gear into the other.

There was still work to be done. We had to move the dump away from the edge of the ridge and put the supplies next to the tents, where they would be accessible in a storm. Qasim and I restacked the food boxes and oxygen bottles and then rearranged the other equipment such as coils of rope, extra crampons, and pitons so that we could find them if they were buried by fresh snow.

I made a quick inventory. There were twenty-four boxes of food and nineteen bottles of oxygen. We were ready for the siege. Up to this point the high-altitude boxes had been a good carrying unit and protected the food well. However, their contents were varied and three boxes numbered in sequence formed a complete unit. Some boxes had breakfast food, others contained lunch and dinner. The boxes had become separated during the different carries and no one knew exactly what was in any of them. From Camp III on we would be carrying only specially selected items of food, so Qasim and I began to break into the boxes to see what we had. The first box contained two pounds of salt! Christmas again! Spurred by this discovery, Qasim and I ripped off lid after lid with our ice-axes. It began to snow. We ignored it as cans of mixed nuts, lemon cookies, meat paste, and other scarce items poured out. There were even two cans of fruit cocktail! We redistributed the food, and the sight of box after box filled with cans of meat, cheese, and hot chocolate made me forget the weather. "Take anything you want, Qasim," I said expansively. He promptly picked up the two cans of fruit cocktail and then took a can of mixed nuts for good measure. I had underestimated our gallant HAP. "Is that all you want?" I said, trying to conceal my chagrin. "Thank you, sah'b," said Qasim as he crawled inside his tent with the loot. I threw some food into the entrance of my tent and joined Rizvi.

It was now snowing heavily. But with plenty of food we felt secure. Rizvi lit a cigarette, his first in many days. He inhaled several times and then went into a paroxysm of coughing. His face flushed and tears streamed from his eyes. I was afraid that he was going to choke and simultaneously set the tent on fire. Eventually he caught his breath and passed the cigarette through the tunnel to Qasim, who finished smoking it. Then Tas and I laughed uproariously.

We got little sleep that night. The storm battered the tent while condensation formed on the inside lining and dropped on our faces. When I tried to shrink down inside my sleeping bag to avoid this frosty version of the Chinese water-torture, I began to suffocate. Tas coughed constantly and I developed an infection in the right ear. In the morning the wind died, but it continued to snow. Rizvi was still gasping and coughing. "Do you want some oxygen?" I asked. His reply sounded like "No." The HAPs passed some hot chocolate through the tunnel. After breakfast Tas felt much better. "I wanted the oxygen, but I couldn't speak distinctly," he said.

About eleven it stopped snowing so I put on my reindeer boots and went outside. It had become stifling hot inside the tent and the fresh air felt good. Tas also got dressed and we discussed trying to push the route over to the snow plateau. We were enveloped in mist, which limited the visibility to a few feet. Route-finding would be difficult in such weather, and as there was no sign of anyone coming up from Camp II, nothing would be lost by waiting one day. We had lunch and crawled back into the tent. I spent the long afternoon bringing my diary up-to-date. It has been said that one's handwriting can indicate the progressive lack of oxygen on a high mountain. This is not true in my case. Even the section of my notebook completed in Karachi looked as if it had been written in a perfect vacuum. We killed more time by prolonging dinner and then lay quietly in the sleeping bags.

The next morning, June 28, the clouds lifted slightly and it stopped snowing. After breakfast we went outside. Rizvi was still feeling weak, but Qasim and Abdul Rahim were ready to push toward the plateau. I was slowly lacing up my reindeer boots when suddenly Schoening, Kauffman, and Hussein arrived. I was astonished. It was only nine in the morning. "What are you doing here at this hour? You must have been really going. What time did you leave, anyway?"

"Yesterday," replied Kauffman.

"Yesterday!"

"Yes, yesterday. We bivouacked on the ridge."

"You what!"

"I'll tell you the whole story in a minute, but first let's get Hussein inside a tent. He's got stomach trouble and is snow-blind."

Qasim and Abdul Rahim took the sick HAP's pack and led him into their tent. Kauffman sat on a food box and took off his crampons. "Yesterday everyone started off to come up here, but McCormack didn't feel too well so he decided to wait a day, and Swift and Nevison stayed with him while Pete, Hussein, and I left Camp II about eleven o'clock. The storm had wiped out all the steps and we had to make new ones. Hussein moved very slowly and we could not get him to go faster. He sat down constantly. When we reached the base of the dome we couldn't tell where we were going without the fixed line. Hussein had refused to wear his goggles and he was snow-blind. We were carrying full equipment, including a tent and a butane-gas stove, so we decided to camp on the spot. We stamped out a platform and spent the night. This morning we got up early, broke camp, and came on. So here we are. The others should be coming up this afternoon." Kauffman got up and went to assist Schoening pitch another tent.

This was an embarrassing development. The others were already arriving and we had not even begun to push toward the plateau. "Qasim. Abdul Rahim. Get your packs and get ready to go." The two HAPs came out of their tent. We would make up for the delay by carrying loads while we were pioneering the route. "Everyone will take a couple of oxygen bottles over to Camp IV." "Gee, sah'b."

We roped up and started out. As soon as we left camp we plunged calf-deep into soft snow. The clouds had closed in again and it was snowing lightly. The ridge dipped for 100 feet, then climbed up approximately 500 feet to the top of the next rise. I could not tell how large the cornice on the right was so I tried to stay as far to the left as that steep slope would allow. A hundred yards out of camp, I had just reached the bottom of the depression when suddenly I plunged waist-deep into a hole. As I threw myself forward and dug in my axe, I thought that I had stepped through the cornice, but how? I pulled myself out and made a careful investigation of the area. It was just a large crevasse running at right angles to the ridge. "That has no business being there," I thought as the HAPs safely crossed it at a different place.

Now we could see only ten feet ahead. A six-inch layer of snow on the slope to our left broke off and cascaded down toward the Glacier du Milieu. We began to plow upward. After great effort we climbed a hundred yards and were above the level of Camp III. The soft snow got deeper. The ridge broadened and the only safe place was exactly on the crest between the left and right slopes, but in the mist I could not distinguish it. I sank in above the knees with every step. Thin surface slides gently hissed down off to the left. We made another thirty yards. There was no place to cache the oxygen bottles. I turned around and signaled the HAPs to turn back. We arrived in camp just as the storm broke. As Rizvi had wanted to talk with Kauffman, he had joined Andy in the new tent while Schoening was in mine. I tried to brush off the snow, and slithered inside. "How far did you get?" Pete asked. "Three hundred yards—perhaps," I answered. "It's snowing, the snow's soft, and you can't see a thing. Also, there's avalanche danger. A small section of the slope near us let go. All I can say is, if Bob, Tom, and Mac are coming up in this weather, they're catching it."

Swift, Nevison, and McCormack were coming up in that weather and they were "catching it." Furthermore, Rahim Khan was with them. When everyone had climbed from Camp I to Camp II, he had been sick and was left behind to recover. However, Rahim Khan knew that the expedition was reaching its critical stage and he did not want to miss the excitement. On June 27, the day that Schoening, Kauffman, and Hussein were forced to bivouac on the ridge, Rahim Khan picked up a full load of oxygen and climbed to Camp II alone. When he suddenly stuck his frost-covered head inside their tent, he gave Swift, McCormack, and Nevison the shock of their lives. Now the four of them were climbing to Camp III.

Once again the track had to be remade. McCormack plowed out the way up to the base of the dome and then Bob Swift led up the ice slope. The wind clutched at them and they had to brace against the sudden gusts to keep from losing their balance. Nevison had brought his magazine camera and, in spite of the conditions, he kept taking color movies. "Look at the snow blow off the ridge. What a picture this'll make. Hey, Mac, stop looking so grim. People will think you're not enjoying this." McCormack's reply was lost in the wind. Step by step they hauled themselves up the fixed line.

Schoening and I were speculating about the snow conditions on the plateau when he said, "Listen, I hear them coming. I'm going to go outside and help them pitch their tent." Pete rapidly began putting on his boots. The party from Camp II arrived to the cheers of Rizvi, Kauffman, and me. All the sahibs except Akram, who had not yet acclimatized and was taking care of Base Camp, were at Camp III together with four HAPs. Nothing would stop us now.

Two more tents were pitched parallel to the first three. Rahim Khan and Qasim occupied one while Swift, McCormack, and Nevison took off their wind suits and went into the other. It took them a while to get their air mattresses and sleeping bags organized, but finally Nevison yelled, "Okay, we're ready for visitors." The rest of us went over to their tent for the final council of war. "Be sure you knock all the snow off before you come in," someone said as, one by one, Schoening, Kauffman, Rizvi, and I squirmed into the tent and crowded the original inhabitants up against the rear wall. After a little effort we got our legs untangled. Rizvi zipped up the front entrance. There being a quorum present, the meeting came to order.

Everyone knew exactly what our situation was and everyone was pretty much in agreement as to our course of action, but just to keep the proceedings orderly Schoening summarized our position. "There are eleven of us here with enough food to last over two weeks. Almost all the supplies at Camp II have been brought here so that camp is now just an overnight stopping-place for parties coming up the mountain. The rest of our supplies are down at Camp I and Base Camp. The fixed line will keep the route open down to the glacier. We are going to need at least two more camps, one where the ridge joins the plateau and one high on the plateau. Now we have two choices: We can methodically build up Camps IV and V, or everyone can carry loads over to Camp IV, leave five men there, and they can establish Camp V for the final assault. What does everyone think?" For the next five minutes we chaotically agreed with each other.

"Our biggest danger is being trapped by a prolonged storm . . ."

"I think everyone wants to spend as little time as possible out on that snow plateau . . ."

"We'll probably have unsettled weather for a few more days but we are sure to have a good spell and it will only take three days from here to climb the mountain."

"Conditions permitting . . ."

"If we are caught by a severe storm, we could immediately retreat, using oxygen if necessary."

"Our safety lies in the oxygen, which gives us mobility, and not in a large stockpile of food, which takes precious time to build up."

"If we waste time stockpiling we will be caught by the monsoon . . ."

"The sooner we climb the mountain and get off it the safer we are going to be . . ."

"Then everyone favors the rapid buildup," said Schoening, trying to put the lid back on his Pandora's box. Everyone did. He continued, "All right. Hussein is out of action so that leaves seven sahibs and three HAPs to carry loads to Camp IV tomorrow. Five sahibs, the two in the first summit team and the three in support, will stay at Camp IV and then establish Camp V the day after. The next day the first summit team goes for the top using oxygen. Then they come down and the support team occupies Camp V to make the second assault. The remaining two men will keep the supply line from Base Camp open and, together with the HAPs, will relay loads to Camp IV until the mountain is climbed. When the second team moves up to Camp V to make the next assault, the third team will move up to Camp IV in support and then if possible make a third try for the summit. I guess we are ready to determine the various teams. Is there any discussion before we start voting?"

By now Schoening should have known better. "I don't think I should vote because this is your expedition and I . . ." Rizvi was cut short in mid-sentence by the rest of us all talking at once. Finally Schoening could be heard over the babel: "You are as much a member of this party as anyone else in this tent. Your vote counts equally and you must participate in making the decisions of the expedition." Bob Swift ripped a blank page from his journal and tore it into seven scraps of paper. "We'll vote for the summit team first. Then we'll vote for the support team. Does everyone have something to write with?"

Everyone had. The scraps of paper were passed around and each man tried to write down his choice as best he could in those cramped quarters. Then we folded our slips of paper and handed them to Nevison. When Tom had collected all the ballots, he unfolded them and read the results while Schoening recorded the vote in his notebook. Neither Schoening nor Kauffman had voted for themselves, but everyone else had. They were to be the summit team. Scraps of paper were handed around again. Swift, Nevison, and Rizvi were to support them. "That's it. We've got an hour before dinner to get everything ready for tomorrow," said Pete.

We squeezed out of the tent like toothpaste out of a tube. There was much to be done. Schoening began filling a plastic bag with a five-day supply of delicacies for Camp V. Swift and Nevison began debating about what food should be taken to Camp IV. "There's plenty of ox tongue," I suggested. They rudely ignored me and kept putting cans of corned beef into their box. Kauffman and I straightened out the ropes and stacked the oxygen bottles. We also sorted the regulators and masks. We would take five complete sets of oxygen equipment onto the plateau and leave one at Camp III for emergency use. Then the loads were organized. The five men staying at Camp IV would carry their personal equipment, food, and one tent. Three men would carry ten bottles of oxygen, one man would carry two seventy-hour butane-gas stove bottles, and the last man would have two tents and other equipment.

Everything was set. It had stopped snowing and the overcast was lifting slightly. If it would only clear. We had dinner and crawled into our sleeping bags.

"Pete, what do you suppose that snow plateau is really like?"

"Don't know, but we'll find out tomorrow," he said, rolling over in his bag.

13

THE PLATEAU

We awoke early on June 29. The bitter cold made breakfast in bed a necessity instead of a luxury. At last, when the rays of the sun finally lit the walls of our tents, we crawled out of our cozy sleeping bags and into our wind suits. The five sahibs who were going to remain at Camp IV rolled up their bags and stuffed them inside their packs. Hussein inside his tent moaned a few times, which was unnecessary for we were not going to make him carry a load. Schoening picked up his pack and led the first rope out of camp with Kauffman, Qasim, and me tied behind him. We moved steadily until we came to the end of the previous tracks. Sinking to his thighs, Pete wallowed forward while Andy and I praised his tremendous effort, hoping he would not stop breaking trail until we reached the top of the first rise. He did not. We took off the rope and wandered around a few feet to look at the view. Five hundred feet below, the second group was starting down into the depression beyond Camp III. We watched them cross the big crevasse. "This is really getting to be a dull trip," said Kauffman in feigned disgust as the last man safely cleared the obstacle.

We languidly tied back into the rope. "Let's put Qasim to work. He's not going to pack a load to Camp V," suggested Andy. The HAP was delighted with the honor and began plowing the track with great enthusiasm. Other expeditions have encountered difficulty in persuading their high-altitude porters to climb, but our only problem with Qasim was trying to restrain him—although we did not try very hard. Originally I had thought that he was single, but Rizvi told us that Qasim's elder brothers had forced him to marry a wealthy widow twice his age in order to get control of her property. So our HAP left Askole on the slightest pretext and turned the sahibs' hair gray with his wild stunts on the mountain.

Now he plunged ahead without hesitation. I was next on the rope and I noticed that he kept edging toward the right. "Stay low to the left. There's a big cornice over to the right," I shouted, motioning for him to proceed in a straight line. Qasim stopped and nodded his head. Then he started forward again. Ten steps later he began angling off to the right. "Qasim, stay low. There's a cornice over there." Again he stopped and nodded his head. We slogged on. The left side of the ridge became steeper and suddenly Qasim halted on a rock outcrop. We joined him and saw that the ridge ahead dipped sharply for thirty feet. It was impossible to continue traversing; the slope was too steep and the snow too soft. There was only one other way. We would have to climb to the top of the cornice and follow its edge down into the depression. Fortunately it was a large cornice so the chances of Irvin and Roberts writing the mountaineering mystery story of the year appeared remote. Qasim stayed on the rock while I took up an intermediate stance and belayed Andy as he climbed to the top of the cornice. Then Kauffman gave Schoening an ice-axe belay as Pete began to kick steps in the loose powder snow down to the gap. Kauffman and Schoening could not see each other and, as I could see both, I was the communications relay. Meanwhile the others arrived and, strung out along the ridge, they watched the operation disapprovingly. "Sorry, no choice in the matter," muttered Kauffman in response to their queries as to whether we knew what we were doing. Schoening reached the depression and decided to return by traversing the slope. "That's no good, Pete. The snow's too rotten. We've got to stick to the cornice," I yelled.

He immediately agreed as his next step went down the mountain. "We'd better put a fixed rope down this," he said. Andy pulled the last four-foot aluminum picket out of his pack. It was one that we had salvaged off the slope below Camp II when we had joined two fixed ropes together. The pole was bent slightly in the middle where the weight of the creeping snow had pushed it in. Andy drove the picket into the top of the cornice. If only the safety committee could see us now, I thought, unkinking our last piece of manila rope. I tossed the end to Kauffman and he tied it to the picket.

A half-hour later we were in the notch spread out along the cornice as Pete tried to find a way off the ridge onto the plateau. Kauffman went to the top of the next rise and gave Pete a belay while I tried to anchor Andy. Schoening continued another thirty feet. "It's hopeless out here. I think we can drop through the cornice back where everyone is sitting," he said. Behind us the members of the second rope alternated sitting high and low on the side of the ridge in a prudent effort to have at least one or two men in a relatively secure position in the event the cornice broke. "You realize where we all are, don't you?" said Swift as Kauffman and Schoening returned.

Pete began cutting away the edge of the cornice. Here it overhung only slightly. The first 10 feet of the slope below was vertical and there was a large cave melted into it; then the slope continued at a fifty-degree angle for over 150 feet and ended in a large open crevasse. To avoid this, we would have to descend for 70 feet and then traverse the slope to the end of a flat space that led toward the plateau. Schoening finished hacking out a passage through which we could descend. I anchored a rope around my axe to serve as a fixed line, and Andy gave Pete a belay as he disappeared over the side to take a look at the situation. Several minutes passed. Then Schoening yelled up, "This is the way. It goes. Let's get the loads down." Meanwhile McCormack, who had been climbing on little except will power since he had become sick at Camp II, unloaded his pack, apologized to Swift for not being able to do his share, untied from the rope, and before the rest of us realized exactly what was happening, returned alone to Camp III.

We began to lower the first pack. It caught on the floor of the cave and we could not shake it loose. Andy and I pulled the pack up again. Nevison descended to the platform and Kauffman handed him the pack, which I lowered on the fixed line. Nevison sent it down to Schoening, who wrestled it into a safe place on the slope. By now several hours had passed. Obviously this system was no good, so we decided to send the HAPs down with their loads.

"Okay, Qasim, down you go," said Andy. Rizvi translated. The HAP grabbed the fixed line and descended, but for once he was unhappy. Upon reaching Schoening he put down his load, glanced back up the slope, and decided that this was enough. At this Rahim Khan and Abdul Rahim refused to go down the fixed line. These men had performed extremely well. They had made the long haul from Camp I to Camp II day after day without resting and had climbed the narrow arête between Camp II and III without complaint, but this was too much. We were high on the mountain and they would have to rappel down the rope and then climb back up it. They were brave men, but this was unfamiliar to them and they refused to do it. All the loads would have to be lowered and a permanent fixed rope attached to the slope.

There were no more rappel pickets, so Kauffman and I dug a U-shaped channel a foot deep and a yard in diameter in the snow and attached a nylon climbing rope to it. "We should pad the thing to prevent the rope from cutting into the snow," said Andy, but there was nothing we could use. "It's big enough. It should hold," I said, hoping I was right.

Schoening had had considerable difficulty in dragging the first load diagonally across the slope to his stance, so Bob Swift joined him and Qasim at the end of the fixed rope. Rahim Khan and Kauffman handed another pack to Nevison and we lowered it down the slope. The sky had become increasingly overcast and we were getting thoroughly chilled. Rizvi, who was arranging the loads, coughed constantly. Finally he turned to me and said that because of his throat he would only hinder our effort out on the plateau and he felt that in the best interests of the expedition he should withdraw. "Besides, I know that you are eager to go to Camp IV," he added.

I had wanted Rizvi to be in the support party, but I also wanted to get out on the plateau very badly so I made only a perfunctory protest. Rizvi gave me his air mattress and sleeping bag. Meanwhile another load had been sent down to Swift and Schoening. Kauffman began to dump yet another pack on Nevison's head. I looked at my watch. It was three o'clock. Rizvi mumbled, "Excuse me," and started back to Camp III as Abdul Rahim and Rahim Khan waited for their packs to be emptied and hauled up the slope. Watching Tas climb off the edge of the cornice and disappear around the corner, I vaguely thought that this was not very safe, but there were other things to worry about. We pulled up Rahim Khan's and Abdul Rahim's empty packs and then pulled up Qasim. He appeared badly shaken. Now only two packs remained to be lowered, Kauffman's and mine. With most of the loads down, Nevison descended to Schoening and Swift and picked up his pack. "Go ahead and find a spot for Camp IV," said Pete, and Tom began trudging out toward the plateau.

Kauffman's pack had all the expedition's flags sticking out of it and we were afraid that they would be lost if we lowered the pack. "Look, let's lower my pack first; then I can give you an upper belay so you can carry your pack down and then I can rappel," I said. Andy agreed. "Here's the last one, Bob," we yelled as we heaved my pack over the side. "Fish her in." Swift fished it in. Kauffman wrapped himself in the fixed rope and rappelled off. "Off rappel, off belay," floated up. I pulled up the belay rope. It was four o'clock and only the three HAPs and I remained on the corniced ridge. "What are they standing around for?" I thought. Then I suddenly realized that they were waiting for a rope. We had brought three nylon climbing ropes: two for the summit and support teams and one for the group that had to return to Camp III. Now with one of the climbing ropes attached as a fixed line, we were short. Reluctantly I cut in half the rope we were using for belaying and gave the HAPs their share. Although there was no harm done since sixty feet of rope was all that any of us needed, I was upset since I had never had to cut a climbing rope before and it was an act I had always associated with the ultimate in mountaineering mismanagement. The three HAPs tied into the rope I gave them and started back. "Salaam, sah'b," said Qasim, and Rahim Khan and Abdul Rahim echoed him. "Salaam," I replied and then, thinking that their efforts deserved something more, added "Baltis zindabad!" I got on the fixed line and rappelled through the cornice.

I reached the place where Andy was standing and got out of the rope. "Don't step in a crevasse," he said solicitously. There was a hole near his pack. Apparently our flat section in the slope was a large crevasse that was covered with snow. Kauffman and I picked up our packs, tied into the short length of rope, and started out along the deep tracks, which led toward the plateau. Schoening and Swift, who had already made two relays, were returning to pick up the remaining two loads. "Nevison is making a campsite a hundred yards ahead," said Pete as we passed. Andy and I descended twenty feet and gingerly picked our way across the bottom of a wide depression, another snow-covered crevasse. We climbed forty feet up the far side and found Nevison sitting on a pack. Other packs were around him and a small area of snow had been tramped down. It was a flat spot, sheltered from the wind by the end of the ridge, twenty feet high to the north, and close to our line of communication. From here we could walk out to the main plateau.

"You picked an excellent spot, Tom," I said.

"It really is," added Andy.

"I didn't really select it," replied Nevison modestly. "I was heading toward the plateau and was sitting here resting when Pete came up and said the same thing, so this is it."

Schoening and Swift returned with the last two loads, and in slow motion we began to tramp down a site for the tents. With a slight kick here, a slight kick there, we packed the snow. Our feeble efforts looked so ludicrous that Nevison summoned the energy to dig out the movie camera and take a picture. We pitched the two tents and connected their tunnels. The bottles of oxygen were carefully stacked upright in the snow and the food boxes were placed next to the tent entrances. Swift and Schoening crawled into the tent nearest Camp III while Nevison, Kauffman, and I squirmed into the other. Then we made a rude discovery. The only matches we had brought were the ones we habitually carried in our pockets. With only two seventy-hour butane-gas stove bottles, things were going to be tight. Also, one of the burners was new and required several precious matches to break it in, but after that the burner would light with one match. As the clouds descended, our five-day supply of food began to look very small.

The comforting purr of the stove melting snow into water dispelled the gloom. Soon the soup was hot and everyone dug out his tin can. We had started the expedition using tin plates and plastic cups, but the plates were never carried out of Base Camp and the cups developed leaks, so after a few weeks we were reduced to eating out of cans. There were only three types that could be used. The powdered milk tin was the worst. It was big and could hold a large amount of liquid, but it had a double lip at the top to hold the lid, which trapped the soup and dribbled it down our shirts. The hot chocolate can was better. It was smaller and easier to handle, but it dribbled, too. Only the mixed nuts can, or "mixed peanuts" as we referred to its contents, was really satisfactory for gracious living at 22,500 feet. But while Base Camp was well stocked with mixed nuts, the man who possessed such a can high on the mountain was indeed blessed. The lip did not hold the heat and it did not dribble. Furthermore, it held exactly the right amount of food in that two canfuls of anything was almost a satisfactory helping. And if it still had the lid, which could be used as a handle, attached to it, the owner had a treasure beyond all value. Other cans were abandoned when we moved to the next camp, but a mixed nut can received the care one normally reserves for a Ming vase. Initials were carved into the cans and each man jealously guarded his prized possession.

Then there was the matter of spoons. In a moment of softheadedness down at Camp III, I had lent my spoon to the HAPs. I never saw it again, and at every meal I was forced to throw myself upon the mercy of my more intelligent companions, who had grimly held on to theirs. I rapidly made the terrible discovery that a man without a spoon on an expedition hovers on the verge of starvation. But my charitable brethren at Camp IV rotated the onerous task of gulping down their food so I could eat mine before it froze. That first evening I am afraid that I did not display the proper gratitude. "Please hurry, Pete, I'm getting hungry," I said as

Schoening choked on a huge mouthful of meat he had swallowed in an effort to expedite dinner.

It snowed lightly during the night. We awoke at seven and made breakfast. Dinner was the main meal but breakfast was the most fun. This was due entirely to the power of advertising. On the back of one of the packages of breakfast food was a picture of an elfin character who was called "Noddy." The box also contained a card showing Noddy engaged in some nefarious activity. This card could be colored merely by adding water. The consumer was exhorted to obtain a complete set of six pictures, and over and over again occurred the phrase, "Noddy is hungry." Somehow the result produced by this combination of American hucksterism and English tradition was devastating to five climbers lying in the sack in the Himalaya. Soon we found ourselves holding out our cans at meal times and chorusing, "Noddy is hungry." Noddy became a symbol for everything that had gone wrong with the expedition and the person who made the mistake of the day was promptly nicknamed "Noddy." One picture of our hero was suspended from the roof of our tent, although it remained colorless, as water was too precious to spare, even for such a noble cause.

After breakfast we crawled out into the mist and surveyed the situation. We wondered what the plateau would be like. Schoening took about fifteen steps through the thigh-deep powder. "You shouldn't be doing that, Pete. Save your strength," I yelled. He returned. I turned to Nevison. "Tom, let's go out to the plateau and see what it's like. We'll be gone only a couple of hours and the track will save us time later. Besides it'll be better than sitting around here," I said. "Okay, we can take willow wands and mark the route," he replied. Swift also was eager to be doing something. At eleven we left camp. A half-mile away the main section of the plateau seemed to be cut off from our camp by a large crevasse; however, there seemed to be a connection to the northeast, so we slowly headed for it step by step. We rotated the lead every twenty minutes, and after an hour we came to the large crevasse that stretched from out of sight on our left to out of sight on our right. Fortunately we had arrived at the only snow-bridge that we could see that spanned the gap. At this moment Nevison had the misfortune to be leading; the bridge held and he became the first person to penetrate what we had considered to be the mysterious inner sanctuary of the mountain. But dragons did not spring out of the earth and devour him and he did not plunge out of sight; he was just knee-deep in the same soft snow as before. We put two willow wands in front of the crevasse to signal a weak bridge, hoping that the markers would remind leaders of future trips to move forward with less lead-footedness, and second men to wake up and stop allowing the rope to drag in the snow.

We continued to buck forward. We could look directly up at the summit through the high col between the ridge of Hidden South and the Urdok Comb. Ahead were a few undulating areas with large crevasses, but it would be only a matter of putting one foot in front of the other, at least as far as the final pyramid. We had found our way past the cliff bands and had turned the defenses of a great mountain. Through the years as we had clung to ice and rock, chopped steps, and dangled from pitons, we had dreamed of climbing an Eight Thousander. Now the culmination of our mountaineering careers was going to be a trudge through soft snow with heavy packs. Just a walk—a walk in the sky. It seemed ridiculously simple. Yet we could barely move.

We were now about a mile from Camp IV and near the center of the plateau. The exhilaration of pioneering new ground was dimmed by fatigue and the cold wind. "How many more wands?" asked Nevison, who again was in the lead. "Two," I replied. He continued plodding. "Twenty-three. Twenty-four. Twenty-five. That's it," I shouted and stuck our last willow wand into the snow. "Let's go home," said Nevison.

We turned around and mechanically began to slog back to Camp IV. It was infinitely easier to return with the trail broken, but even so we had to rest twice on the way. During these brief halts, the stupendous beauty of our surroundings slightly penetrated the dull fog in our minds, but our consciousness always centered on returning to our tents. As we climbed the final short uphill stretch into camp, Schoening called, "How was it?" "It goes if we can," someone replied. The three of us took off the rope and sat down on some food boxes.

"Guess what?" said Andy. "About an hour after you left we heard Qasim and Rahim Khan yelling from the top of the fixed rope. They had made a run over from Camp III by themselves. When Pete and I heard them, we went over to the base of the slope and they lowered their loads down to us and we brought them back to camp."

"They actually made the run unescorted? That's tremendous! How much food did they bring?" I asked.

"That's just it. There were three oxygen bottles, a seventy-hour stove, one Thermos bottle, and your down pants," said Andy disgustedly.

"I gave them a message for McCormack requesting matches, food, and stoves in that order," said Schoening.

"Well, it could be worse. Next time they'll bring the food," I said cheerfully, for after all, I now had my down pants.

The weather remained unsettled for the rest of the afternoon. One by one we walked up to the crest of the ridge twenty feet above camp and gazed at the fantastic scene. The perpetual loneliness of the human soul merged and dissolved into the vast grandeur of the Karakoram. Across the plateau Urdok Peak rose for 2,000 feet, a parody of a mountain. Although it was over 25,000 feet high, its base was 23,000 feet and it seemed like a fraud. To the south beyond the Conway Saddle was Saltoro Kangri, impressive if for no other reason than that one did not expect to see such a high mountain in that direction, just purple hills with light snowcaps. But dominating the scene was Masherbrum, the queen of the lower Baltoro, which rose above its mere 22,000-foot neighbors, a constant reminder that there will always be one more to climb. If Masherbrum were farther east, it would be lost in the concentration of Eight Thousanders at the head of the Baltoro Glacier, just as Gasherbrum III is, but instead it is isolated from its peers and is famed for its beauty and majesty. Looking at those mountains it was impossible to realize that few men have ever seen that magnificent array. Perhaps professional explorers can accept the fact that they are in some remote part of the world, but after expeditions in Canada, Iceland, and Peru, I am still overwhelmed on every trip by a sense of unreality.

As we swung our gaze to the north, we were jolted back to the problems of our situation, for beyond the ridge of Hidden South was the summit pyramid. Why didn't we have skis? Skis would make at least the first three miles easy. Perhaps even more. The first ski ascent of an Eight Thousander. The thought was intriguing, especially if we climbed the mountain on skis using oxygen. Sacrilege! But the summit pyramid would require climbing, so Hidden Peak was protected from such an ignominious fate. Besides, the whole question was academic as we had neither skis nor snowshoes. I thought bitterly about a letter we had received from a climbing friend in California who had urged us to get our "glorified ski tour" over with and get back to some real climbing. I was beginning to wish that all we had to do was some "real climbing" rather than a ski tour without skis at 23,000 feet. But we would get to the top. We would get to the top even if we had to dig a five-mile trench shoulder-deep.

It grew colder and started to snow again. The five occupants of Camp IV crawled back into their tents. Kauffman began to heat a pot of soup. Reindeer hair floated around on the surface of the liquid. Our reindeer boots were our pride and joy. When we put them on in the morning we almost felt like intrepid explorers instead of "shirkers of responsibility." Truly, the boots were wonderful, but also they shed hair like an alley cat. Not only did they shed hair, but also the hairs were able to sneak through the zippered wall of the outer vestibule, march down the full length of our sleeping quarters, and climb up the stove into the soup pot. It was uncanny, frustrating, and, when we drank the soup, most unpleasant.

After dinner we were still ravenously hungry and everyone discussed the effect of altitude upon appetite. We were supposed to lose our desire for food, but if at that moment Pegasus had wandered through camp, he would have been devoured on the spot and his bones would have been making soup.

It snowed all night and the next day. If we did not get more food we would have to return to Camp III for supplies at the first break in the weather instead of pushing forward, which might jeopardize our chances to climb the mountain. So far our only contact with the support group had

been Qasim and Rahim Khan. Just what was going on down there anyway? Then someone thought of Dick Irvin and Gil Roberts. They should
be approaching Base Camp by now. Perhaps they were already there. Our
morale rose. As soon as Irvin and Roberts learned of our situation
everything would be all right. Dick and Gil would not let us starve. Good
old Dick and Gil! The thought of our splendid companions arriving fresh
and eager filled us with renewed hope. Even the dour remark of one person
whose mind was functioning more clearly than the rest—that Irvin and
Roberts were unacclimatized and could do little to help us—failed to dim
our enthusiasm. On to the summit! Outside it continued to snow.

Three that afternoon was one of the highlights of the trip for me. Bob
Swift finished his volume of *The Short Stories of Bret Harte.* I quickly
grabbed it and in a few minutes I was back in the Mother Lode country of
California. Until then the only reminder I had had of home was a few
small boxes of raisins, which somehow did not inspire any nostalgia. In the
opposite corner of the tent Nevison made some butterscotch pudding.
Everyone else just dumped powdered milk and butterscotch mix into
water, stirred the mixture until it had the consistency of quicksand, and
served it to the victims, but not Tom. He took pudding-making very
seriously and his concoctions were works of art. Unfortunately, in the
camps where there were plenty of ingredients there was no Nevison, and
vice versa. Now everyone looked forward to the delicacy.

We prolonged dinner for two hours and then tried to go to sleep.
Several days earlier Kauffman's face had been badly sunburned. His lips
were still swollen and bleeding and he could not sleep. Nevison gave him
some pain-killer, but Andy tossed, turned, and moaned all night.

It was still snowing lightly on July 2. About noon the inactivity had
become intolerable. I just had to walk around. I put on my reindeer boots
and wind suit and went outside. I was passing some pots filled with snow
inside the tent when I heard a faint cry. The HAPs were at the top of the
fixed line with more supplies! "S-a-h'-b! S-a-h'-b!" "Okay, we're coming," I
yelled, hoping they would not get discouraged and leave. Kauffman, who
had been lacing his boots when the porters called, popped out of the tent.
We roped up and started for the fixed line. We were in a whiteout and it
was almost impossible to determine directions, but we wallowed toward
the impatient shouts of Qasim and Rahim Khan and eventually reached
the bottom of the fixed line.

The HAPs lowered the first pack. Kauffman retrieved it and imbedded
the contents securely into the slope. As the HAPs hauled the rope up,
Andy leaned against his axe and complained about his lips. I joined him
and saw that they had become worse; the blood was oozing through the
protective coating of zinc oxide and he was in great pain. I gave him a Dar-
von tablet and he went back to belay me. Above, I could barely see two

fuzzy dark shapes as Qasim and Rahim Khan began to lower the second load. The pack came down the slope to a point even with me and several feet away. "Bas, bas, enough," I yelled and gingerly stepped out to recover it. It took a while to untie the knots on the pack and transfer its contents into my rucksack without dropping it down the slope and into the waiting maw of the omnivorous crevasse below. I put a note for McCormack inside the empty pack and signaled the HAPs to pull it up. I thanked them and started to leave when Qasim began to yell at me and relower the pack. It took me a moment to realize that the reason for their action was that McCormack must have put a note in the pack. I had looked for one but had not found it. This time I discovered a piece of paper stuffed inside a hollow tube of the pack-frame.

"June 30. Tas and I have to descend to Camp I with Hussein and Abdul Rahim to recover. Qasim and Rahim Khan will continue to relay to Camp IV. Mac."

So there was no one at Camp III to read our note. But Rahim Khan and Qasim had brought sixty pounds of food, which would allow us to continue forward. Now if we only had some more matches. The two HAPs pulled the pack up again, and said, "Salaam, sah'bs." "Mihrbani, Qasim, Rahim Khan, salaam." Our contact with the rest of the expedition was over.

Andy and I carried the food back to the tents. Everyone was greatly cheered. If it would only stop snowing. We crawled back inside our dank tents. The interior was a mess. Moisture condensed on the inside of the nylon inner lining and the reindeer hair found a temporary resting-place on the wet sides during its march from the boots to the kitchen.

Later that afternoon we went outside again and watched the clouds form over the mountains and drift by. "It's the monsoon. It's the monsoon," repeated Kauffman. "We're going to be trapped. We'll all perish."

"This isn't the monsoon. The monsoon would be a lot worse than this. This is just a premonsoon storm. It will clear up for at least a few days before the monsoon hits," I said.

"How do you know it isn't the monsoon?" said Andy.

"How do you know it is?" I said.

With this brilliant display of empirical proof our scientific probing into the secrets of the local meteorology came to a halt. The argument would have continued except that Andy never believes his own pessimistic statements.

It was still overcast on July 3, but it had stopped snowing and the wind was shifting away from the southeast. By now everyone was impatient to be doing something, so we decided that all five of us would carry oxygen bottles out to our previous high point on the plateau and establish a dump. This would rebreak the trail and give us a fast start the next day for Camp V. We each picked up two bottles of oxygen and at ten we started out. After two hours of slogging we reached the last willow wand, dumped the bottles out of our packs, and stacked them into a high pyramid so if another storm suddenly arose we could find them. Then we returned to camp.

The next two days were going to be crucial, and as we sat around camp we tried to devise methods for coping with the deep snow. Schoening improvised a pair of snowshoes by putting his crampons through some plywood tops from our food boxes. He waddled around the camp on his new invention. "I think it helps—somewhat," he said after completing his circuit of the tents, and promptly began to tear apart another food box in order to make a second pair for Kauffman. Meanwhile Andy got the idea of having the man breaking trail on the way to Camp V use oxygen. He would carry a special pack, which would be slightly lighter than the others and have one bottle of oxygen in it. Thus the lead man could break trail at a steady pace and the rest of us could follow in the track without the added help. It was an excellent suggestion.

We made final arrangements for the loads. Two men would carry three bottles of oxygen each, four for the summit assault and two for sleeping purposes the night before. We were not planning to sleep two men on one bottle as the Swiss had done on Everest in 1956. Marmet had succinctly described the result of that operation, and we decided to avoid arguments over who was getting what out of the bottle. Another man would carry the tent and community gear, and Schoening and Kauffman would carry their personal equipment and food. Kauffman untied the various flags from the guy ropes of the tents and put them in his pack. We ate dinner outside under a clearing sky and then went to bed.

July 4. At long last the weather was perfect. We were up at five in the morning and off by six. There was little wind and the bitter cold did not penetrate our wind suits and down clothing. We thought respectfully of our predecessors—not those who had climbed the other Eight Thousanders in the last decade for they, too, had modern clothing and equipment, but the early British climbers on Mount Everest with their leather boots, tweed jackets, and pipes at 26,000 feet. They were a rugged breed. We were able to use the tracks made the day before, which were uncovered and hard, and within forty-five minutes we arrived at the oxygen dump. We untied from the rope and sat down. After taking a few pictures, we added the six bottles of oxygen to our loads, which now weighed over fifty pounds, and rerigged the rope. Instead of tying directly into the rope, we made small loops in it and clipped waist slings into these with carabiners. This way we could change positions on the rope without untying. From the dump the plateau stretched horizontally for another half-mile before it began to climb upward through a series of large crevasses toward the

"Tomorrow and tomorrow and tomorrow." Pete Schoening
adjusts the oxygen equipment before starting to break trail.

25,000-foot col between Urdok Peak and the ridge of Hidden South, where
we hoped to place Camp V.

Schoening was elected to try the first thirty-minute spasm using oxygen. He shouldered the specially prepared rucksack, put on the oxygen
helmet and mask, adjusted the equipment, and, using a flow rate of two
liters of oxygen a minute, started off. He sank in almost up to his knee at
the first step. Slowly we dragged across the level stretch and the col faded
farther and farther away. We had no trouble keeping up with Schoening's
pathetic one-step-at-a-time pace and I wondered what was holding him
back. After all he was incredibly strong and he was using oxygen. What
was going to happen to the rest of us when it became our turn to lead?
Pete's effort covered two-thirds of the distance to where the plateau began
to rise. Then he sank into the snow. Kauffman continued until he reached
the spot where Schoening was sitting and collapsed in the track, while the
rest of us did not even bother to close up the remaining distance. We just
sat down where we stood. Pete and Andy exchanged packs. Then Andy
clipped into the first loop on the rope while everyone else unclipped. The
rest of us pulled the rope back and reclipped into the loop just ahead of our
prior one. We sat in the snow for a long time.

"Everyone ready?" said Andy. We nodded and, except for Schoening, hauled ourselves up on our feet and braced ourselves over our ice-axes. Andy took his first step, then his second, and the rest of us followed. Schoening just sat there as we passed him one by one. There was no point in standing up; it would take several minutes for the line to pass him. As Bob Swift, the last man, approached, Pete pulled himself to his feet. Bob silently handed him the coil of rope that contained the end loop and plodded on. Pete clipped in, adjusted the wrist sling on his ice-axe, payed out the coil of rope, and fell in at the end of the line without causing a second's delay.

Exhaustion alone is not the most distinguishing feature of high-altitude climbing. There are many more mundane ways a person can push himself to the verge of collapse. Crawling on hands and knees with an eighty-five-pound pack through the swamps, slide alder, and brush of British Columbia is an excellent exercise in total fatigue, and mountaineering offers many others equally delightful. But the biggest characteristic of Himalayan mountaineering is frustration. The most extreme efforts produce such meager results. It takes everything one has to make one step, and progress is measured in yards. I began to wonder what had happened to Schoening, Kauffman, and Nevison, as they acted as if every step breaking trail would be their last. I felt absolutely exhausted just carrying a load through the broken track, but that was just because I was carrying such a heavy load without oxygen. I could hardly wait until it was my turn to carry the light pack and breathe the gas.

"Time," I called and Nevison dropped on the spot. With great effort I closed the gap and collapsed beside him. He gave me the oxygen pack and I gave him mine. There had been three leads of thirty minutes each. Three hours had gone by and we had climbed 400 feet up the steepening slopes of the plateau. After the usual prolonged rest I strapped on the oxygen mask, turned the regulator dial, and checked the flow indicator. The breathing bag filled up. I took a couple of deep breaths and pulled myself to my feet. Everyone was standing up except Nevison, who was following the standard practice of waiting for the end of the rope to come by. I started off. One step. I was up to my knees. Another step, the same thing. I breathed deeply and took another step forward. I was determined to increase my pace but it was impossible. All the oxygen did was enable me to keep going forward while breaking trail. It was a heartbreaking discovery and I wished I were again at the back of the line. Step. Step. Step. Step. "Boots— Boots—Boots—Boots, movin' up and down again!" "Tomorrow, and tomorrow, and tomorrow,/Creeps in this petty pace from day to day . . ." I began to angle to the right to find more consolidated snow. I did not. Then a crevasse barred the way and I cut sharply to the right to pass it. The going seemed to be infinitesimally easier. "Time," yelled Nevison and a split second later I was lying on the slope. The thirty minutes went by fairly fast after all, I thought. At least they did after my mind retreated as far back into unconsciousness as it could and still allow me to realize what I was doing. Swift flopped down beside me and we exchanged packs. "Now we'll go. Bob's strong and fresh," I thought. Swift stood up and started off. I lay in the snow until Nevison handed me the end loop, and with his helping hand I staggered to my feet. I clipped my carabiner into the loop and fell into the end of the line in time, just like everyone else.

Swift plunged forward with grim determination, but he went neither faster nor slower than the rest of us had. By now it was past noon. Could anything be worse than this? Then the oxygen regulator jammed. The regulators for the summit team were buried deep in someone's pack. Why bother to fish them out; that would take forever. We decided to go ahead without oxygen and alternate leaders every ten minutes. That also would take forever. Fortunately the cold prevented us from lying around too long in our comatose state without getting the urge to undertake some activity to warm up. The urge always completely vanished when we got back on our feet.

Schoening led off. He put forth a tremendous effort, and ten minutes later, when we all collapsed, we had gained a hundred feet of distance and thirty of elevation. Another victim, another ten minutes, another hundred feet, another rest longer than the period of moving. Soon it was my turn again. One step, again up to the knees, and I bent double over the axe, gasping. One does not sweat at high altitude, but I could almost feel the water in my body departing through my lungs every time I exhaled into the dry air. Part of me seemed to stand aside and revile the inert figure hunched over the axe. "Don't stand there, take another step, take another step, NOW." But it was impossible to move until I caught my breath. Another step, more gasping, and a wave of remorse swept over me as I knew I was letting everyone down. "Time," yelled Nevison, and as I sank into the slope the agony of failure was blunted by fatigue. Another hundred feet.

We reached the base of a steep slope that climbed upward for a hundred feet or so. "We'll put our camp somewhere up there," said Schoening, confirming a fact we all knew. However, the formalized thought revived us slightly and Swift threw himself forward with renewed vigor. He actually got halfway up the slope before his time was over. Schoening took the next lead and we arrived at the top. A thousand feet above us was the col with the summit pyramid behind it, but it was now three in the afternoon and we had to stop. There was a small flat spot behind a large crevasse, which provided protection from possible avalanches off the Urdok Comb. "This looks like a good place," said Schoening, and the rest of us signified our assent by throwing down our packs.

With our lead-footed shuffle we trampled down a site in the snow and pitched the tent. It was amazing how adept we had become at avoiding unnecessary work, for the tent exactly covered the prepared area with not an

"We dumped the equipment out of our packs...and sat down on the snow." Camp V is established. From left, Swift, Schoening, Clinch, Nevison.

inch to spare. We dumped the equipment out of our packs, stacked the oxygen bottles, and sat down in the snow. We looked down at the two tents of Camp IV 1,500 feet below and several miles away. We had come a long way. Then we looked up at the summit. It was several thousand feet above us and miles away. There was a long way to go. And up to the col and beyond stretched those interminable slopes of soft snow.

It was getting late. Schoening and Kauffman had to make preparations for the morning, and Nevison, Swift, and I had to get back to Camp IV. We all pulled ourselves to our feet and Tom, Bob, and I wished Pete and Andy good luck.

"Don't worry, Andy, you'll make it," I said.

"If we do, it will be because of the three of you," said Kauffman.

"Not us—everyone in the expedition," said Swift. We shook hands all around and then Nevison, Swift, and I slowly left our comrades and the piece of cloth that was euphemistically called Camp V.

"Let's stop every thirty minutes," said Swift as we started down, aptly expressing what both Nevison and I were thinking. But what a difference it was to be coming downhill without heavy loads, and using solid tracks. We looked at the closely bunched splotches in the snow that marked our resting-places at the end of each ten-minute spasm on the way up. Pathetic. As the sun approached the horizon, we became aware of the wildness and beauty of our environment. At five we staggered into Camp IV as if we had been out on a three-week binge. We crawled inside the tents and left the flaps open so we could gaze up the plateau toward Camp V and Hidden Peak. Pete and Andy were going to have their work cut out for them tomorrow. But it was clear and cold and few clouds were in the sky. The weather would be good. Then we rediscovered the two most precious things in the world—water and sleep.

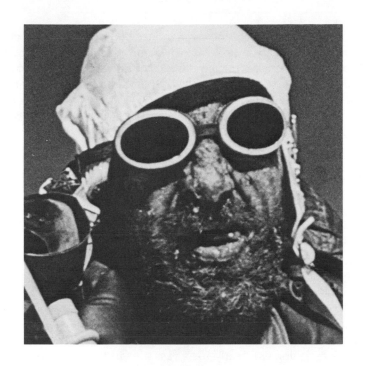

14

THE SUMMIT

by Peter K. Schoening

With a feeling of stark solitude, Andy and I watched our companions plod across the flat near Camp V and finally drop down out of sight. Minutes passed. It was almost lonely now, isolated in snow and ice at 24,000 feet. Thoughts flashed across my mind—the past, other experiences, the possible, the future—and then they were erased by the duties of securing camp.

A huge ice crevasse split the slope immediately above us, which provided a sense of security from avalanches and reduced the possibility of other crevasses underneath the tent. Also, the crevasse was very convenient for the disposal of garbage, although this seemed to be a minor problem under the circumstances.

While I went inside the tent and began to arrange our equipment and start the stove, Andy arranged our ice-axes immediately outside the entrance and draped our crampons over them. The nine-by-nine-inch plywood panels that we intended to use as snowshoes were stuck in the snow next to the axes. Then he made a final check of our oxygen cylinders and came inside the tent. Each of us would carry two bottles of oxygen, which at our planned flow rates of two to three liters a minute would furnish us with a continuous supply for approximately twelve hours. Besides the oxygen, we would carry the usual essentials—food, extra socks and mittens, compass, first aid kit, matches, candles, spare goggles, and some other survival items in a small bag. Other articles that we used constantly, such as goggles, sunburn ointment, and an ear protector, were kept overnight in our parka pockets. By nine we had finished our dinner of, primarily, soup and tea and had melted a pot of snow into water to facilitate breakfast the following day.

After everything was ready for a fast start in the morning we began the task of sleeping. It is always difficult to sleep at high altitudes, especially the first night in a higher camp. Based upon the experiences of previous expeditions, we had hoped to solve this problem at Camp V by breathing a small amount of oxygen during the night while we slept. We laid the two extra oxygen cylinders that had been brought for this purpose inside the tent. Then the regulators were attached to the bottles and set for a flow rate of one liter per minute. It was uncomfortable to wear the masks, so we merely laid them in front of our faces. This bled the oxygen near the vicinity of our noses and with luck we would be able to suck some of it into our lungs. Apparently this technique was successful for we slept soundly until 3:00 A.M. when the alarm wristwatch we had borrowed from Nevison sputtered.

Despite all our careful preparations the evening before, it still took us over two hours to prepare a small breakfast, lace up reindeer boots, strap on crampons, and handle the other infinite details involved in living in such a place. Then we set the oxygen regulators for a flow rate of two liters per minute and stamped our crampons through the plywood squares. A final check: rope on, prusik slings for crevasse rescue adjusted, safety cords to the down mittens attached, and pack belly-strap fastened. At five o'clock we moved out toward our first goal: the col, more than 500 feet above us and more than a mile away.

Several feet east of the tent a snowbridge spanned the huge crevasse.

We walked softly over this gateway and entered a large, gradually ascending flat that led toward the complex of snow and ice that dropped sharply from the col. Debris was scattered about the area from avalanches that had fallen off the ridge between Hidden South and the west side of the col. As the slope steepened, our progress became slower and slower. The plywood snowshoes became more and more useless as it required increasing effort to keep them from slipping off the small snow ledges that we pounded out with every step. Finally, just below the top of the first rise, we had to abandon them completely. From here it was just plain plowing. With every step we sank into the snow between the ankle and the knee, sometimes deeper. After the first rise there was another small flat section where a huge crevasse had formed and then had been refilled with snow. Beyond this there was an exhaustingly steep section, 300 to 400 feet high. Slow, but we could not fight it—we just kept going. Directly above us now was a cornice that extended along the entire edge of the col. Fortunately a section of the cornice had broken out a few days before, which made a passageway to the top and eliminated the necessity of having to tunnel through the overhanging lip. We meandered through the ice blocks of the broken section, muscled our way for thirty feet up the last block, and reached the col.

The col was obviously a cold and windy place. So far our route had been on the lee side, but here, only a few feet beyond the cornice, a strip of rock rubble 200 feet wide had been blown bare by the intense wind that funneled through the gap. The snow of the west glacier was on the windward side, but it was low enough to withstand the prevailing gales.

We had been climbing for five hours since leaving camp and the summit looked a long, long way off, so we stopped for ten minutes and had a quick snack. We speculated about the climb ahead and established our mental attitude. "We'll just keep moving and see how it goes," which under the circumstances seemed more appropriate than the "fight and drive" approach.

East of the col the ridge joins the main ridge from the Urdok Comb, which in turn curves north and then west to terminate at the summit of Hidden Peak. This circular ridge forms a cirque, which is the origin of the huge glacier that cascades down the west side of the mountain. The summit was due north across this cirque from our position. We decided to cross by ascending slightly up and to the right in order to gain altitude continually, which would bring us to some steep snow below the summit. Above this snow there was ice-covered rock and then a bare rock wall that began 400 feet below the crest of the summit ridge. Fortunately, a narrow snow couloir just east of the summit provided a passage through the rock barrier. This was our objective, the key to the climb.

We reset our regulators for a flow rate of two and a half liters per minute and started across the cirque. Soon each step became part of a mechanical plodding process and we exchanged the lead every ten minutes. Even so, crossing the cirque went rapidly and we took another short but rewarding rest at the base of a large serac. Now the glacier rose steeply, with the summit slightly to the west. From here the final ridge did not look too far away, and although we knew that this was due to foreshortening, our attitude of "just seeing how it goes" began to change. It was a harmless self-delusion.

The steepening snow became icy and the two claws of our ten-point crampons, which projected in front of our boots, became extremely useful as we toed directly up the slope. But even under these favorable conditions we moved slowly. One step; two, three, four, gulps of air and oxygen; another step, more gulps of air and oxygen. And then for some reason we hardly moved. Above the wind I could faintly hear Andy mumbling through his mask about having difficulty in breathing. Minutes passed and we climbed only a few feet. Andy yelled for a halt so he could survey the situation. Then he discovered the trouble—his oxygen cylinder was empty. Mine was almost empty, also, so we both changed to our second bottles and allowed the first ones to slither off down the slope.

We increased the flow rate to three liters of oxygen per minute. Rocks that began to protrude through the snow and ice served as a guide to our progress. The couloir that we had seen from the col was now to our left and we had to make a climbing traverse over snow and ice-coated rock to reach it. The climbing was not too difficult, but the footing was slippery and occasionally we belayed each other. Eventually we reached the edge of the couloir and took another short rest while we evaluated this next problem.

The couloir was bounded by steep rock walls and its snow was windslab. We decided to climb up the snow while keeping near the rock of the right-hand wall. This would enable us to establish good belays if necessary and reduced the danger of disturbing the equilibrium of the snow. We started up. The summit was only 500 feet above us and, barring some unexpected difficulty, we knew that we would make it. We still set our methodical pace, but now we could have made it even with an exhausting "fight and drive."

The snow in the couloir was quite hazardous, typical for such a cold and windy spot. The small crystals had been packed by the wind and laminated in layers and there was very little bonding between laminations. Its sugarlike consistency took crampon points well, but it had a tendency to fracture suddenly and slide over the smooth underlying layers. As we neared the top of the couloir, we traversed left again toward the summit and finally gained the crest of the ridge. An icy wind was blowing out of the north, but the sky remained almost cloudless. We could not have expected a finer day for such a high mountain, although when we removed our down mittens for even a few moments our fingers became numb.

At three o'clock we topped the rounding ridge and there was no place higher to go. We had reached the summit of Hidden Peak, the terminus of months of planning, teamwork, and constant effort. It was exhilarating and beautiful.

To the north and some fifteen miles away rose the distinctive pyramid of K2, the second highest mountain in the world, and I could see the location where our Camp VIII had been in 1953. Between us and K2 were more giants—Broad Peak, and Gasherbrums II, III, and IV, all over 26,000 feet, all slightly lower than Hidden Peak. To the northeast, barren rolling hills extended endlessly toward the horizon. It looked warm in that direction. Elsewhere we were surrounded by masses of gigantic peaks covered with ice and snow, with rock faces and pinnacles on their steeper sides. Eight thousand feet below were the South Gasherbrum and Abruzzi glaciers. Beyond them and Gasherbrums V and VI we could see the Baltoro Glacier, definite proof that Hidden Peak is not really "hidden" after all. I descended a few feet down the north ridge to get a full view of the South Gasherbrum Glacier. A thin line in the snow indicated the track of the Italian expedition to Gasherbrum IV. A small black speck was one of their camps. Across the

"Have we vanquished an enemy? None but ourselves." (George Mallory)
Andy Kauffman on the summit of Hidden Peak, July 5, 1958.

cirque and beyond the col were other small black specks, our Camps III and IV. Suddenly there were mirror flashes from Camp III. We promptly flashed back, using a lid from a can. For the brief period that we were on the summit, the members of the expedition were in contact with each other.

Then we began the duty of taking photographs. First we took the panorama along the horizon, then I shot a movie of Andy reaching the summit, and finally we photographed the numerous flags that Andy had carried all the way from Skardu for just this occasion. There were the flags of the United Nations, Pakistan, and the United States. Then there were the British and French flags, in commemoration of those who had contributed their knowledge and efforts in making this ascent possible. Unfortunately the Swiss flag had been ripped from Kauffman's pack when he had struggled over the last obstacles below the col and we did not find it until the descent, but it was certainly with us in spirit. Finally there was the Free Hungarian flag, in memory of some very courageous people.

After having accomplished the chore of photographing the flags, I took a last look at the scene. I was quite happy to be there and I never considered just why I was there. The reason was taken for granted and I seriously doubt that anyone who has just reached a major summit feels the need to justify his presence there. It was time to descend. It was four o'clock and Camp V was miles away. We replaced our oxygen masks, adjusted the regulators for a flow rate of two liters per minute, and started down. We moved rapidly along the ridge, but when we reached the couloir we slowed down. We were extremely tired and this snow was treacherous. We reached the point where we had traversed the ice-coated rocks but thought that we could find a better route lower down. We descended and tried a new way. The first one had been better.

Step by step we retraced our tracks around the cirque and reached the col by seven-thirty. There were only eighty atmospheres of pressure remaining in the oxygen bottles and we decided that they were more of a hindrance than a help, so we dumped them and continued on. It was getting dark and we moved very slowly, carefully following our old footprints as we tried to avoid even the slightest unnecessary effort. A half-hour later we stopped and shared a Dexedrine pill for the final push into Camp V. At nine we stumbled up to our little tent and with great effort took off the rope and our crampons and crawled inside. After taking off our reindeer boots we struggled inside our sleeping bags. We had had nothing to drink all day and were extremely thirsty, so we melted down a pot of water. It disappeared instantly and we craved more, but we were just too exhausted to melt more snow. I reached out of my bag for the stove, turned it off, and we immediately fell into a deep sleep.

15

EVACUATION

Nevison unzipped the tent flap and stuck his head out into the cold morning air. "There they go," he said. Looking out the entrance I could see two black specks on the snow above the location of Camp V. The specks were moving slowly but steadily upward. We watched them until they went behind a hummock of snow and were lost from view.

We were still feeling the effects of yesterday's exertions, but at eleven we finally left for Camp III to get some more food. We reached the steep slope leading up to the ridge and with the aid of the fixed rope, Nevison kicked and cut a line of steps to the little cave underneath the lip of the cornice. As Tom struggled upward, Swift, who was belaying him, turned to me and said, "What do you suppose this slope will be like after the monsoon comes?" It was a good question. Swift climbed to the cave and gave Nevison another belay as Tom, with great effort, pulled himself over the roof and onto the top of the cornice. Meanwhile I realized that I would have to rest if I was going to carry another heavy load to Camp V tomorrow and try for the summit the day after. Swift and Nevison assured me that they would be able to bring up adequate supplies, so I wandered back to Camp IV while they watched to make sure that I did not break through the snowbridge on the way. Then they descended to Camp III.

With the track already made, Swift and Nevison reached Camp III within a half-hour after leaving the top of the fixed line. Just then McCormack and Akram also arrived at Camp III after climbing up from Camp II. In an expedition composed of determined invalids McCormack and Akram were two of the unluckiest members. They were also two of the most determined. Akram had not fully acclimatized and McCormack was still suffering from respiratory trouble, but that did not stop them. The plan called for them to move up in support of the second assault so they moved up in support. The previous day they had climbed from Camp I to Camp II, and now when they met the delighted and astonished Nevison and Swift, McCormack said, "We'll be coming over to Camp IV tomorrow." And they did not intend to quit there either. The plan provided for a third summit assault and McCormack and Akram were firm believers in the plan. The expedition was back to normal. Once again it was climb or get run down by someone who would.

McCormack and Akram had some interesting information. So far during the expedition we had heard only a few weather broadcasts and these were prepared for the Austrian expedition to Haramosh. The reports were uniformly depressing, and one reason we continued to push on was that we were unhampered by any knowledge about how bad conditions were in the Karakoram. However, our lack of information as to the location and progress of the monsoon made us uneasy. Just before leaving Camp I to come up the mountain again, McCormack had been fiddling with the shortwave receiver when suddenly, for the first time, he picked up the weather broadcast that Radio Pakistan beamed to our expedition. The monsoon was a week away.

Also McCormack and Akram had brought up the pair of binoculars that had been left at Camp I. The four sahibs kept passing them around until they spotted Schoening and Kauffman climbing the final couloir toward the summit ridge. Nothing would stop them now. Camp III broke into celebration.

At Camp IV I was sitting on a food box absorbing the warm after-noon sun and reading Bret Harte when Nevison and Swift arrived and put down their loads.

"How was it?" I asked.

"Fine," said Nevison. "McCormack and Akram have come up to Camp III and will be coming over here tomorrow."

"That's wonderful. Any other news?"

"The British have climbed Rakaposhi," said Swift.

"Alaska's the forty-ninth state," added Nevison.

"Anything else?" I asked.

"No, that's about it," said Nevison. "Here's some mail that Akram brought up."

So we were still hijacking the Italians' mail runner, I thought, taking the letters. We had told the Italians that we could not afford to pay for mail run-ners, but the postmaster at Skardu gave the Italian runner mail for both expeditions and our party would waylay the runner on his trip to the Ital-ian camp. The Italians never complained about these depredations, and when the expedition was over they generously declined our offer to pay for our use of their mail service.

I tore open the first letter and discovered that it was safe for me to come home. I had passed the bar examination. I informed Bob and Tom about this and after they had duly congratulated me, Nevison held out the binoculars and said casually, "You may want to use these. Pete and Andy have been standing on the summit for the last half-hour." While Swift and Nevison sat there grinning, I grabbed the binoculars and scanned the summit pyramid. Silhouetted against the blue sky Schoening and Kauffman were descending the summit ridge. It was a pleasant five minutes in my life.

I was extremely happy, but I was not so wildly exultant as I had thought I would be if this moment occurred. Then I realized that I had been expecting it to happen. We had all worked so hard for this goal that I always felt that somehow we would climb the mountain. I knew that Schoening and Kauffman would get to the top, not because they were supermen but simply because they would not quit until they had.

"They're moving very slowly," said Nevison looking up with the binoculars. "Well, I guess we had better get things ready for the morning," he added. We decided that Swift would carry the food and his personal gear while Nevison and I would carry the oxygen. We could use Schoening and Kauffman's sleeping bags at Camp V. Only two more days of good weather and we would be on the summit ourselves. Swift prepared a din-ner that was equal to the occasion and then we went to bed.

It was now seven-thirty and getting dark, and we could see that Schoening and Kauffman were not yet back to Camp V. We began to get concerned for their safety, especially Nevison, who lay with his head out-side the tent entrance, carefully following their progress. Finally he lost them in the evening shadows, pulled his head back, and closed the flap. "Hope they get in without any trouble," he said quietly.

It would be only a one-way trip to Camp V so we did not leave our tents until seven, a relatively late start. As we slogged toward the plateau we kept looking for signs of activity at Camp V. It was cold and a high wind scourged the snow. Just as we reached the oxygen dump we spotted Schoening and Kauffman getting ready to descend from Camp V. In unison we tried to shout to them to leave their sleeping bags and air mattresses, but our voices did not carry over the wind. They obviously did not hear us and began to stagger down the slope below Camp V in a direct line. Nevison and I added more oxygen bottles to our loads and, with Swift in the lead, we plodded forward.

Slowly the two parties came closer and closer, but no one said anything and no one gestured. There was no use in yelling in that wind and everyone knew that everyone else knew about the climb. As Schoening and Kauffman drew near, Swift stepped off to one side to photograph the "dramatic" reunion according to the plan that we had devised at Camp IV. But Schoening, who was in the lead, came right up to us and silently collapsed into the snow without even attempting to shake hands. "Nice going. How was it? Did you leave your sleeping bags up there?" I said. "It's a long climb. No, we've got our sleeping bags with us," said Schoening.

Kauffman staggered in, coiling the rope as he came, and crumpled beside Schoening. Andy caught his breath. Then very deliberately he said, "Pete Schoening climbed this mountain. Pete broke trail over two-thirds of the way." For once in his life Schoening did not vehemently object to such a statement. He was too tired to care. On an expedition everyone ages ten years, but the change in Pete and Andy's appearance in just one day described their ordeal more eloquently than any words. They were exhausted.

"What are you going to do? Are you going to try for the summit?" said Schoening.

"What do you think?" asked Nevison.

"That's a decision the three of you have to make," was the reply.

We glanced up at the summit, the ambition of a lifetime only one day away. Cloud streamers whipped past the final pyramid. Other clouds were forming over nearby peaks and white streaks lined the sky around us. There was going to be a storm, but what kind of a storm? Would the bad weather last for a day or so and then clear up or would it be a prolonged siege that might strand us in Camp V? The wind had filled Schoening's and Kauffman's tracks to the summit, so we would not be spared that burden; however, with three of us rotating at the task of breaking trail we could probably make it. Also we had a four-day supply of food and plenty of oxygen, but our support was diminished as Schoening and Kauffman could not help us. And exactly where was the monsoon? The summit was within our personal grasp and yet we had achieved our objective. We had climbed Hidden Peak. Today would remain good, and if we immediately evacuated the mountain we would be off the plateau by nightfall and tomorrow everyone would be safe on the Abruzzi Glacier. Despite our mistakes and many people's predictions, we had accomplished a near-perfect expedition. Should we jeopardize our success by making another summit attempt with the weather changing? There was only one correct decision, and Bob, Tom, and I knew it. Again we glanced up at the summit and reluctantly and unanimously agreed that it would be unwise to make a second assault. "I'm sure glad to hear you say that. It's a big load off my mind," said Schoening.

Although Schoening and Kauffman had brought down their sleeping bags and air mattresses, they had left the tent behind, as well as Nevison's movie camera and the oxygen regulators. We quickly decided that Bob Swift, who was carrying his personal gear, should escort Pete and Andy down to Camp III while Nevison and I continued to Camp V to retrieve the equipment. "We'll pack up Camp IV and take everything down except your sleeping bags, air mattresses, and one stove so in case you want to spend another night before coming down to Camp III all you will have to do is repitch the tent," said Swift. "Fine, but we'll probably come on down to Camp III tonight anyway," said Nevison.

Nevison and I dumped the oxygen bottles from our rucksacks and left them lying where they fell. So this was their end. It had taken the combined efforts of Jean Couzy and Jürg Marmet to obtain those bottles, we had nursed them all the way to the base of Hidden Peak, and with great difficulty we had hauled them up to this point above 23,000 feet just to drop them into the snow, with the protective aluminum foil wrappers still on them. Think how much work we could have spared everyone if we had just known how things were going to turn out. But we could not have known, so we had had to obtain the bottles and carry them up the mountain. Yes, we even had to carry them to this desolate spot between Camps IV and V. Swift started off on the long walk home, rebreaking the trail for Schoening and Kauffman, for already the wind-driven powder snow had drifted over our tracks. Nevison and I began to punch our way upward toward Camp V. We moved slowly, but having empty sacks and being slightly more acclimatized than two days previously, we set a steady pace. By noon we reached the tent of Camp V, a particle of foreign matter on the plateau. Nevison and I immediately crawled inside to escape the wind.

The tent and its contents represented the ultimate in our equipment and supplies. All previous camps and their equipment existed for the sole purpose of allowing this camp to be established, the lonely culmination of the expedition's supply line. Several cans of mixed nuts were untouched.

The two oxygen bottles used for sleeping still contained plenty of gas. There was a stove and we promptly melted snow for a pot of water. "Have some tea," said Nevison, handing me a can of hot tea and a half-full can of nuts. "Have some oxygen," I replied and thrust the mask into his face with the regulator turned to full flow. He took it and breathed deeply. "This is the life," he said. Then his eyes caught sight of something else. "Look! An unopened box of lemon cookies!"

We gorged ourselves until we could hold no more and sadly looked at the rest of the delicacies, which would have to be abandoned. There still remained one can of mixed nuts and, while I knew that within a couple of days we would be in Base Camp and could have all the mixed nuts we wanted, the last two weeks of privation had so affected me that I automatically threw the can into the pack. "Can't waste mixed nuts," I said in response to Nevison's bewildered look.

The wind rattling the sides of the tent reminded us that we had work to do, so reluctantly we cleaned out the interior of the tent, put the equipment into our packs, and then collapsed and rolled Camp V. We were ready to go. We paused for one last look. Cloudcaps covered the various mountains like thatched roofs on peasants' huts. Urdok Peak II looked ridiculously simple. "It's too bad we don't have a few extra days up here. Just think what we could do," I said. Then slowly we started down. The wind whined in our ears as it instantly obliterated our tracks behind us, impatient to eliminate the offensive signs of man in this sublime region in which he does not belong and cannot live, but which if he is lucky and persistent he may visit just long enough to absorb some of its mystery before being forced to depart from it forever.

Meanwhile McCormack and Akram had arrived at Camp IV in time to greet Schoening, Kauffman, and Swift. They had a quiet reunion and sat around discussing the summit climb over a pot of tea before they finally reconciled themselves to the task of breaking camp. They packed the tents, cached the two sleeping bags belonging to Nevison and me, and left for Camp III. As it was still early in the afternoon when they reached that camp, it was decided that Swift, McCormack, and Akram should remain in Camp III to serve as support until Nevison and I got off the plateau while Schoening and Kauffman went on to Camp I. Although Pete and Andy were very tired, the fixed ropes were in place and they wanted to get off the mountain as quickly as possible. Also, Kauffman's feet were numb and he wanted to put the last difficulties behind him before the feeling in his toes returned. They shouldered their loads and moved with great caution down the fixed ropes. They reached the end of the ropes and wallowed down the lower slopes of the buttress to the Abruzzi Glacier and into Camp I. Rizvi and Abdul Rahim rushed out to meet them as they stumbled into the base camp tent and collapsed.

At three-thirty Nevison and I reached the remains of Camp IV. We were tired and thirsty, and for a moment we considered pitching the tent and spending the night, but it would take about as much mental and physical effort to pitch camp as it would to climb the fixed rope up to the ridge so we compromised with ourselves. We melted a large potful of snow and made tea saturated with sugar. Time passed rapidly. "It's four-thirty. We'd better get out of here before it gets too late," said Nevison.

We stuffed the sleeping bags and air mattresses into our packs and started off. We reached the base of the fixed rope and discovered that the steps kicked by the previous party were still in, as the slope was on the lee side of the ridge. This saved us considerable effort, but there still remained the roof of the cave. I gave Nevison a half-hearted belay as he straddled the gap and then with a great heave pulled himself on top of the cornice. I passed up the two packs, untangled the belay rope from the fixed line, and followed. Nevison untied the nylon climbing rope that had served as our fixed rope, and sitting in the snow he slowly coiled it. The sun was sinking low on the horizon, casting a reddish hue on the gathering clouds, and the lengthening shadows gave the surrounding mountains depth and made them stand out from their background of sky and glacier.

With the removal of the fixed rope our last link with the plateau was gone. We were the last men down and everyone was safely out of a position where we had constantly expected the worst. Yet we had a feeling of remorse rather than relief. The lofty, lonely snow plateau capped by the summit pyramid of Hidden Peak would be only a memory and the fantastic sea of mountains dominated by Masherbrum would be gone forever. An hour later we skirted the last crevasse and climbed the few feet into Camp III. Qasim and Rahim Khan, beaming from ear to ear, charged out of their tent and enthusiastically hugged the breath out of us. After we had been incapacitated by their greeting, they carried our packs into camp.

July 7 dawned overcast and cold. There would have been no summit assault that day. At nine Swift, McCormack, and Nevison left for Camp I while Akram and I remained behind for another hour to ensure that everything we wanted to save was packed up. Rahim Khan and Qasim wanted to take their time on the descent and come down last on a separate rope. As they had proved themselves to be highly competent, there was no objection to this, so after the loads were arranged Akram and I started down. By now the clouds had closed in and we could see only a few yards ahead through the blowing snow. The fixed line seemed to plunge downward through a white wall. Occasionally a strong gust of wind would part the mist temporarily, and we could see that the plateau and summit pyramid were caught in the fury of the storm. My snow goggles fogged constantly, but I was afraid to remove them for fear of becoming snow-blind. Akram and I reached the flat area on the ridge where there was no fixed line and waited for Abdul Rahim and Qasim to catch up, as we were beginning to worry about them. Soon they appeared and again we started down. Just as we reached the narrow arête and began our balancing act, the clouds lifted and it stopped snowing. Halfway across the traverse I noticed that the loose piton we had always stepped on was missing, together with a large portion of the rock it was in. Later I learned that McCormack had had the fun of removing it, but the fixed rope had stopped him.

We reached the remnants of Camp II (Nevison, Swift, and McCormack had already stripped it of most of the equipment) and stopped to rest. I screwed a stove burner I was carrying into a butane-gas bottle that was lying in the snow and began making hot chocolate, then soup, and then tea, which we consumed along with large quantities of lemon cookies. By this time Swift, Nevison, and McCormack were on the lower slopes of the ridge. They were moving extremely slowly and suddenly I realized that they were sinking waist-deep in soft snow. We watched their struggles with grave misgivings, and after fortifying ourselves with another pot of tea and two more boxes of lemon cookies, we resumed the descent.

We had gone less than 500 feet below Camp II when it became apparent that our work on the mountain was not over. On the upper slope we were able to extract our legs out of the morass by leaning out against the fixed rope. The real difficulties began when we reached the end of the fixed line. In the past we could heel down or glissade these lower slopes; now they were a crusted quagmire of rotten snow. Every few steps we sank in to our waists and with our heavy loads it required every ounce of strength we had to roll out of the holes. It was almost impossible to help each other because when someone went forward to assist a floundering comrade by taking his pack, he plunged in also. We almost began to wish that the slope would avalanche. It would have been the easy way down. We were alternately furious or resigned. Sometimes we angrily tried to crawl out of the hole as soon as we broke through. Other times we just rested, wishing we could stay there forever. Worst of all, we did not break through with every step, so we could not make a track. A cautious step would put us up on the surface. We would tentatively shift our weight forward a few times, gain confidence, relax our guard, and plunge back waist-deep again, our feet churning in a vacuum. Frequently all four of us were in holes simultaneously, struggling like ants in a puddle of honey. After much effort we reached the main slope leading to the Abruzzi Glacier and discovered it was covered with snow debris four feet thick. So it had finally avalanched. We passed the site of our reconnaissance camp and noticed that the debris had barely missed it. Our little side couloir had had no diverting effect at all.

Akram and I stumbled into Camp I and joined the rest of the expedition in the big tent.

"What did you think of the avalanche?" said Nevison.

"It really must have been something. It was big enough," I replied.

"I saw it come down," said McCormack. "It happened about a week ago, around five in the afternoon. It was big but it moved slowly. I think a person probably could have run out of the path. It was more like a slide than an avalanche."

"Well, there goes another story," said someone in the back of the tent.

Unfortunately we had not escaped completely unscathed. When Kauffman took his boots off at Camp I the big and middle toes of both feet were black with frostbite. Nevison took a serious but unalarmed view of the situation. He put Kauffman on a diet of antibiotics and assured him that drastic treatments were now frowned upon. "The main thing is to get out of here as quickly as possible so Andy's feet can be properly treated. All we can do is soak them in warm water, keep them clean, and make sure that they don't get infected," he said.

The big question was how far Kauffman could walk on those feet. In 1953 on K2 George Bell's feet had been so badly frostbitten that he had to be carried out on a litter and on porters' backs, something we wanted to avoid if at all possible, for none of us ever doubted the truth of Bell's classic statement concerning his ordeal, "I would have walked if I could." Riding a litter out of the Karakoram is a most effective cure for hypochondria. Andy preferred to walk.

Except for Kauffman's feet and a pervading weariness, we were in good shape. We were safely off the mountain and it slowly began to dawn on us what we had done. Already Rizvi had sent a message to Brigadier Habib-ur-Rahman Khan by the Italians' mail runner, which said, "The 1958 American Karakoram Expedition climbed Hidden Peak on 5 July 1958."

We ate a huge dinner of Italian spaghetti and then gathered in the big tent to broach the small flask of rum that we had brought for such an occasion. A thimbleful was carefully doled out into each man's tin can, there were a few comments about our inadequate planning for all eventualities, and then it was gone. Victory was sweet. We thought about our friends who had helped to make it possible: Coveney, Hall, Couzy, Marmet, Gurtner, Roch, Frank, and the rest, and wished we could see their faces when they got the news. Chauvinistic English, French, and Swiss mountaineers had worked around the clock to furnish and ship equipment for a foreign expedition; Pakistanis who could not climb had climbed; superstitious Baltis who were afraid of the mountains had carried loads alone between high camps; lazy Americans had crawled out of the sack day after day; the weather had remained excellent and Hidden Peak had been climbed. We had broken many cherished stereotyped concepts and were absolutely delighted. "Twenty-five days out of Base Camp. Slow, but what can you expect from a 'marginal' party?" said Kauffman, referring to

The long road home. Starting down the upper Baltoro Glacier with the Muztagh Tower in the background.

one of the more optimistic adjectives that had been applied to our expedition. Everyone roared with laughter.

Just then we heard the scraping of skis on hard snow and saw two bobbing lights out on the glacier. We yelled but there was no answer. Then as the figures drew near we recognized Dick Irvin and Gil Roberts. They had left Skardu on June 21 with seven porters, probably one of the smallest parties in the history of Karakoram mountaineering, and had marched in part of the way with the Japanese expedition that was going to attempt Chogolisa. Irvin and Roberts had been in our base camp for several days, and as the Italian liaison officer had told them that our Camp I was only an hour up the glacier, they had borrowed two pairs of skis from the Italians to visit us before dinner. That was three hours ago and now they would have to spend the night.

Dick and Gil crowded into the tent. They were delighted at the success of the expedition of which they were an integral part, but they were a little chagrined to have traveled halfway around the world and marched for two weeks to reach this remote spot only to discover that the mountain had just been climbed and that they had arrived in time to turn around and march back out again. We tried to conceal our overwhelming joy in seeing our two friends by calling them the "Upper Baltoro Hiking and Knapsack Club." "Are you sure you don't want to climb something else?" said Gil plaintively. Actually it was an appealing idea, but we were very tired. Besides, Kauffman's feet effectively settled that question.

"And not only did you climb the mountain but it was well timed, too," said Irvin.

"Oh?" said Schoening.

"Yes, you climbed it on the fourth of July," said Irvin.

This came as an unpleasant surprise. Sitting around Camp IV we had had only a vague recollection of time, but we were under the impression that we had climbed the mountain on July fifth, which was Bob Swift's birthday, and the first message we dispatched gave this date.

"Are you sure about this?" asked Schoening.

"It had to be the fourth of July," said Irvin. "We arrived in Base Camp the day you climbed the mountain and we have been marching for fifteen days." He began to rattle off the days and the various stages of the march. We realized that it is as easy to keep track of days when you are on the march as it is to lose count lying around inside a tent, so Irvin must be right. At first the rest of us were unhappy about this since it made our expedition seem like a publicity stunt. "It'll sound like a put-up job," said Schoening. But after we reconciled ourselves to this fact, it did not seem so bad after all. The first ascent of an eight-thousand-meter peak, and on the fourth of July. That should cause a mild stir. We gave Irvin and Roberts eight different foothold-by-foothold versions of the climb and then it was time for bed. We dug up two spare sleeping bags for our welcome guests and as there was not room for everyone in the base camp tent, Akram and I went to our separate high-altitude tent.

The next morning as I started to crawl out of my sleeping bag Akram said, "The light hurts my eyes. I can't open them." He was snow-blind, but how? "I did not wear my goggles between Camps III and II yesterday," he said. I was stunned, not because Akram had not worn his goggles, but because I had not noticed it. We were on the same rope and at rests we always sat together and talked. I must have looked him right in the eye. Why didn't I remind him to wear his goggles, especially when I had worn mine? Normally I would have noticed such a thing instantly. Then I realized to my shock that perhaps my mind had not been functioning properly because of the effect of altitude and fatigue. It was hard to believe, but there seemed to be no other explanation for such an inexcusable oversight. I went over to the big tent and broke the unhappy news.

Nevison gave me a tube of ophthalmic ointment for Akram's eyes and we decided that Akram and I should stay behind a day while everyone else would descend to Base Camp. Abdul Rahim and Qasim would also remain at Camp I to retrieve the remaining equipment that had been left behind at Camp II. Irvin and Roberts strapped on their skis and the others started trodding down the glacier. It was still early in the morning when they reached Base Camp. Meanwhile the Japanese expedition had just arrived at the base of Chogolisa, so Schoening sent Ghulam Razul down to the Japanese base camp to obtain thirty-five of the porters that they would be releasing to carry our baggage. This would save us at least ten days, for otherwise it would have been necessary to send a messenger to Askole and wait for the needed porters to come up the Baltoro Glacier.

Earlier Bob Swift had written Dick Irvin that we urgently needed a box of cigars as a present for a maharaja. Irvin and Roberts had faithfully carried out their delicate diplomatic mission and had nursed the box all the way to Base Camp. Now Swift introduced himself as the maharaja in question and confiscated the cigars. However, His Highness distributed his bounty with a lavish hand, so there was no ill feeling. Nevison brewed a huge pot of lemonade while Gil Roberts, for the benefit of everyone's camera, staged a one-man style-show of what the well-dressed Himalayan mountaineer will wear. Then they pitched the big base camp tent. Irvin and Roberts produced the one bottle of rum that they had brought for medicinal purposes, and throughout the afternoon, evening, and under the light of the butane-gas lantern, many a fortune in hard candy was won, lost, regained, and lost again in a marathon poker game.

At Camp I, I put ointment into Akram's burning eyes every six hours. He was blind and in great pain but he never complained. Meanwhile Abdul Rahim and Qasim made the run to Camp II and returned by noon. The last equipment was off the mountain.

July 9 was a beautiful day. Our storm had lasted only one day and then the weather was perfect for a week. We could have put the entire expedition on the summit without any trouble. Unfortunately, in such matters it is easier to be a historian than a prophet. Abdul Rahim and Qasim left for Base Camp while Akram and I folded our tent. It was still early in the morning and the surface of the glacier was frozen, but the old tracks sunk deep into the snow warned us what would happen as soon as the sun rose and we increased our pace. There had been radical changes in the glacier during the last two weeks. Opposite the French buttress a large lake occupied our former route. We began to lose our race with the sun and started breaking through the crust in places. We came within view of the Italian base camp and by now Akram, who had started earlier than I had, was out of sight. Our new base camp was supposed to be below the Italian camp somewhere. I crossed a surface stream, climbed up the opposite side, and there it was, only fifty yards and one rushing river away. I would have to climb back to the Italian base camp, cross the river there, and come down the moraine. This information was gleefully shouted to me by all the lounging loafers in Base Camp. While they sipped lemonade, took pictures, and laughed, I began plunging my way back toward the Italian camp. Abdul Rahim was more merciful. He met me and took my pack. I

That's not the hand I dealt you! McCormack, Rizvi, Nevison, and Irvin play poker for "a little something."

stumbled into Base Camp looking forward to a nice rest. "You'd better start packing. We'll be leaving here in three hours," said Irvin.

Earlier the remaining loads at our original base camp site had been brought over and everyone was sorting gear. Just outside the packing area were our thirty-five porters, who were eagerly waiting to descend upon our camp and pick it clean. The food was stacked in one big pile, Swift and Schoening carefully took out the amount of rations we would need during the march out, and then the HAPs were allowed to take what they wanted. They also got first crack at the equipment we were going to abandon. The HAPs took so much that Ghulam Razul had to hire his own private porter to carry out his loot. Rahim Khan even took an empty oxygen bottle. "He wants to make a butter churn out of it," said Tas. After the HAPs had taken everything they wanted, the remaining unwanted food and equipment was stacked, the porters were allowed inside the packing area, and the scramble was on. The porters dived into the pile and came away with anything. Occasionally a can of mixed nuts or a spoon would turn up and we would be treated to the amusing sight of a sahib-versus-Balti battle over some dirty item. Also, the Baltis began to pick up some articles that were not being disposed of, but we quickly put a stop to that practice. Finally everything that was supposed to be packed was packed and everything that was supposed to be left behind was also packed—by the Baltis.

We wanted to say good-bye to our Italian neighbors and thank them for all their kindness and hospitality, but they had already established a camp on the col between Gasherbrums III and IV and were getting into position for the final assault, so no one was at their base camp. I was especially sorry to have missed Fosco as I had not seen him since we had left Skardu, but all we could do was leave a note, which Kauffman took over to the Italian base camp.

After lunch we lined up the Baltis, called off their names, and assigned numbers and loads. One of the porters was Issac, the HAP we had dismissed at Askole. Despite that incident, he was always cheerful and polite and proved to be one of our strongest men. At one o'clock the last porter had received his load. Gil Roberts unfurled the umbrella he had brought, and Razul's "Shabash" rang out on schedule. One by one, Baltis and sahibs started down the moraine, leaving behind only a few empty boxes to testify to the existence of the 1958 American Karakoram Expedition.

16

RETURN

For three hours we casually strolled down the Abruzzi Glacier until we reached its junction with the upper Baltoro Glacier and the moraine curved sharply to the right toward Concordia. Here we stopped and pitched camp. Ahead and to our left about a mile away we could see the tents of the Japanese base camp. Their leader, Professor Takeo Kuwabara, had sent us a very nice note of congratulations, and as we had heard that they were using kerosene stoves,

A leisurely breakfast. Nevison, McCormack, Irvin, and Roberts postpone breaking camp.

Schoening, Rizvi, Rahim Khan, and Abdul Rahim went over to their camp to pay a courtesy call and to give them the ten gallons of kerosene that Irvin and Roberts had brought. Just before Pete and Tas departed on their visit, we posed for the inevitable group photographs with Hidden Peak in the background. Such expedition portraits are usually taken at the end of the trip for the simple reason that two months' dirt and beard makes even the most callow of academic types resemble the popular conception of "rugged mountaineers." Also, McCormack had brought a telephoto lens the size of a grenade launcher and now he mounted this on a tripod and aimed it at the defenseless Muztagh Tower. "How's it coming, Sella? Have you captured its mood yet?" said Roberts. Then he added, "And while you're at it, take one for me."

The next day we hiked to Concordia. The Muztagh Tower slowly grew larger and larger as we marched down the moraine. However, the mountains no longer overwhelmed us; we were adjusting to the gigantic scale of the Karakoram. Then K2 suddenly appeared from behind an intervening ridge, a splendid isolated pyramid rising high into the sky. We were not prepared for this! It seemed a shame that K2 is not the highest mountain in the world, for in shape and size it is the embodiment of everything a great mountain should be.

That afternoon as we sat at Concordia and waited for the porters to arrive, we succumbed to the occupational disease of all mountaineers. After initially absorbing the beauty of the scene, we automatically began to select routes up the surrounding peaks. It is amazing how much harmless passion can be generated in arguing over routes that you not only are not going to climb but that also will probably remain unclimbed for years to come. "Except for the fact it is constantly racked by avalanches from the summit slopes, I think the left-hand rib looks pretty good," someone would say, pointing at some horrible wall. Everyone else would violently disagree and pick out alternate routes, equally useless. During our discussion of horrible routes, we looked up at Gasherbrum IV and wondered how our Italian friends were doing. "They'll probably climb it in a day or so if they haven't climbed it already," said Schoening. "Probably so," I agreed, "but if they don't get up now in this weather, they'll never make it."

Later we learned that we were wrong on both counts. The Italians did not climb Gasherbrum IV during that spell of perfect weather, but what they eventually did was even more incredible. They failed on the first attempt, retreated back to their base camp, rested, and then made a second assault, which was successful. On August 6 Walter Bonatti and Carlo Mauri stood on the summit of one of the hardest mountains that has ever been climbed in the Himalaya. It was a magnificent and well-deserved victory by an outstanding party of mountaineers and gentlemen. Also, on August 4, after a rapid and efficient campaign, the Japanese expedition climbed Chogolisa, completing the most successful season in the history of Karakoram mountaineering, for all three expeditions to the upper Baltoro had achieved their objective without a man getting seriously hurt.

Except for my original attempts to obtain financing, we had followed a successful policy of avoiding publicity so we would not be under outside pressure to climb the mountain. Also, we had felt that it would be preferable for people to say, "Where did they come from?" rather than "What ever became of them?" That evening after dinner we decided that perhaps we should send news of the climb to our friends and families and the outside world. Accordingly we prepared a brief message saying that we had climbed Hidden Peak on July fourth. This was to be sent to Henry Hall, Lawrence Coveney, and Jürg Marmet. A longer message was prepared for Radio Pakistan and the news services, and a copy of this was to be sent to my father in Dallas together with a request that he notify the families of the members of the expedition. Finally there was a question as to whether cables to presidents Mirza and Eisenhower would be presumptuous or polite, since we knew that neither of them had ever heard of us. After some discussion we agreed that to send messages to the president of

The embodiment of everything that is excellent.

Pakistan and the president of the United States would be the courteous thing to do. We gave the seven messages together with a covering note to Rahim Khan and told him to deliver them to the Brigadier Habib-ur-Rahman Khan at Skardu. The next day Rahim Khan and Haji left ahead of the expedition to carry out their mission.

Schoening wanted to go to the base of K2 to visit the memorial he and the other members of the 1953 expedition had erected to their comrade Art Gilkey, and I agreed to accompany him since I had always wanted to visit that great mountain. Also it was important that in our moment of success we remember our predecessors to the Karakoram who had paved the way. We would make a round trip between Concordia and K2 one day and then catch up with the rest of the expedition at Urdukas the following day.

That night Rizvi and I slept in a separate tent to relieve the population pressure in the main one. About midnight I finally made up my mind that my head was definitely downhill, got up, and turned my air mattress and sleeping bag around to discover that the original position had been right after all. However, this useless activity had some compensations. When I went outside the tent, there was K2 bathed in moonlight, a silvery wisp of the imagination that would disappear with the dawn. Broad Peak, Gasherbrum IV, and lesser mountains also shimmered in the cold light while in the foreground little groups of Baltis huddled underneath their blankets inside the crude stone windbreaks that they had so hastily constructed. It was

194

one of the most impressive scenes I have ever witnessed, and I stood there for some time before the cold air drove me back to my sleeping bag.

Schoening and I left early the next morning for the base of K2. Our primary problem was to find a way across the three large surface rivers at the main conflux of glaciers that meet at Concordia. We decided to go up toward Gasherbrum IV and cut through the seracs and pools that are the source of the rivers. Up and down, in and out, we tried to find a route through the watery maze. An ice tower barred the way and Schoening started to cut a line of steps. He smote the ice vigorously and the head flew off his ice-axe, an old one that Nevison had brought as a spare. With great reluctance I handed mine to Pete and he finished the steps. Then I grabbed my axe back before he could increase his score. After several hours of wandering that would have done credit to a white rat in a psychologist's testing box, we emerged on the other side of the broken area and hiked steadily up the Godwin Austen Glacier. Soon we reached the junction of the Savoia Glacier and the 200-foot-high rock promontory on top of which stands the memorial to Art Gilkey. We scrambled up to the cairn, which commands one of the finest mountain scenes in the world. Next to it was the grave of the Italian climber Mario Puchoz who had died of pneumonia on K2 in 1954. Two pieces of board that had formed a cross were lying a few feet away. We added a few rocks to the Gilkey Memorial Cairn, remade the wooden cross, wrote Puchoz's name on it, and reerected it at the head of his grave. Then beside the Gilkey Memorial we built a very small cairn. We dug out a piece of notebook paper and Schoening wrote, "In memory of all the brave men whe have died on K2: Dudley Wolfe, Pasang Kikuli and his two Sherpa companions (Pasang Kitar and Pintso Sherpa), Art Gilkey, and Mario Puchoz." We put the piece of paper inside a waterproof match container and stuck it into the small cairn. It was not very much, but it was tangible proof that they had not been forgotten. The history of mountains is told in terms of men, and at this moment we felt like a small but integral part of the continuing sweep of human history in this remote region, a link between the past and the future.

It was time to leave; our pilgrimage was over. On our return we visited the location of the Italian base camp in 1954. Old cans of food and tent pegs covered a wide area. Below it we found several cans, which marked the site of the American camp in 1953. We set a rapid pace back to Concordia and after some rather exciting stream crossings that involved step-cutting to get up the steep sides of the channels, we reached our campsite just as it became dark.

The next morning we got up with the first light, rolled our sleeping bags, and started marching down the Baltoro Glacier. For ten hours we moved steadily down the moraine. Then as we approached Urdukas we saw the Bramani boot tracks of our companions, which led toward the left side of the glacier. Soon we were climbing up and down on loose scree over melting ice. It was extremely slippery footing and the seats of our pants began to show signs of wear. In desperation we cut over to the dirt slope beside the glacier, where we found more Bramani tracks. A cliff barred the way and we skidded down a crumbling couloir back to the glacier. For the next hour we scrambled up loose lateral moraines, balanced along their tops, traversed dirt slopes, and finally turned the corner of a buttress on a series of narrow ledges and at five in the afternoon arrived at Urdukas. The big white tent was in its proper location.

"Pretty good," said Irvin. "We didn't think you would make it."

"How did you come?" said McCormack. "Along the side?"

"Were those your tracks that led us through that mess?" I testily inquired as I flopped in the grass and reached for the cup of tea that Abdul Rahim had brought.

"Yeah," said Gil. "We were about an hour ahead of the porters when we cut too far to the left and were struggling up and down through that junk when we saw them go by out in the middle of the glacier."

"They got here an hour before we did," said Irvin, "and were they ever laughing at us! By the way, we have some other news for you, too."

"What?"

"June has only thirty days."

"So?"

"We climbed the mountain on July fifth."

"You're joking," I gasped.

"Don't you wish I were?" said Irvin, handing me his diary. There in ink was an entry under the heading "June 31st."

"Wonderful. Now what do we do?" I said. "We've already got messages dispatched saying we climbed the mountain on the fourth and no one is going to believe this story." I was beginning to wish that Rahim Khan were not so reliable. He would deliver those messages to the political agent all right. We could count on that.

"And we can't even rationalize it by U.S. time, since we missed the fourth of July back there by three hours," said Kauffman. Like everyone else, he was grasping at straws. "Let's face it, we've had it," said Schoening, glowering at Irvin.

"Any other bad news?" I asked. There was not. Andy's feet were slowly recovering under Nevison's careful supervision and lack of treatment. Even now Kauffman was soaking his toes in a *dekshis* of hot water.

That night Irvin had difficulty in getting to sleep. "Does anyone have a sleeping pill?" he asked. "Here, take this," said McCormack, handing Dick a capsule in the dark.

"Thanks, Mac," said Irvin, swallowing the pill. An hour later Irvin was still not asleep. "Say, I don't feel sleepy at all. Just what was that pill you gave me, McCormack?" he said. "Dexamyl," came the reply. Irvin's friend in need had slipped him a "happiness pill." While everyone else roared with laughter, Irvin said, "I'll get you for this," and for the rest of the night whenever the rest of us woke up we could hear Irvin whisper, "Wake up, McCormack," as he jabbed his elbow into his benefactor's ribs. Neither of them got much sleep that night.

Urdukas was wonderful after six weeks on snow and ice. Blue and yellow flowers were sprinkled throughout the grass, a few birds hovered about in the warm air, and about a hundred feet from our camp a stream from the snowfields above trickled through the idyllic scene. But the relatively low altitude and heat made the inside of the tent seem oppressive, so I threw my sleeping bag outside on the ground and slept soundly until morning when Abdul Rahim stepped over me on his way back from the stream with a dripping pot of water.

Three hours after we left Urdukas we arrived at the pleasant little stream we had hopped over during the march in. Now it was a raging torrent of swirling, silt-laden water. Schoening, Swift, and Irvin locked their arms and waded out into the current, which almost knocked them off their feet. But they managed to keep their balance and discovered that if they angled upstream, the bottom was not excessively deep. McCormack, Roberts, and I were next. We grabbed each other and started off. Two men braced while one man moved and finally we reached the opposite bank where we spent a half-hour trying to wash the sand out of our boots and socks. Meanwhile Kauffman and Nevison decided to look for a better route out on the Baltoro Glacier. They found one.

While the others waited to make sure that the porters got across the stream safely, Schoening and I went on. We still wanted to see as much of the country as we could, and since Dr. Charles Houston was considering organizing an expedition to attempt Payu Peak, Schoening had suggested that we reconnoiter that mountain for him. From the Baltoro Glacier a ring of diamond-shaped granite walls a thousand feet below the summit seemed to eliminate any possibility of a route on that side. However, Pete wanted to climb up a gorge about two miles west of the stage of Payu and try to get a look at the mountain from that side. I had agreed to the scheme provided that Pete would "take it slow and easy," and now we had to make a double stage down to Payu, climb the gorge the following day, and catch up with the expedition again on the third day.

At noon we passed through Liligo without stopping. It was hot and dusty and we felt sorry for our comrades who would have to spend the night there. Below Liligo we followed the small cairns that the Baltis had built to mark their path over the moraines of the lower Baltoro and by five we arrived at the woods of Payu. On the approach march it had been the garden spot of the trip; now the passing of three expeditions had made it the cesspool. We stopped only long enough to cook dinner, and after eating our meal in the smoke of the fire to discourage the flies, we quickly washed the pot and left.

The rushing Biaho River, swollen with the glacial melt, covered the sand flats we had previously used, so now we had to take the high road, a narrow trail winding along the crumbling cliff banks 500 feet above the river. We had hoped to reach a flat shoulder that led up to our canyon, but as darkness fell we were still a half-mile short. We found a tilted section of dirt, the flattest place in sight, scooped out two semilevel platforms, lined the outside edge with large rocks that would awaken us if we tried to roll off the mountainside, threw down our air mattresses and sleeping bags, and went to sleep.

The next day we climbed 5,000 feet up the gorge in blistering heat, the first 3,000 feet on the wrong side, over sand, high-angle mud, and crumbling rock and moraine. But that evening we had our reward for we reached a grassy campsite near a beautiful glacial cirque underneath Payu Peak. Also, we found a possible but probably dangerous route up the mountain. The ring of diamond shields continued around the mountain and protected the summit, but there was one weakness. A long snow couloir led up to the crest of the ridge opposite us. It was subject to avalanches, but it provided a route to the top of the ridge. From there it might be possible to link up with snow couloirs on the other side of the ridge or even to climb a diamond of rock that rose above the ridge. It would not be easy, but it was the most promising side of the mountain that we had seen.

The next morning we skidded down the gorge up which we had so slowly struggled and by nine had regained the trail near the Biaho River. There were fresh Bramani tracks; the expedition was ahead of us. An hour later we found their campsite beside the river. So they had gone beyond Payu yesterday. The expedition was far ahead of us. We maintained a steady pace and reached Bardumal by noon. No expedition. They were double-staging it all right. The horses were heading for the barn. We reached the spot where we had forded the Dumordo River and scanned the opposite side. There was still no sign of the expedition. We knew we could not have caught up with the sahibs, but we had an innate faith in the slowness of the porters. "The rope bridge we have to cross is a mile and a half upstream, and they are probably camped there," said Pete.

We were extremely tired. Nevison had been right. Our tremendous psychological momentum concealed our true physical condition and now it was beginning to wear off. As every cut and scratch became infected, we realized that we were worn out physically, if not mentally. But we still had one advantage. Success made the miles seem shorter. We came to a clear stream and halted briefly to eat our last chocolate bar to give us a final spurt of energy. From here we could see the rope bridge. There were no tents. Suddenly Pete shouted, "There they are, across the river!" Our column of porters had crossed the bridge and were coming back along a trail above the cliffs on the opposite side of the river. Just then we saw a man fall! He slid forty feet down the mountainside and barely stopped on the brink of a cliff. We could see Ghulam Razul running toward the scene of the accident, but the porter picked himself up, climbed back to his comrades, and the column moved forward.

"We should catch up with them soon," I thought, as we started for the rope bridge a short distance away. Then we came to another stream. It was in full flood and our first attempt to wade the torrent failed as the channel suddenly deepened. Finally after forty-five minutes we found a passable ford, reached the far bank, put on our boots, and hurried on.

It had been my firm belief that the terrors of rope bridges had always been exaggerated in mountaineering books and lectures, perhaps in an unconscious effort to pay for the trip. Now as I stood before my first rope bridge I unhappily realized that the descriptions were understated. First of all, a rope bridge is not made out of rope; it consists of twisted vines, twigs, and other forms of vegetable matter. This bridge had a narrow foot-rail and two handrails that were connected by thin vines, a third of which

"According to popular legend, rope bridges are not repaired until they break." Crossing the Dumordo River.

had rotted and were dangling down below the structure. To reduce the strain, the bridge had to sag considerably, so it was suspended from rock cairns erected on high walls at a point where the Dumordo River was narrow, deep, and swift. According to popular legend, rope bridges are not repaired until they break, but on the approach march we had seen men repairing them, so we felt better about that. However, they do turn upside down. One had done so in 1953 with a porter, but he had hung on and was saved. The entire structure swayed in the wind about thirty feet above the water, and while it was only 200 feet in length it seemed to be a mile long and a quarter-inch wide.

Schoening grabbed both handrails and started across. "Don't slip or you've had it," he said. It was the most unnecessary warning of the entire trip. I waited until Pete was halfway across in order to reduce the bouncing, and then I started. I clung grimly to the handrails and carefully placed each foot on the bottom strand. In mountaineering one learns to see only his immediate footholds when he looks down. On a mountain this prevents dizziness. On a rope bridge with a river underneath, this makes you think that the bridge is rapidly moving upstream. As we made each step forward we had to push the handrails out, which disturbed the equilibrium of the structure. I was two-thirds across when I noticed three Baltis who had been gathering wood approach the bridge. Just then Schoening reached the end and one of the Baltis, a boy about fifteen years old, came out and began spreading the handrails with his back and feet, stabilizing the bridge. When we reached the far end, I gave him a rupee. He was delighted and it was the least begrudged baksheesh during the entire trip.

"What did you think of it?" asked Schoening.

"If you went into that river, you'd come up twice: once at Askole and once at Skardu," I said.

"You should have seen George Bell come across that bridge sitting on the bottom rail so he wouldn't injure his feet," said Schoening.

"As far as I'm concerned, Bell can hold the record for that event," I replied.

Just as it was getting dark, we arrived at the expedition's camp, which had been pitched beside the Dumordo River near our original ford. Kauffman, Akram, and Qasim were not there. Despite his sore feet, Andy had gotten far ahead of the caravan and, accompanied by Akram, a prodigious hiker, he had made the detour up to the rope bridge, crossed it, hiked back down the river, and was disappearing from sight when the main party arrived at the river. Obviously Kauffman and Akram were not going to stop at the planned destination, so Qasim was sent after them with two sleeping bags. The HAP caught up with them that night at Askole.

We got another early start the next morning and after traversing narrow ledges, crossing the Biafo Glacier, and traversing more narrow ledges, we arrived in Askole. There in our old campsite under a tree sat Akram and our frostbitten cripple. After that only Nevison worried about Andy's feet. Somehow it was difficult for the rest of us to feel sorry for a person we could not keep up with.

We spent the remainder of the day resting at Askole. Akram and Kauffman had just ambushed another Italian runner and had gotten our latest mail. McCormack, however, provided us with the principal entertainment of the afternoon. On the back of his neck he had a large boil that had to be lanced. First, of course, came the penicillin shot. "Hold still, Mc-Cormack," said Roberts, getting ready for the grand prize dart throw. "Now listen, Gil, if you . . ." was all McCormack could say before the needle was rammed home. Still feeling the effects of the shot, McCormack was propped up on a box and Nevison opened the ugly sore. McCormack grimaced but said nothing. "Just like a Balti. I do believe the local people are having a beneficial influence on him," said Irvin. When the afternoon spectacular was over, we went back to rereading our mail.

The next morning's walk was a short and pleasant interlude in our dash out from the mountains. We had decided to follow the right side of the Braldu River, stop at the village of Chongo, and climb over a high shoulder the next day rather than retrace our original route, which would require crossing two rope bridges. "Anything is better than two rope bridges," said Roberts, expressing the consensus.

A mile short of Chongo we reached the hot springs, took off our dirty clothes, and jumped into the pools. We spent over an hour in the warm water, washing away the grime and obeying the first law of human motion, that a body at rest tends to remain at rest until it becomes hungry or thirsty. Finally we got dressed and went into Chongo.

Our campsite there was a bucolic place. The grass was green, the cedar trees were green, and so was the water hole. We left at five the next morning.

The trail climbed out of Chongo in a series of steep switchbacks, but in the cool of the morning we reached the top of the 2,000-foot shoulder just as the rays of the sun hit the valley. Then we dropped down the opposite side and wandered along the edge of the Braldu River. The trail disappeared, and, strung out, we followed the Bramani tracks of the man ahead. Irvin was in the lead. He had put some cans of choice meat in his pack and everyone was hurrying so as to be with him at lunchtime. Soon we were on a first-rate training course. We crossed streams of oozing mud, climbed vertical dirt banks that afforded the most difficult and desperate climbing of the entire trip, and even went into the river. Surely the porters who were behind us could not come this way. Later we found that the Baltis went much higher and avoided all the difficulties. Only the foolish sahibs would force a way through such obstacles. Finally after I had climbed up 300 feet to gain entrance to a steep gully and then had followed it back down to the river before I could find an exit out the far side, I came upon my companions who had stopped for lunch. I was in time for my share of the meat.

"Good route, isn't it?" said Irvin. "Which variations did you use?"

"Did you climb up that last wall? The one with the overhang at the top?" asked Nevison.

"At that point I went into the river," I said.

"Coward," said Nevison.

"Did you climb it?" I asked.

"Of course not."

Soon Rizvi appeared. He did not have his ice-axe and he looked very unhappy. "What happened, Tas?" I asked.

"I got halfway up one cliff and the axe was in the way so I threw it over the top of the bank, but it hit wrong and went into the river," he said.

The remaining distance into Chokpo was not very exciting and we arrived there by two.

Once again the following morning we got an early start. By now we automatically swung one leg past the other. We were like toy soldiers—wind us up and we would walk forever, but we seemed to be hollow inside.

Just outside Dasso Schoening exclaimed, "Look! Mulberries!" There was a large tree near the trail and Pete went up it like a starving goat. "They're not ripe yet, but . . ." he said, his fingers flying rapidly from the tree to his mouth. "Aren't we encroaching on someone's property?" said I, stripping the lower branches. "In Baltistan all the village trees are community property and the fruit belongs to the person who gathers it," he said between mouthfuls. Soon the porters arrived. We pitched camp and spent the rest of the afternoon gorging ourselves on apricots and mulberries. The political agent was right. Baltistan has the finest apricots in the world.

At Askole we had sent a runner ahead to have *zahks* brought from Juno to Dasso so we could save a day's march. However, when we arrived at Dasso the rafts were not there, but as we were assured that they were awaiting us only three miles down the river, we left at four-thirty in the morning. Ten hours later we were in the Shigar Valley sitting on the opposite side of the river from the village of Juno waiting for the rafts. "Longest three miles I have ever done," said Irvin.

Soon two large and one small *zahk* appeared. The porters were to be ferried across the river by the small *zahk* in order to continue the march to Skardu under the supervision of Ghulam Razul and the assistant police constable, who had been sent by the political agent to assist us. The ten sahibs would ride down the river in style on the two large *zahks*. "This is the first means of water transportation used by man," said Rizvi. "The skin raft is older than the log raft." Looking at the two *zahks* we were going to use I readily believed his statement. They consisted of thirty cowskins blown up like balloons and lashed to thin poles, which formed the frame. Four Baltis, *zahk* wallahs, guided each raft with long poles. Two of them sat on the front corners and two of them about halfway back along the sides.

Swift, Irvin, Kauffman, Nevison, and Akram got aboard one raft and the rest of us climbed onto the other. Then Irvin hoisted a large black flag, the *zahk* wallahs leaned into their poles, and the race was on.

"Just think what they could do if they had oars," said Roberts as we went twisting down the river. "Yahoo!" yelled McCormack as a wave sloshed over our feet. In the back of our raft Schoening took movies with the Bolex while Roberts leaned against the pack-frames and sang over and over again a charming ditty of the sea that began, "SOS, SOS, Captain, we are lost." Every time the other *zahk* hit a large wave we would cheer loudly. When we hit one, they reciprocated.

Our course into the waves followed a regular pattern. The *zahk* wallahs always tried to hit the first oncoming wave with the right front corner of the raft. We would ride over this wave, but the impact would turn us slightly around to the left. This threw our timing off and the second wave would break over us slightly. By the time we hit the third or fourth wave we were usually broadside in the trough so the water would pour over us, threatening to dump us into the river. One wave in particular was almost a disaster. It crashed over us so hard that it put the Bolex out of action. We grabbed for each other and the cowskins, so nothing was lost.

We were having a fine ride down the Shigar River when suddenly a large rock loomed ahead, splitting the current. The Baltis on each side of the raft began shouting at each other. "What's going on, Tas?" I yelled. "They're arguing about which way to go. The men on the right side want to go right; the men on the left side want to go left," he replied. They were still arguing when we struck the rock head on. We ricocheted off without undue damage and continued down the river.

During the more peaceful interludes the two *zahk* wallahs in the middle of the raft would inflate the cowskins that had slow leaks. They accomplished this by blowing air through a leg of the cowskin and then tying it with a piece of vine. The *zahk* wallahs worked hard, but finally when we had almost reached periscope depth they had to beach the two rafts, unload them, turn them over, and blow up all the cowskins. Then we continued on. We had hoped to reach Skardu that night but were forced by darkness to stop at Shigar. After beaching our rafts, we hiked into the village. This took us quite a while because the route was blocked by apricot trees. Irvin showed up at the police station twenty minutes after everyone else. He had found a ripe tree.

"SOS SOS. Captain, we are lost!" Pete Schoening and crew go "zahking" down the Shigar River.

The police constable who had accompanied us to Askole was at the station, and he prepared a large pot of hot tea for us. This was very welcome although we were not very thirsty, since we had been drinking out of the river. Our drinking habits on the march out had slowly deteriorated with the increasing scarcity of clear streams, and finally we just drank out of the muddy Shigar itself. Nevison said that the garbage of the upstream villages would be sufficiently diluted so as to make the water reasonably safe. We suffered no ill effects.

The next day we resumed our scenic cruise down the river and after some fun with the waves at the confluence of the Shigar and Indus rivers, we beached our *zahks* and hiked the last two long miles into Skardu. At noon, July 21, 1958, exactly two months after we had left it, we arrived at the rest house and collapsed in the chairs and sofas. Our long walk was over.

Once the expedition reached Skardu it dissolved as informally as it had formed. Afraid that the weather might change and strand us indefinitely, Kauffman, Irvin, Roberts, and Nevison flew out to Rawalpindi the next day, followed by Swift and McCormack a day later. Then the six of them went to Karachi and, heeding my advice about the fabulous hospitality of the Swiss Foundation for Alpine Research, left Pakistan for their respective homes by way of Zurich. Akram, Rizvi, Schoening, and I remained for several more days in Skardu to organize the loads for the flight out, handle last-minute details, avoid the heat of the Punjab, and savor the delightful hospitality of Brigadier Habib-ur-Rahman Khan.

At an impressive ceremony Brigadier Rahman Khan presented the medals we had brought to our six HAPs. The HAPs were proud of these medals, which they had so richly earned. They were the best high-altitude porters in Baltistan and on Hidden Peak they had turned in their finest performance. Without them the mountain would never have been climbed.

Four days after we had arrived at Skardu, we thanked the brigadier for everything he and the people of Baltistan had done for us, said good-bye to our valiant HAPs, and caught the plane to Rawalpindi, the last plane that would be flying there in the next two weeks.

Unfortunately we were not able to fly our baggage out. The days passed. Akram had to report back to his regiment at Lahore, and Rizvi, Schoening, and I saw him off on the train. Then Rizvi took Schoening and me on a privately conducted tour of Peshawar and the historic Khyber Pass. The weather still remained bad in the mountains. Schoening presented me with the community bottle of paregoric and left. His wife, Mary Lou, was expecting to meet him on the beach at Waikiki. Finally the equipment arrived at Rawalpindi. I said good-bye to Tas and climbed aboard the Khyber Mail. Once again the 1958 American Karakoram Expedition was only a letterhead.

EPILOGUE

When I wrote this book in 1959 I concluded by writing, "Epilogue to follow." It was my intention to explain the cosmic significance of the expedition, but that was too imposing a task to undertake without the assurance that the book would be published. As the years passed, the task became more and more difficult until it became impossible, at least for me. However, with the passage of time, it is appropriate to put some of the references in the book in perspective and to review what has happened to the participants in this story, including the mountain, since 1958.

It would require another book to update all the information that I have presented in the preceding story. However, a few comments regarding various chapters are in order. In Chapter 1, the reader is right if he gets the impression that a little naiveté is indispensable in getting one's first expedition started. One's second expedition is the result of the erroneous belief that one has learned to do it right by struggling through the first expedition.

Today it is easier to get the necessary permissions for an expedition and it is much easier to obtain the food and equipment than it was for us as described in Chapter 3. In contrast to all the effort we spent in 1958 getting our food and equipment from many different countries, in 1974 we packed the supplies for an entire expedition in one weekend in the basement of the Recreational Equipment Co-op in Seattle. However, one thing will seldom change. Fund raising will always be difficult. It is helpful to know a good pawnbroker.

Things are much more organized now in Pakistan than Chapter 4 would indicate. The biggest problem today is the large number of expeditions into the Karakoram. At least we felt we had the mountains pretty much to ourselves. Also, it was unusual for us to forget about the cooking pots. Most expeditions forget the toilet paper.

There is now a jeep road almost to Dasso, which saves the three days of time, money, and sore feet I described in Chapter 5. Present expeditions no longer have to do the Skardu to Dasso march, just as we were spared the fourteen-day march from Srinagar to Skardu that the pre-World War II expeditions had had to do.

The dispensing of the coins in Askole as described in Chapter 6 had a most interesting sequel. In 1960, after the completion of the Masherbrum

"Something lost behind the Ranges. Go and find it."
(Rudyard Kipling)
ANDRÉ ROCH

expedition, Dick Emerson and I visited Brigadier Habib-ur-Rahman Khan in Gilgit where he was then the political agent. Brigadier Rahman told us many stories about the difficulties he had in getting prompt action from his superiors in his efforts to help the local people. One serious problem was the lack of coins in Baltistan. Because the country was so poor and prices were so low, coins in small denominations were badly needed to accommodate simple commercial transactions. Brigadier Rahman made numerous attempts to get the necessary coinage but to no avail. The economy was slowly grinding to a halt. Suddenly coins in vast numbers began appearing all over the country. He could not understand where the coins had come from, but the crisis was solved. It was a great pleasure to inform our Pakistani friend about how we had saved the economy of Baltistan.

In 1974 our porters set up the same chant at the snout of the Baltoro Glacier that I mentioned in Chapter 7, and we confirmed from our Pakistani companions that they were indeed praying. Also, many of those "incredible pinnacles" of the lower Baltoro now have been climbed by mountaineers of many nationalities, even Americans.

The discussion about the route and the philosophy of route-finding in Chapter 9 is outdated in an era when the most difficult aspect of Himalayan route-finding is done before the expedition departs, as one tries to determine if one's proposed route has ever been done. Anything goes: rock, ice, and avalanche chutes.

Professor G. O. Dyhrenfurth in his revised edition of *To the Third Pole* objected to our calling our final route the Roch ridge since, as he correctly pointed out, André Roch and Hans Ertl had climbed the ridge together, and he suggested that it be called the IHE (International Himalayan Expedition) ridge rather than be named after some individual. He probably was right, and the original edition of his book was the one that first pointed out the route to us. However, André was our friend and the one we talked with about the route, so it was natural for us to refer to it as the Roch ridge. Besides, the concept of a Roch ridge that was primarily snow was irresistible.

The "pneumonia" about which we were so concerned was, of course, pulmonary edema. The title of Chapter 11 should be changed to "The Pulmonary Edema Patrol." Dr. Charles Houston discovered what the illness really was in 1959 and we knew about it in 1960 on Masherbrum. The antibiotics were useless as treatment.

The discussion in Chapter 15 about the potential consequences of the frostbite to Andy Kauffman's feet and the description of George Bell's return from K2 in 1953 emphasize one major difference between climbing in the Karakoram then and now. If you got hurt in 1958, a helicopter would not come in to get you.

Our trash disposal practices left a little something to be desired. Although the Baltis took most of it, we did not give much thought to what was left. Except for a sardine can on the summit of a supposed first ascent, it was always interesting to find a few indications of one's predecessors. With the large number of expeditions today, such an approach would be intolerable. The difference between an ancient relic and garbage is volume.

Modern scholarship has subsequently revealed that the point reached by the Japanese was not the highest point on the Chogolisa summit ridge, as everyone then believed and as I stated in Chapter 16. The highest point was attained by a later expedition. I trust we will be forgiven if we continue to think that our Japanese friends "climbed" Chogolisa.

Having briefly reflected on the past and present state of Karakoram mountaineering, let us move on to the main point of this epilogue. In writing it, I cannot help but think first of friends who are no longer here. Othmar Gurtner, the distinguished editor of *The Mountain World*, who was so encouraging to us, died before the expedition had returned from Pakistan. Even more of a shock was the unexpected death of Jean Couzy, who was killed in November, 1958, by a falling rock while belaying his second on a climb of the Crête des Bergers in the Alps. Not only was Couzy one of the finest mountaineers in the world, he also was a very warm person with an encyclopedic knowledge of mountaineering. He was a great loss and I felt cheated that I would not have the opportunity to know him better.

Fernande Spichiger of the Swiss Foundation for Alpine Research repeated her tremendous efforts in regard to the Hidden Peak expedition by doing them all over again for our 1960 Masherbrum expedition. She died in 1972 of cancer. She had energy, efficiency, and a marvelous sense of humor that almost made crises worthwhile just to have the pleasure of working with her while trying to cope with them. Karl Weber is gone, too. I never met him. He created the Swiss Foundation for Alpine Research and thus made possible all the good things that they did for us.

If I had been more efficient in writing this book, I would not have to include Lieutenant Colonel Eric (Buster) Goodwin, our host in Rawalpindi, and Brigadier Habib-ur-Rahman Khan, the political agent in Baltistan, both of whom died within the past two years. There are not many genuine legendary figures in this world, but they were two of them.

There also was Mohd Akram, our companion on the expedition. Akram died suddenly in November, 1959, just before the Masherbrum expedition in which he was to participate. I was stunned. I wrote a memorial about him in *The American Alpine Journal*, which concluded, "Some day Pakistani mountaineers will stand on the summits of the greatest mountains in the world. Mohd Akram will not be there; but he will have led the way." It was fitting that his replacement, Captain Jawed Akhter Khan, reached the summit of Masherbrum the following year. Since then, Pakistanis have climbed Payu, Rakaposhi, and even K2. But Akram did, indeed, lead the way.

Finally, Lawrence Coveney died in August, 1981. Not only was he one of my closest friends, but with hindsight it is apparent that he also saved the Hidden Peak expedition from its biggest hazard—discouragement. I stubbornly refuse to change the original writing in this book, including the dedication, but if I were to change my mind, the first words in this book would be a tribute to the man who taught me the meaning behind the words Dr. Charles Houston found written in English on a Sherpa village's school blackboard on his way to reconnoiter Mount Everest in 1950: "Gather courage. Don't be a chicken-hearted fellow."

Then there are those with whom we have lost contact over the years. The leading person in this category is Tas Rizvi. I saw him in the United States in 1959 and never heard from him again. I do not know if he is alive or dead. When one's friends are officers in an army that has fought in several wars since one last saw them, it is difficult to speculate.

Ghulam Razul, Qasim, Rahim Khan, and Abdul Rahim were four of our six high-altitude porters on Masherbrum, who turned in the finest performances ever done up to that time by Balti high-altitude porters in the Karakoram. Ghulam Razul had a bad knee on Hidden Peak, but when he was healthy, as he was on Masherbrum, he climbed with the best of them. He also was our sirdar in 1974 when a few of us reopened the Baltoro with an attempt on Payu Peak and later made the first crossing of the Masherbrum La. He now runs the K2 shop at the New Bazaar in Skardu. If you ever go there, drop in and say hello to the man who was the finest sirdar in Baltistan.

I have not seen Rahim Khan or Abdul Rahim since the 1960 Masherbrum trip. I did see Qasim again in 1974. When we reached Askole he was there. Qasim and I ran full speed into each other's arms as the men of Askole cheered.

What about the effect of the expedition on the American participants? It did not make us rich or famous. Pete Schoening and Andy Kauffman are not exactly household words except in their own households. The rest of us are known only to a few mountaineers who are over forty-five and have either very good memories or a penchant for scholarly research. But we did not go on the trip to become rich or famous.

With hindsight, we recognize an important side benefit of the expedition, a benefit that we all most appreciate: it made it easier for us to go climbing. We settled into our professions and careers, but we continued to climb, so much so that the public should be grateful we are too lazy to write books.

Gil Roberts practices and teaches emergency medicine in Berkeley, California, and is medical director of Mountain Travel, USA. He was the medical officer for the successful 1963 American Everest Expedition and spent most of that expedition in the western cwm. He skis, climbs a little, and gets to the Himalaya frequently as a trek leader. He returned to the Baltoro in 1978 with his fifteen-year-old son, and spent the fall of 1980 doing the high passes of the Everest area. He is probably best known by the younger climbing generation for his practical and pungent remarks at mountain medicine seminars.

Dick Irvin is working on his Ph.D. in environmental studies at the University of California at Davis after many years of teaching high school mathematics and science. He has continued to climb all over the world—Koshtantau, Mount Saint Elias, Huascarán, and hundreds of summits in between. He is leading a few treks in the Himalaya in his declining years, but I suspect that today he is doing the highest standard of technical climbing of any of us.

Tom McCormack is still farming and ranching in Rio Vista, California. He went on the 1960 Masherbrum expedition where he made the first ascent with Abdul Rahim of Serac Peak (22,000 feet). A recent climbing publication listed Serac Peak as unclimbed, and as none of us bothered to write in to correct the error, we are awaiting the second first ascent of Serac Peak at any time, as unclimbed peaks in the Karakoram become scarcer and scarcer. With his family he has been doing more and more trekking in Nepal, an almost universal sign among us of advancing age. Even so, he gently keeps offering to go rock climbing with me in the Sierra, but so far I have managed to avoid his generosity.

Tom Nevison is now practicing anesthesiology in Vail, Colorado, after many years of doing medical research in New Mexico and Virginia. He was a member of the 1960–61 Himalayan Scientific and Mountaineering Expedition led by Sir Edmund Hillary and climbed without oxygen to within 400 feet of the summit of Makalu (27,825 feet) when his companion, Peter Mulgrew, became critically ill with a pulmonary embolism. Tom then participated in the heroic struggle to evacuate Mulgrew down the mountain. While Tom may not be so active in climbing as some of us because of his involvement in hot air ballooning, sailing, skiing, and life in Vail, such endeavors make us think he might have stolen another march on the rest of us as usual.

Bob Swift is in San Diego teaching in primary school. Probably the best rock climber in our party in 1958, Bob was the chief guide at the Palisade School of Mountaineering in California for many years and led clients up mountains all over the world.

Andy Kauffman, the "old man" in the expedition, is now retired and living in Washington, D.C., after a distinguished career in the Foreign Service. His assignments included posts in Calcutta and Honduras, among other places. His Calcutta assignment was most fortuitous in that it permitted him to assist the 1963 American Everest Expedition with Indian custom formalities. Like most of us, he did his best climbing in the years after the expedition, including some very fine seasons in the French Alps. In the last decade he has climbed almost every year in the Selkirks and the mountains there are not safe from him yet. Andy has also been active for years in the work of the American Alpine Club.

Pete Schoening is the president of Chemical Proof Corporation in Seattle. I used to say that I did not know what would be the second thing I would do if I were ever called upon to rob a bank or cross the Antarctic on foot, but the first thing I would do is call Pete Schoening. I have not yet entered into a life of crime, but in December 1966–January 1967, Pete and I were in the Antarctic together. It was my turn to play leader, and I sat back and laughed as Pete matched the young "tigers" step for step up the highest mountains on the continent. In 1974 he was the leader of an expedition of nineteen American mountaineers to the Pamirs on the first Russian-American climbing exchange. He still has that "aw shucks" grin when he says he is taking it easy these days, but if you tie into a rope with him you deserve what is coming.

After practicing law and being the executive director of the Sierra Club Foundation, I am now living in Palo Alto, California, with my wife and two daughters. I reached my climbing peak in 1966 just before going to the Antarctic. That leisurely expedition plus the moral obligation to spend the following year talking at the annual dinner of almost every climbing group in the United States rapidly started me on a downward spiral. What little ability I had left was finished by my becoming president of the American Alpine Club. It was not that I felt responsible to uphold the general belief in the lack of climbing ability in a president of the American Alpine Club, although I performed that function admirably; it was that the position demanded all of my spare time.

But what about the mountain? During the expedition it seemed to become more than a stage upon which we acted out our vanities; it seemed to become one of us, the dominating one of us. Hidden Peak today has a history similar to most high mountains in the Himalaya. Climbers have run up it, struggled up it, and died on it. The second ascent was made on August 10, 1975, by Reinhold Messner and Peter Habeler, who ushered in an era of alpine-style climbing on the highest mountains in the world by going from their base camp to the summit in three days by a new route up the northwest face. Remembering the controversy we had over the route in 1958, I could almost hear Bob Swift laughing, but he was too gracious to pick up the telephone and do so. Perhaps it was because the northwest face, while climbed in just three days, was harder than our route! I was filled with admiration over Habeler's and Messner's brilliant feat, but I had the vague wish that they had picked some other mountain upon which to demonstrate their prowess. The lead article in the *Reader's Digest*, which related this exploit, mentioned only that the mountain had been climbed previously and did not state when or by whom. Somehow this seemed not only appropriate but also even fortunate. Happily for us, Messner and Habeler in subsequent years did such things as make the first ascent of Everest without oxygen, and Messner did solo climbs on Nanga Parbat and Everest without oxygen, a rapid climb of K2, and so on, and so on. Thus we can feel that we have been outperformed by a brilliant younger generation, an inevitable fate, rather than think we did not do too well on the world's easiest mountain.

One day after Messner and Habeler had climbed Hidden Peak, Robert Schauer, Hanns Schell, and Herbert Zefferer reached the summit by way of our route. They said they found the ridge more difficult than they had expected, which made all of us feel a little better.

In 1976 two Frenchmen, Louis Audoubert and Marc Batard, made an attempt on the 1936 French route. They got to almost 23,000 feet before being turned back by severe snowfall and continuous bad weather.

A Yugoslavian expedition led by Janez Loncar made the fourth ascent of the mountain by a new route in 1977. They went up the southwest ridge from the South Gasherbrum Glacier. They put in four camps and on July 8, after climbing up windslab snow and icy rocks, Nejz Zaplotnik and Andej Stremfelj reached the summit. The snowstorm in which they were climbing grew worse, but by four in the afternoon they had reached their tent at Camp IV, where later that afternoon they were joined by their companion Drago Bregar. The next day the summit pair continued their descent, but Bregar remained behind in Camp IV to wait for better weather in which to attempt the summit. On August 10 there was no further radio contact with Bregar and attempts to reach the upper slopes to look for him failed. The weather grew worse and avalanches poured down the faces. Finally the expedition was forced to give up their search for him and returned to Skardu. It was a marvelous effort up a new route and it was unfortunate that the Yugoslavs lost one of their companions.

The history of climbing on Hidden Peak came full circle in 1980 when two Frenchmen, Maurice Barrard and Georges Narbaud, reached the summit on July 10 by the original route attempted by the 1936 French expedition. They first climbed Hidden South on July 2, but were forced to return to their base camp because of bad weather. Then they climbed Hidden South again on their way to the summit. It was most appropriate for the French to finish the climb they had begun back in 1936 and do it in the best modern lightweight style. There were only the two climbers and they had no fixed camps. They also used skis on the upper part of the mountain. The French deserved this stunning success.

Recently a British magazine reported that in 1981 a Japanese expedition climbed our route on Hidden Peak using "siege" tactics. For those who are unfamiliar with modern climbing terms, that is a slightly unfavorable way to describe the methods we relied upon to climb Hidden Peak in 1958—by attaching fixed ropes.

Thus Hidden Peak continues to attract mountaineers from many countries. I was glancing through *Pyrenaica*, the magazine of the Basque Mountaineering Federation, and read an item about the efforts of some Spanish climbers to raise money to climb Hidden Peak. Fund raising for an expedition to Hidden Peak! What a flood of memories! Buena suerte, amigos!

So how can one best characterize our expedition? I think Bob Swift expressed it best when he wrote, "Underlying the mush of ephemera that can so easily bury an exploit lies a principle that I think the 1958 trip exemplifies. The idea of our particular group climbing Hidden Peak during that specific summer lay at the precise limits of the equipment, finances, physical endurance, and imagination we then possessed." Exactly.

But perhaps I should close this epilogue by letting my late grandmother, as she so often did, have the last word. Dallas, Texas, in 1959 was not exactly the crossroads of world mountaineering. In fact I laughingly used to call myself one-half of the nonexistent Texas Alpine Club. (I considered Orrin Bonney in Houston to be the other half.) However, that December Jürg Marmet came to Dallas to give a talk at the local Rotary Club. He stayed at our home and while he was there he gave an impromptu slide show in our living room for my parents, my grandmother, and me on the first ascent of Lhotse (27,923 feet), the fourth highest mountain in the world, and the second ascent of Mount Everest, which he had made. Two weeks later the British climber, George Band, and his wife, Susan, visited us from Midland, Texas, where George was working. The Bands also stayed with us, and one evening George gave an informal illustrated talk on the first ascent, which he had made, of Kangchenjunga (28,028 feet), the third highest mountain in the world, and on the first ascent of Everest, in which he had participated. As picture after picture of Everest and then Kangchenjunga flashed on the screen in our living room, my grandmother turned to me and asked, "How high is Hidden Peak?"

"26,470 feet," I replied.

"Oh," she said. "I thought it was higher than that."